From the ends of the Earth

'This is the story of my Living Plant Museum:
a garden that represents plants found by my chosen plant
collectors and which is dedicated to them all: intrepid,
pioneering, solitary, enduring, but eternally enterprising
young men who brought from the ends of the earth the
treasures which have given us passionate gardeners such
endless pleasure.'

PUBLISHED IN 2004 by

Bene Factum Publishing Ltd
PO Box 33, Honiton, Devon EX14 9YD
Tel: +44 (0) 1404 831080 Fax: +44 (0) 1404 831090

ISBN 1 903071 08 9

Designed and produced by Spring O'Brien

Editor: Liz Cowley

Art Directors: Tony Eckersley and Rosemary Gooding

Most plant photographs taken by the author in her garden

Printed and bound in The European Union on behalf of Compass Press Limited

From the ends of the Earth

by

Christian Lamb

Dedicated to
Sir Joseph Banks

BENE FACTUM PUBLISHING

ACKNOWLEDGEMENTS AND CREDITS

Thanks are due to many people in making my text into this book. First to Mike Phillips, without whose cheerful and patient instruction I could never have vanquished my computer, and who could always find what it lost and control its obstructive behaviour. He also helped with the photography. To Alan Wilkinson, reader for Rebecca de Saintonges' Literary Consultancy, who gave me much good advice; I am most grateful to him for his constructive criticism.

There would have been no book without the O'Briens; Liz who oversaw the whole project and handled all aspects of text, proof reading and editing; Donough who masterminded the marketing, and their splendid team of Tony Eckersley who designed the book page by page and created the cover design, and Rosemary Gooding who did the typesetting and picture placing. Thanks also to Meriel Thurstan, artist, who made my garden plan, Clare Travers who took the sensational photographs of the *Echium wildpretii* and the *Rosa banksiae*, Anthony Weldon of Bene Factum Publishing for his skills and good advice, and to my grandson Jamie Rollo who introduced me to the world of mega-pixels.

Acknowledgements to Charlotte Brooks, Picture Librarian, for helpfully supplying the illustrations from the Lindley Library; to the Lincolnshire County Council, the Usher Gallery, for the portrait of Joseph Banks by Benjamin West; to the Société Jersiaise for the portrait of William Mesny; to the British Library for permission to reproduce Dr Parrot's drawing; to Heather Angel of Naturalvisions.com for the photo of the Chusan Palm; and to the Natural History Museum for the picture of *Clianthus puniceus* (water colour by Sidney Parkinson).

I must also thank Annie Barclay (Paintings, Sculpture, Photography) for her photograph of the *Bougainvillea;* to Jack Scheper of Floridata.com for the photo of the *Illicium floridanum*, and to Charles Francis, photographer of the Eden Project whose name appears by his excellent photographs.

CONTENTS

Echium wildpretii – the red echium in my garden

THAT
MAGIC MOMENT

'Spotting the red echium was a turning point, high noon, a coup de foudre. I decided there and then that it should be the first exhibit in the Living Plant Museum that I planned to create in the small Cornish garden that was my domain.'

There I was, prowling through a rather pedestrian garden in New Zealand. The weather was foul; I was cold, having expected to be hot; illness had tied my hostess to her bed; and the only volcano in New Zealand had chosen this moment to erupt, covering everything within its reach with fine grey dust. Then I saw it – the red echium, a perfect miniature – and I knew at once I absolutely had to have it – it was my coup de foudre.

It dawned on me, also at this precise moment, that I had become one of those highly eccentric, rather recherché species – a plantaholic: usually quite normal people except for their one weakness – which is luckily only a spasmodic affliction, the symptoms of which appear when a totally irresistible, deeply desirable plant flies into sight and you know instantly, that to satisfy this passionate need, you may have to sell your house, your soul, even your grandmother. Everyone mentioned in this story has become an involuntary addict, but the fatal attraction is only for nature's creation and has nothing to do with those who spend a lifetime trying to make delphiniums red or carrots square.

In my ignorance, I had thought all echiums blue and classified them among the outsize freaks brigade, because of their wild and uncontrollable behaviour. Their normal pattern of growth is from seed, germinating in their chosen spot – not yours, and flowering huge, fifteen feet, azure-coloured, pyramidal spikes, scattering the next generation

Echium wildpretii by J N Fitch, Curtis's Bot. Mag. 1902

wholesale, totally regardless of where their enormous offspring will come up. The red echium would stand out as an aristocrat in any company. With all the enthusiasms of its blue cousins – save its jumbo size – its exotic, silver-blue, silky foliage rosettes, crowned by the hundreds of tiny, brilliant vermillion florettes which constitute its panicle of flowers, I decided then and there it should be the first exhibit in the Living Plant Museum that I planned to create in the limited Cornish plot that was my domain.

HIGHWAY ROBBERY?

Because of its mad behaviour you can't just dig up an echium and rush off with it, tempting though this might be. It must have a chance to finish flowering where it is and set seed. In spite of hunting high and low, it wasn't until I made a visit to the Chelsea Flower Show that I ran it to earth again; there it was, placed in splendid isolation on the Chelsea Physick Garden stand. This time it was in a pot, so travel to Cornwall in my car would present no problem. I made a stealthy reconnaissance, circling the stand while assessing the situation – could I kidnap it?

Even if I could divert the somewhat forbidding guardian of the display for long enough to abduct it, carrying this tall, spiky construction would alert unwelcome attention on this rather stately Members Day, and its sudden absence would certainly be noticed. I was reminded of a friend in Cornwall

A close up of my red echium

who caught a visitor to her garden pulling up a camellia by the roots, and making off with it. Her reaction was to jump into her Porsche, pursue the thief at furious speed and finally make a citizen's arrest. Returning to the dilemma, I abandoned the rash but enjoyable prospect of highway robbery, and tried the boring, legal method. Naturally it was not for sale; the seed from which it was grown had been given to the Chelsea Physick Garden by the Royal Botanic Garden at Kew, and would certainly not be given to me.

However, once you are a plantaholic nothing, but nothing daunts you in acquiring the 'must

3

The silvery rosettes of the Echium wildpretii

have' of the moment. Somehow I needed to get hold of some seed of *Echium wildpretii,* the ravishing and most suitable name for my pet. It was named after Wildpret, Curator of the Oratova Botanic Garden in Tenerife. He sent it to Kew under the name of *E. candicans,* the blue variety, but when it flowered in 1897, it was seen to be quite a different plant with red flowers, and was then renamed after its discoverer.

PLANT FINDER TO THE RESCUE

The obvious way to acquire the seed would be to go to the Canary Islands and stand over the plant until it obliged, but when pondering this rather extreme course of action, I had one last look in the RHS Plant Finder and found one nursery, in Cornwall, that actually listed it. Forget about seed – these people had germinated seedlings in stock – I was on my way hotfoot.

The silvery little echium rosettes were in pots, outside, in a type of frame, where the nursery man intended to leave them to see if they made it through the winter, and they would then be for sale in the spring. I took two with me and ordered two more for May, doubling my chances of their survival. I knew that to get them to flowering point would take at least two years, so I risked planting them out to get them established their first autumn. This meant the construction of a bespoke, designer, made-to-measure winter-tunnel for them, using 15mm polypropylene water piping for the curved frame, with a wooden base, covered in a very special kind of fleece I found in France, which I had noted protecting the vines from cold winds; not only much stronger than the fleece we can buy here, but sold in huge rolls at the Agricole supermarché. The tunnel was made in such a way that the fleece could be rolled back for most of the winter, when the prevailing climate is mild, damp and very good growing weather. But the minute there is a frost warning, the precious plants could be tucked up tightly in bed; it was easy to insert the thin, wooden poles into the hems, which made it possible to roll the protection up and down. Now, I had done my part, everything within my power, and it was up to *Echium wildpretii* to choose the psychological moment to shoot up the precious pyramidal spike and burst into its scarlet brilliance.

In our daily musings (I frequently communicate with my plants) I must have mentioned the publication date of this book. My echium treated me proud when in May 2004 it triumphantly reached its zenith to become the Flower Star of the garden.

MY LIVING PLANT MUSEUM

My Living Plant Museum was to be my collection of historic exhibits, chosen not only for their exceptional beauty, but in remembrance of the people who found them and brought or sent them home. I had never had the chance to make a garden from scratch, having spent most of my life as a dutiful Naval Officer's wife, bound by the Admiralty to live in other people's houses all over the world. Now anchored firmly in Cornwall for the foreseeable future, with a garden (albeit only a third of an acre), I could indulge my vision, an ambitious fantasy, recording my favourite plants and seeing them grow before my very eyes.

Cornwall is a microcosm of gardens – there will hardly be a known existing plant that is not represented in the county. My addiction to special plants began on my travels abroad, but became obsessional during the delightful and enlightening experience of helping a friend and neighbour reinvent and restore her 300 year old garden, only a few miles from where I live, which had become a virtual wilderness since the war. Established by several generations of knowledgeable gardeners, it was full of luscious rarities.

It was only when she died and I could no longer go and play in this romantic setting, that I really got down to my own. With such limited space and such grand ideas, I had to discipline myself both as to number and size; I would plant specimens as true to the original species as possible. I went so far as to physically follow some plant collectors round the world, looking for where the indigenous specimens had first been found. This aspiration sometimes became a myth as I failed to find the plant I had come so far to see. I invented lectures, which I used as a method of helping to finance my travels.

I learnt how to wrestle information out of our best botanic libraries, quite a feat when each has its own arcane methods, which you need an extra A level to penetrate. Getting into them is an art in itself with their obsession for security. I also struggled with a computer.

My museum garden represents plants found by my chosen plant collectors and is dedicated to them all: intrepid, pioneering, solitary, enduring but eternally enterprising young men who brought from the ends of the earth the treasures which have given us passionate gardeners such endless pleasure; particularly Sir Joseph Banks, who as a collector himself, inspired, trained and sent so many of them, but also to some earlier enthusiasts and many later Victorian hunters such as Robert Fortune, the Veitch family and others whose exploits we shall follow in these pages.

—MY GARDEN— ARRANGEMENT

'William Robinson (author of English Flower Garden 1883) inspires when he says: 'the really artistic way is to have no pre-conceived idea of any style but in all cases to be led by the ground itself and the many things upon it.'

With one primadonna after another clamouring for pride of place in my garden, it was impossible to stick to any plan. All proper gardens are, of course, designed on graph paper with set square and compass, Gertrude Jekyll looking over one shoulder and Vita Sackville-West the other. It was quite a relief to stray from this formula, and with no-one breathing down my neck to start creating from what might be considered the wrong end of a telescope. The whole garden would just evolve with constant changes, plants being tried out in different places, suitable for their needs and to show off their charms.

However, one can't help being influenced by the many writers on the subject, and by exploring hundreds of successful gardens which sometimes inspire useful ideas. I have a great admiration for William Robinson who echoes all my gardening instincts.

His *English Flower Garden,* written in 1883, abounds in descriptions of the cottage gardens he admires for '*the absence of any pretentious plan*'. He says '*one can get good effects from simple materials, the absence of complexity and pretence of 'design' aids these pictures very much. Many things are not needed for good effect, and very often we see gardens rich in plants but not artistic because too much is cut up into dots; there is no reason why gardens should not be rich in plants and pictures too, but such are rare*'. He has no time for the absurdities of carpet bedding or mosaic culture and says, '*the ugliest and most formally set out and planted gardens ever made in England have been made in Victorian days*'. He sounds extremely cross when he writes about '*bedding out fever and the tearing up of bedding twice a year*', but ends the chapter by telling us '*the really artistic way is to have no preconceived idea of any style but in all cases to be led by the ground itself and the many things upon it*'.

Russell Page's *The Education of a Gardener* is constantly at my elbow; his words are wisdom: '*I never saw a garden from which I did not learn something and seldom met a gardener who did not in one way or another help me… I have always tried to shape gardens each as a harmony, linking people to nature, house to landscape and the plant to its soil.*'

THE PRESENT DAY PLANT HUNTER

Plant hunting has a very different connotation in the present day. The acquisition of new and unknown species to dig up and take home is no longer the object of the exercise. Not only would you be constantly arrested by conservationist fiends, but desperately do not wish to harm the environment by diminishing any habitat of some beautiful plant, but just to observe it in its natural background, to judge as nearly as possible its requirements and know, having seen where it comes from, the likelihood of its prospering in a particular chosen setting.

No longer do many of us endanger life and limb, or suffer the indignities of 18th century travel. We are lucky not to be Francis Masson, who when he wasn't in a bullock cart falling into hippopotamus holes in flooded rivers, was riding over slippery tracks in torrential rain, or trekking through semi desert, broiled by the intense heat of the sun and dealing with poisonous snakes.

By contrast, my problems in finding a particular plant would seem very tame to Francis Masson. To begin with, I know exactly what I am looking for. Nevertheless, the very same plants that he found and I search for, are not discovered without considerable exertion and stress. Extreme methods are sometimes called for.

Modern botanists seem fully employed in changing the names of plants, we thought we knew. The many new varieties and hybrids which make such popular garden plants are often at the expense of the original species, which is no longer obtainable.

Scouring the *RHS Plant Finder* is a start, but the acquisition of well-grown plants of a particular variety is no sinecure. You may travel hundreds of miles of solid motorway and curly country roads in vain pursuit of some highly recommended nursery, and endure endless telephone calls, which fail to locate a real human being, but which deafen and enrage you with symphony concerts and unmentionable recorded messages. After that, you may feel that perhaps you will go and dig up your plant in darkest Africa after all.

THE POSSIBILITY OF A GARDEN AT LAST

It wasn't until our children stopped playing French cricket and parking their scooters and old bangers here and there around the house and garden, and finally left home for their various careers – at the same time freeing us financially of the school fee burden – that I noticed the possibility of making any sort of real garden.

The previous owner's efforts had been limited to flower beds with absolutely nothing in them but thrift or sea pink – was there ever a fashion for this plant? If so, it passed me by. It didn't take long to dispose of these and put back some grass. This now left me with a *tabula rasa* – the perfect foundation for my Living Plant Museum.

It is extremely lucky that my south west facing little plot – you could hardly call it a garden at first – on a hill, about a mile from the sea, is blessed with wonderful acid soil. It is rich and black, and a pleasure to run through one's fingers. I nurture it annually with my own compost – trace elements, cow manure, trailer loads of leaf mould, and of course seaweed.

My last seaweed foray was combined with going out to dinner with friends, whose house was practically on the beach; the slippery, bulky stuff was much heavier than I expected, and all the dinner guests had to come in their finery and help me drag it up the shore, before I was overtaken by the incoming tide.

The Cornish climate is ideal for the plants I want to grow, so much so that one of my anxious endeavours is to prevent the whole garden disappearing under the enthusiastic growth of the much too large plants, which, as the all-time plantaholic, I keep on buying.

VISITING MY EX PLANTS

Perhaps I should say now, that at my age, (definitely one of the ancients), there is little point in buying small plants, so where I have chosen trees or shrubs which I cannot live without, and I know will grow too big, I plan to grow them for a few years, just to have a taste of them, then give them away to a more suitable garden. One of my favourite invitations is to visit my ex plants.

One of these was a much beloved *Rhododendron x 'Winsome'* – such a tiresome name – with wavy-edged, salmon pink flowers and very beautiful coppery young leaves, one of the reasons I chose it. But it simply grew too big, and jammed against one of my many camellia hedges, it had nowhere to go. I gave it to some friends restoring a huge old garden, and now when I visit, there is this happy-looking plant, greening up where it was dying back, and twice the size.

Unplanned as it is, the garden seems to have fallen into several natural divisions, emphasised by my hedging and fencing. The central area facing the house is the largest, and from the west side of this, the ground slopes down to the road forming a shady grove, dominated by a big old conker tree.

On the east side of the house are the glasshouse and terrace, divided from the garage section by a myrtle hedge. These sections at least prevent one from taking in the whole garden at a glance, adding the possibility of finding something unexpected. It is quite difficult to produce uncontrived surprises in so small an area, but very desirable to do so.

SECURING THE BOUNDARIES

Mine is an early Victorian, square house, with two centrally placed bay windows, and is protected from my north neighbours' view by a twelve foot wall behind it and which runs along the length of the property.

Another wall, at right angles to it, runs along the road at shoulder height, and the top of this is at ground level in the garden. An informal hedge of overflowing camellias looked good from the outside, and disguised and muffled the busy little minibus which rushed up and down on its way from Fowey to St Austell; however, one or two of these stately camellias did not care for this public exposure, and had to be replaced with more common varieties.

The house was large enough to fit us all in when the three children were still at home, but not big enough for me to feel that I rattle about in it, now that I am on my own. There are houses quite close surrounding it, so barricades are provided in all directions, by planting hedges of myrtle, drimys, camellia, griselinia and some inconspicuous dark green fencing, covered in mostly, evergreen climbers.

These excellent hedges (in my garden just two plants can be a hedge) and fences, most of which have trellis attached to the tops, also provide me

The greyhound beneath the palm trees

Bill, dwarfed by the camellia hedge

with the perfect background for the beds, which are my show cases.

THE INDISPENSABLE BILL

The original barrier to our southern neighbours was marked by a huge (about eight feet thick) privet hedge, the entire length of the property. This seemed to be advancing relentlessly towards the house, and it was one of my first major undertakings to get rid of it.

No such projects could possibly take place without my indispensable, part-time gardener Bill, who is the epitome of the word 'handyman', and makes all the tents and tunnels for winter protection of my most precious tender plants that I am determined shall acclimatise eventually. He is adept at neatly restoring an area I have been working, which, however hard I try, looks as if wild pigs had been rootling. He has a selection of obliging grown up sons of varied ability, on call if required to help with manpower problems. Bill trained as a mason after his national service, then became an agricultural worker and occasional gardener, (having absorbed gardening lore from his most valuable father), before he fell into my hands.

He is the hardest worker I have come across, a mine of information on basic horticultural things I know nothing about such as grass and weeds, and is one of those rare gardeners who does not always know best.

Instead of looking horrified when I have a brilliant new idea, he simply drops everything and invents practical ways of achieving whatever it is – pointing out any drawbacks I had not thought of. Because of being a 'now'

10

Mitraria coccinea

person I can never wait sensibly for his help, but move impossibly heavy pots about as if I were fifteen. Inevitably there has been an ominous moment when I realised I had overdone it, since I can't bend as fluently as I did, so the planting has had to be a shared operation.

At least, this gives us a double chance of remembering what I have put where. I am not averse to labels; indeed I am maddened by important gardens which do it badly, but masses of them in a very limited space intrude and make it look like a nursery, so I tend to keep to the minimum and record in my diary what I plant as a back-up.

It took Bill and all his sons to dig up my frightful hedge, and together they towed it out of the garden by car. I only call upon the extended family for such major activities, when sons Patrick and Andrew are the pick of the bunch. Patrick is extremely nimble and seems to balance on a twig with his chainsaw, removing some offending branch, or persuading some climber to reach for the sky. He is a natural, among other things, at undoing in a trice the tortuous knots that clematis manage to tie and which take me hours to undo.

Andrew is covered in magnificent tattoos, and every visible orifice has some sort of earring attached. He will turn his hand to anything.

I replaced the privet boundary with some curved, dark green painted fencing, giving it a slightly theatrical look, and providing the space for my main centre stage showcase behind two majestic palm trees. The evergreen climbers lined the background, and I rearranged the camellias with a large plant of *C.* 'Cornish Spring' in the centre, and two small osmanthus in front, to cover the lower bare limbs of the camellia, *C. japonica* 'Bob Hope', very dark red on one side, with *C.* 'Water Lily', luscious, well-named, deep pink, adjacent.

On the other side I put pale pink, large single flowered *C.* ' Jenefer Carlyon', with most elegant leaves, next to *C.* 'Nuccios Cameo'. Prostrate plants occupy the spaces here, with low growing, spreading camellias, which flower in the autumn, taking pride of place.

Sub-shrubs *cornus* and *gaultheria* help to make mats, whose purpose is to beat the weeds and provide an attractive setting for the grander shrubs. I sprinkle *Anenome blanda* all over the place and these are followed by species geraniums, which weave their way in and out, and, if left to their own devices produce a decorative and labour-saving spread in seasonal succession. They are helped by another very adaptable Chilean shrub *Mitraria coccinea*, which has brilliant, scarlet tubular flowers,

Chusan Palm, Trachycarpus fortunei

very late, and has the obliging feature of thin manoevrable branches, which resemble a Rastafarian hairdo, and can be spread out over the bald patches.

Two old stone urns with dwarf rhododendrons add an extra gravitas, as does my couchant greyhound, who lies between the Chusan palms, looking very responsible.

THE CHUSAN PALM BED FACES THE HOUSE

The largest exhibits in this bed were planted long before my day, but fit very well into my museum. They are the two Chusan palms, *Trachycarpus fortunei,* named after Robert Fortune, one of my favourite collectors, whose exploits will be described in the camellia chapter.

They are now about 20 feet or so tall, and have probably been there for about a hundred years. Their large attractive fan-shaped leaves top the straight trunk, which is covered in furry brown, fibrous matting which keeps them warm in the winter. In many countries this is stripped, but my birds find it invaluable for their nests and its shaggy look is both unusual and exotic.

On the other side of my ex privet hedge lives a thespian family who runs a small theatrical company, and its musical rehearsals are often an asset to my garden atmosphere.

One particularly vivid rehearsal resulted in the children setting fire to a structure, which leaned against, and then burned a hole in my new fencing During their apologies they revealed to me that I was under-using my own space – good news indeed, so I presented them with a tent to make up for their loss.

On the west or road side of the house I have converted an old lean-to shed into an office, from which I peer out of the window on to some of my exhibits which grow against the back wall. The *nerines* flower exactly the same dusky pink as the autumn flowering *Camellia sasanqua* 'Sparkling Burgundy', and in November they

Camellia sasanqua 'Sparkling Burgundy'

complement each other to perfection.

This is also my show-off, tree-paeony bed, followed by the autumn lilies. Where this west side of the garden slopes down to the road, (one of the natural divisions), it is shaded from the south by a large conker tree, planted in the distant past and besieged by small boys during the season, after school.

There used to be a gate in the wall along the road from which you stepped out into the traffic. Removing it made the property less accessible – one of my aims – and added marginally more space. The conker tree and the Chusan palms are the only plants in the garden for which I am not responsible, everything else has been chosen by me.

My conker tree is a mixed blessing; I employed a tree surgeon to take out a whole layer of branches, to let in as much light as possible, but to shape it elegantly, so now it looks like a huge mushroom.

Whereas before, its hairdo had been a really thick, untidy, shaggy mop, it now had a splendid neat bob; the potential underneath it was unbelievable with room and light for my special little trees, more camellias and many of the shrubs which have particularly spectacular autumn colour. They perform best in this shady atmosphere and act as extra protection for some wild orchids, autumn crocus, shrubby clematis and a variety of plants which I am always discovering and desperately trying to find a home for. I shall delve into why they are called what they are, and

some of their histories, as we proceed.

The flowering season of plants is as important as the size and shape or colour, but emphasis must be on late flowering plants to replace the spring riot. The camellias are at their best in March, though some do continue flowering until May.

Euchryphias from Chile are most valuable in August, with their thousands of small scented white flowers – there are five varieties here and more than one of each.

I decided that every inch of this museum must be utilised with suitable and decorative exhibits, which have other attributes besides flowers: autumn coloured leaves, bright fat berries – even new growth.

That of a particular Japanese rhododendron comes to mind – the new growth is almost better than its flowers: the pale silvery, velvet-soft, young leaves are covered in a sort of down; the underside turns fawn as it matures, and the whole plant shimmers its bi-coloured foliage.

Under the conker tree is a witch hazel, another example of varied attraction. Around Christmas, its most unusual, squiggly, yellow flowers

13

smother the bare branches, scenting the air; after this display it produces large elm–like leaves, which last all summer long, turning paler and finally brilliant yellow before they fall. (More about this in the 'must have' chapter).

Here, also, the evergreen foliage provides wonderfully different shades and shapes, such as the pinnate mahonia leaves, the willow-like podocarpus, and the rather dramatic feathery tree fern, all of which stand out against the shiny, almost black green of the many camellias.

When demolishing the old garage, which stood against the back wall, to the east of the house, (another natural division), a wooden structure was revealed which appeared to be asking to be made into a sort of pergola. Here I was able to adapt and grow, in very narrow beds, some interesting climbers and more autumn flowering camellias. At right angles to this, north and south, I planted a myrtle hedge, with a scallop shaped top; this hides the gravel area in front of the new garage, which is pressed up hard against the eastern boundary.

That side of the myrtle provides another evergreen background for climbers, late flowering clematis and ginger lilies – the cinnamon red bark of the myrtle and summer scented flowers do all and more than one could desire. An arched way through the hedge, with stepping stones through the mown grass, provides a path towards the house.

My biggest camellia hedge, now about 12 feet tall, marks the southern boundary of the garage section. It is sometimes tight clipped, when I must say it does look rather smart (see p.10).

MY GLASSHOUSE STARS

The glasshouse leans to against the east side of the house, where the wall is 4 feet thick. Behind it, the outside flue from the Rayburn cooker adds a little extra warmth. Lately, some laminate was added to the glass roof for shading, and a strip bulb to replace our lack of light and sunshine in the winter. There is also a small electric heater for frosty nights.

There used to be a battered old greenhouse with an enormous vine, very prone to mildew, which produced delicious grapes, however the insurance company became tired of paying out for storm damage and in replacing it with the present structure I managed to kill the vine, (sort of by mistake on purpose).

It is no good attempting to grow anything in it which really needs heat, but there are mouthwatering plants with which to have a go.

It has been my particular interest to grow plants, first seen on any Joseph Banks inspired expeditions, such as exquisitely scented boronia, and rather unpleasantly scented hibbertia.

Some of these Australian introductions are the greatest challenge, many of them being much too delicate to be reliable outside.

Among my other glasshouse inhabitants there are varieties of passionflower, also lapagerias, and some tender clematis, as well as mandevillas, a few hardy orchids, and most favourite, the Malaysian rhododendrons (see p.19). These, not having seasons where they come from, flower when they feel like it, and are a splash of unexpected colour.

The greenhouse is intended for me as well as plants; it adds an extra dimension to the house, and one can spend a lot of time in there, which is just as well as it is easy to miss a flower which only spends one day showing itself off.

THE IMPORTANCE OF POTTING

The plants in it are all in terracotta pots; the first thing to do when a new treasure appears is to repot it in its chosen mixture. I do not have a proper potting shed, so we mix the required recipe in the wheelbarrow and I can manage with that instead. The pots stand on wooden slatted staging, which is painted white or on the tiled floor.

Pigwire covers all the inside surfaces, which is ideal for climbers. Indeed, every inch of wall or fencing in the whole garden is covered in it, being cheap, unobtrusive, and not providing quite such desirable and easy housing as the plastic-coated kind for the many pests queuing up to move in.

The war against these intruders is waged relentlessly – it takes a really wily insect to escape Bill's eagle eye – we both examine their favourite

haunts daily, but Bill is better at it than I am, being more agile upside down on a ladder. Visiting cats are another menace. These greenhouse plants are by no means always successful and if, after fair warning, anything looks less than decorative, it is banished, either to the bonfire or to a small area of garden kept for invalids, where surprisingly some of them recover.

Another wall extends behind the greenhouse. You can't have too many walls; this one just allows my car to squeeze through the pergola on its way to the garage; any visitors don't usually attempt this chicane, but park in the road.

Beyond this wall is a small gate, the only way in; giving such priority to the garden makes the whole place extremely inaccessible. I live with the illusion, that surrounded as I am by my walls and camellia hedges, in splendid isolation, that I am also happily invisible.

The bed on the greenhouse side of this wall is planted with my very best lilies. Climbing up it are two very special evergreen climbers: a trachelospermum and a hibbertia and several clematis, (all described in the climber chapter), which have got to the top and are now coming down the other side, as requested.

In front of this bed is the square terrace, which has stone pots and troughs on it, to enliven the garden furniture. It still looked a bit bare, so larch poles joined by arches decorate the edges, and on the south side support a really enthusiastic akebia from China, which flowers little purple scented blooms in the spring; a *Berberidopsis corallina* from Chile, another favourite, produces lookalike, miniature bunches of cherries, which have decided to grow in elegant festoons, all among and hanging below the akebia; these are its flowers.

The other poles on the east side of the terrace have three different honeysuckles, a vigorous one from Burma, *Lonicera similis var delavayi,* with fragrant white trumpet tubes, an evergreen one from America, with flowers of rich orange scarlet drooping spikes, and another variety with large, coppery yellow flowers. These climb along ropes which join the poles, being flexible against the

Lonicera similis var. delavayi

lesser prevailing, but still sometimes fierce easterly wind.

The problem of how to show the exhibits to best advantage is a constant anxiety. Part of my gardening operation is to sit on my terrace and criticize my handiwork; any excuse will do for this activity,

indeed it is why I have a garden – not to spend hours upside down weeding (I don't have an obsession about weeds, except to smother them in something more interesting), but to rejoice in how lucky I am, not to be driving round Cornwall in five or ten mile traffic jams, but comfortably relaxed in a very well designed garden chair. It is then that I see how things can be improved: for instance, it is not always apparent that a plant such as the embothrium with its violent, scarlet racemes, will flower before its pink camellia background has finished; another brilliant vermillion to beware of is the mitraria which kills almost any other colour within range stone dead.

THE CHALLENGE OF COLOUR

Talking of colour, there are no taboos about it in my museum. Perhaps I am colour blind, but even where I have a mass of three different, clashing, scarlet pieris, I exult. *Streptosolon jamesonii,* the marmalade plant, and a Vireya rhododendron called 'Java Light', which flower at the same time in the greenhouse, can be trying when their neighbours are bright purple and pink, but one can move their pots about and at the very worst put on dark glasses.

In my efforts to fit in more varieties of camellias, I had made a bank of them in a corner, pressed into the myrtle hedge; at their peak is a very

Right: Berberidopsis corallina by W Fitch – Curtis 1862. Inset: photo of the same plant in my garden.

16

Vincent Brooks, Imp.

Prunus 'Shimidsu Sakura'

valuable volume, which I often refer to), described as *'one of the loveliest of Japanese Cherries, a small tree, with wide spreading branches, forming a flattened crown; its large and fimbriated, double flowers are pink tinted in bud, opening to pure white and hang all along the branches in long stalked clusters',* seemed the answer to prayer.

It is supposed to grow to 15 feet, and now at about 14 feet I have cheated slightly, by cutting some of the single pink camellia off the top to give the cherry clearance, until it reaches its full potential. It has more than fulfilled its obligation, by spreading over, not only the group, but embracing as well a large Australian camellia, 'Margaret Waterhouse', facing the other way behind it.

The very words *'secret garden',* seem to have been purloined by Frances Hodgson Burnett, so that one cannot use them without being reminded of Dickon in that most seductive story, but I like to think that all my barricades, walls and hedges have created just such a tranquil retreat.

tall bush with single pink flowers, that I grew from seed; in front of that is a double white camellia 'Sabina', which has an occasional red stripe, and that old favourite camellia 'Lady Clare', a plant with huge, luxurious, rose pink, double blooms with glorious, dark green serrated leaves, which sweep decorously to the ground.

There was a space behind this collection, where a Japanese cherry could queen it, and eventually form an umbrella over them. *Prunus Shimidsu Sakura,* according to *Hillier's Manual of Trees and Shrubs,* (a most

'It wasn't until our children stopped playing French cricket and parking their scooters and old bangers here and there, and finally left home for their various careers that I noticed the possibility of making any sort of real garden. This now left me with a 'tabula rasa' – the perfect foundation for my Living Plant Museum.'

Vireya rhododendrons - see page 15

19

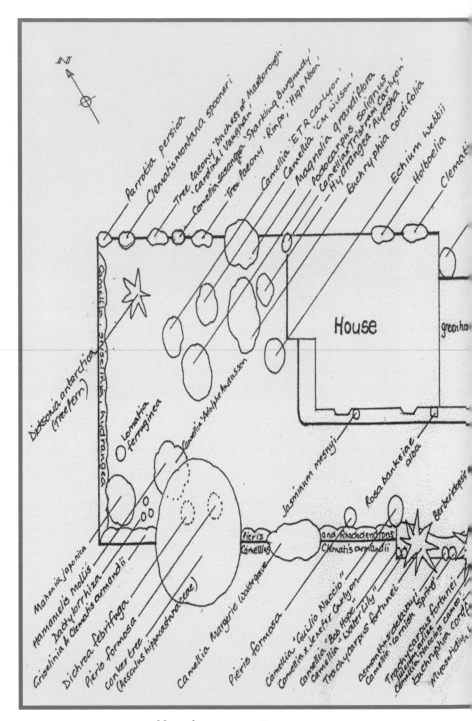

My garden arrangement

20

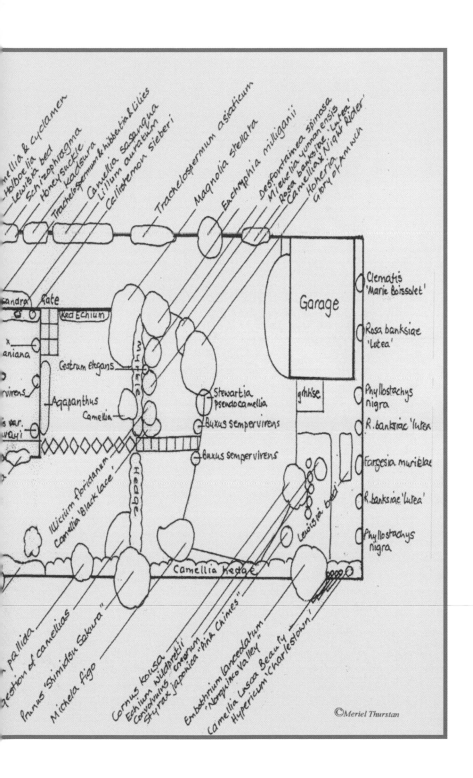

REMEMBERING SIR JOSEPH BANKS

'Joseph Banks was a one-off from the start, who managed to be educated at Eton, Harrow, Oxford and Cambridge.'

My plantaholic state necessitates digging into the background, not only of every special plant I grow, but also into the darkest secrets of the plant collector who found it. For example, one of my earliest choices was the lobster claw, *Clianthus puniceus.*

This delightful climber was admired in New Zealand by Joseph Banks, on his famous voyage with Captain Cook to the South Seas in 1768, and he chose to call it the 'Glory Pea'. It will ramble up anything, its pretty feathery foliage displaying to perfection the

Left: Joseph Banks, surrounded by artefacts from New Zealand, painted after his return in 1771 by Benjamin West

pendulous racemes of scarlet or white parrot bill. I managed after several failures to get both coloured forms growing together against the old wall that I can see from my office window, unaware that snails could, and did, strip every elegant, pinnate leaf from the branches overnight. It is not very long lived at the best of times, so my rage was great and my revenge swift. I had a sharp-eyed, eight year old grandson staying with me at the time, and as soon as it was dark, ignoring bedtime, we prepared for battle with a torch, some pincers and a large jar of salt. In the silence you could almost hear the armies of teenage gastropods emerging from their safe, walled haven, crunching their way through

23

24

other precious plants, as they went about further destruction. Unsuspecting slugs were moon-bathing all over the grass. The massacre ensured there was blood on the carpet that night.

I hardly knew anything about Banks until I plunged into his life story with such enthusiasm that it led me to the Open University, and a year-long course called 'The Age of Enlightenment.' This riveting indulgence took me thirty hours a week instead of the fifteen anticipated, and writing eight essays during the year was considerably more than I had bargained for.

My convent education had left me with School Certificate credits including Latin and Botany – and entrance to Oxford, but the war prevented this and left me with the untrained mind which is responsible for all my academic failings.

Nevertheless my recent OU study of Voltaire's *Candide* and letters to Catherine the Great, and having to write essays on Haydn's *Creation* and the Noble Savage, not to mention Diderot, David Hume and Rousseau, added greatly to my knowledge of Banks' background and explained many of his interests and activities. That year, I had also arranged my lecture trip to Australia, which very nearly clashed with my OU exam, curiously taking place in the St Austell Rifle and Pistol Club. Honour was satisfied when I scraped through.

Left: Clianthus puniceus – watercolour by Sydney Parkinson, 1770, from Banks' Florilegium

BANKS, A TRUE ORIGINAL

Joseph Banks was a one-off from the start. First, he managed to be educated at Eton, Harrow, Oxford and Cambridge.

His father removed him from Harrow when he was thirteen, as he had learned nothing there since he was nine. He was decribed in his school report as '*so immoderately fond of play that his attention could not be fixed upon his studies.*' In truth, he was bored to death at Eton by the heavy, classical curriculum, and spent his time gathering plants as he wandered along the banks of the river Thames. This was his introduction to botany, a lifelong passion, and his entry to the company of plantaholics. It was also the start of his natural history collections.

When he entered Oxford he discovered that the only Professor of Botany had given one lecture in twenty years and was not prepared to give another, so he went to Cambridge, where he recruited Sir Israel Lyons, Master of Astronomy and Botany, to teach him – and they became lifelong friends.

He was just twenty one when his father died, leaving him his ancestral home Revesby Abbey, near Lincoln, and a vast fortune which included thousands of acres of land. He continued to feed his addiction to natural science at the British Museum in London, by studying the rigours of botanical diagnosis and Latin description and working under Daniel Solander, who was a favourite pupil of the great Carolus Linnaeus. The Swedish naturalist, who appears later, was responsible for the binomial nomenclature which remains the basis of all plant classification, standardising taxonomic procedure and giving plants two Latin names, one for the genus and one for the species, such as *Clianthus puniceus.*

Museum Banks was much occupied settling into his new estates and responsibilities in Lincolnshire, never missing an opportunity to add to his knowledge of natural history. But then came the time for his first field expedition to Labrador, Newfoundland and back via Portugal, travelling as supernumary in *HMS*

SIR JOSEPH BANKS
(1743-1820) Baronet 1781

Born London 13 February 1743, died Spring Grove Isleworth, Middlesex, 19 June 1820
MA Oxon 1763, DCL 1771, FRS 1766, FLS 1788.

A British botanist, Banks established the international role of Kew Gardens. His wealth enabled him to be a munificent patron of research and exploration for the advancement of science, and he accompanied (and later wrote about) Captain Cook's great voyage round the world on the Endeavour (1769-1771), thereby becoming recognised throughout Europe as an authority on Australia.

Banks made other voyages of scientific exploration, and from 1778 until his death was President of the Royal Society. He played a leading role in the foundation of the Ordnance Survey, the astronomy of Edward Herschel, the breadfruit voyages of William Bligh, the origins and progress of the convict settlement at Port Jackson, NSW, the importation and improvement of the Spanish Merino sheep that became the basis of the Australian economy, Mungo Park and the exploration of Africa, the Royal Botanic garden at Calcutta and the botany of India, scientific relations with France during the revolutionary and Napleonic wars, the protection of Iceland and the search for the north west passage.

Here, Banks must have made his mark as he was elected a Fellow of the Royal Society when he was just twenty three, of which he was to become the President at thirty five, and remain so for forty years, the longest ever incumbent.

BANKS' FIRST FIELD EXPEDITION

Following his time at the British

Niger on Fishery Protection duty, with his friend from Oxford days, Constantine Phipps. Together, they went on prolonged trips ashore at every opportunity to study and collect the native plants. His letters home to his sister have some moments of humour. Characteristically written without much punctuation, he describes St John in Newfoundland:
'For dirt and filth of all kinds St John may in my opinion reign unrivald as it far

exceeds any fishing town I ever saw in England….as everything here smells of fish you can not get anything that does not taste of it; hogs can scarce be kept from it by any care and when they have got it are by far the filthiest meat I ever met with; poultry of all kinds, ducks, geese, fowls and turkies, infinitely more fishy than the worst tame duck that ever was sold for a wild one in Lincolnshire. The very cows eat the fish offal and thus milk is fishy…'

He then goes on to describe their entertainment:

'We all felt great pleasure in returning to society which we had been so long deprived of; St John tho the most disagreeable town I ever met with was for some time perfectly agreeable to us….we were all invited to a Ball given by Mr Governor, where the want of ladies was so great that my washerwoman and her sister were there by formal invitation but what surprised me most that after dancing we were conducted to a really elegant supper set out with all kinds of wines and Italian liqueurs to the great emolument of the ladies who ate and drank to some purpose dancing it seems agreed with them by its getting them some excellent stomachs'.

BANKS, COOK – AND LEGEND

On his return Banks heard about the proposed voyage of discovery to the South Seas, under the command of Captain Cook, and desperately wanted to be involved. He therefore persuaded the Royal Society to ask the Admiralty to take him at his own expense, so he could study the plants and wild life of the countries visited. It would be the first time an educated naturalist had accompanied such an expedition, and he made himself the blueprint of all the plant collectors he was to mastermind for the rest of his life.

Banks sailed in August 1768 with Captain Cook in *HMS Endeavour,* as naturalist for the three year voyage. He chose his own party of nine scientists, artists and assistants, among them his friend Daniel Solander, all on his payroll, plus his two favourite pet greyhounds. This set him back about £10,000, almost half a million in today's money.

The story of this Voyage of Discovery is well documented, their adventures and achievements legendary. The immediate purpose of the voyage was to track the transit of Venus across the sun's face, which was due to take place June 3rd 1769. This would help establish the earth's distance from the sun, which would be an advance in astronomy, known to be the key to more accurate navigation, rather a hit or miss affair in those days.

Cook had secret orders to search for the Southern Continent, *Terra Australis Incognita,* which scientists believed existed. During their search they found and then went on to circumnavigate New Zealand, discovering New South Wales on the East coast of Australia, and finding and recording many hundreds of new species of plants everywhere they stopped.

On the Great Barrier Reef they wrecked their ship and were lucky to get her to Batavia, an island of the

Dutch East Indies, for repairs. It was here on this low-lying island, full of stinking canals and rife with the terrible fevers of malaria and dysentery, and on the voyage home that many of them died. Out of the 94 men who sailed, tragically only 41 returned.

LOSS OF LIFE – AND ART

Added to this catastrophe all three of Banks' artists died, and only 280 of the 900 watercolours begun by Sydney Parkinson, the botanic artist of the voyage, were completed. Parkinson had developed a technique (required by his often being overwhelmed by fresh new material, produced for him daily) of making sketches, sometimes coloured, with detailed notes on the back, which he could finish later. During the thirteen years after his return to England, Banks employed five more painters and eighteen engravers to complete the paintings and make copper plates, which were to be the basis of his *'grand and stylish publication', Banks' Florilegium.*

Sadly it was never published but lay in Solander boxes, designed for the plates, at the British Museum for over 200 years.

It was not until 1988 that the magnificent collection was at last printed in colour, under the aegis of the British Museum, (Natural History), as a limited edition of 110 sets with 723 prints in each, at a cost of £150,000 per set. They were all sold long before the nine years it took to complete the work. The Museum offered a rare treat for anyone interested, when they promised to produce for comparison, Banks' herbarium specimen, Parkinson's original painting and the new coloured print – I asked for *Clianthus puniceus* and was delighted at the sight.

BANKS, THE PERFECT SUBJECT FOR A LECTURE

There was a splendid exhibition of *Banks' Florilegium* at the Chelsea Physic Garden in March 1988, which coincided with my newly-invented lecture on Sir Joseph Banks. Never having lectured in my life, I was persuaded by a friend that any fool could do so – all you needed was a good beginning and a good end, because no one ever listened to anything in the middle.

I couldn't believe it was quite as easy as that, but I started with a talk on camellias, about which I know something. Then, after all my detailed discoveries about Banks, I decided to make him into a lecture too, partly because he made such a good subject, but also because this marvellous man was so fascinating and so little remembered. I made friends with the specialist printers at Historical Alecto, who were kind enough to give me a selection of slides, which illustrated the making of these brilliant prints, and I acquired a list of the purchasers of the 110 sets, mostly universities and botanic gardens, many in America. Choosing half a dozen of these illustrious names, partly for where they were, (I particularly wanted to go to California to see the redwoods and other plants, in whose origins I was interested), but also for the least intimidating institutions, I wrote a carefully worded letter, suggesting that when I was in the States the following year, they might like to hear my lecture, giving some background to their magnificent purchase, and enclosing my leaflet.

I was thrilled to have one answer with the offer of an engagement for $500 for the following autumn at the Filoli Centre, Woodside, near San Francisco, and another to address a banquet in Redwood City. How on earth did one do that? I decided rather nervously to accept everything, and using my real engagement as a lever, I managed to arrange three more dates with the Garden Club of America. If I couldn't lecture before I went, I would certainly be a dab hand by my return.

INCOMMUNICADO

Banks would have known as he set out in 1768 that he would be completely incommunicado, and that only on his return would he be able to tell his tale. The voyage had the same dazzling impact as when we shot a man to the moon in a rocket, but we are so used to instant communications by satellite that it is hard to imagine the deafening silence that had to be endured by those anxiously waiting at home for news. A daily account on CNN would have electrified his audience.

Their dramatic return in July 1771 with such a success story must have astonished and delighted the many who had despaired of their safety, and their pleasure was only tempered by the tragic loss of life. King George III, (who had been closely involved in the venture, subscribing £4,000 for the very expensive, scientific instruments), sent for Cook and Banks so he could hear at first hand what they had discovered. From this first meeting Banks made lifelong friends with the King; the two were much the same age and had many scientific interests in common. Banks became his adviser on all such matters and unofficial director of his Royal Botanic Gardens at Kew; the King made him a Baronet in 1781.

Banks dispersed plants worldwide, both to prevent famine and for commercial reasons. For example, it was at his instigation, and he took personal charge of all the arrangements (Bligh's voyage), to send the breadfruit from Tahiti to Jamaica, intended to alleviate our slaves – supposed to be harvesting sugar, but who were dying of starvation.

He also sent cotton from India to America, hemp from China to Europe, and the cocchineal insect on its cactus from South America to India, Australia, and to his own green-house in London, among other ventures. Banks wanted Kew to be much more than just a collection of exotics; it was to be a living encyclopaedia, the great exchange house of the Empire, testing plants for their acclimatisation and practical usage in horticulture, medicine and commerce.

One of Banks' ideas was that some varieties of plant could be grown under very different conditions from where they were found, if they were acclimatised, and in 1805 he published a major paper on *'inuring tender plants to our climate.'* In this he wrote that *'several valuable shrubs, that used to be kept in our stoves, are now to be seen in the open garden'.* He was convinced that over successive generations, plants could adapt themselves to differing climatic conditions. *'If we could make the Myrtle bear the climate of Middlesex,'* he hoped, *'as well as it does that of Devonshire, or exempt our laurel hedges from the danger of being cut down by severe frosts, it would be an acquisition of no small consequence to the pleasure of the gentleman, as well as to the profit of the gardener.'* This is a Banks idea that I can and do try out, with some of the tender plants that I grow, which readily propagate by seed. For instance, the Chatham Island forget-me-not, the commelina, even the echium if I can control it, might evolve and be able to do without their very expensive winter tenting; they will certainly be candidates for this experiment.

THE HUB OF NATURAL HISTORY

Banks was determined to dedicate his life and a great deal of his vast fortune to the advancement of science, with England always to be in the van – he was a passionate patriot.

He bought himself a large house in London, at 32 Soho Square – and he rented another at Spring Grove, on the other side of the Thames to Kew, where he had his own small botanic garden in which he carried out his experiments.

He acquired a copy of every book published on scientific subjects, and had special bookcases built to house them, as well as cabinets for his collections.

He describes the study at Soho Square, in which he did most of his work as *'the unarranged regularity of my little den',* and it became the hub of the natural history world, with an unending stream of friends, philosophers, naturalists, botanists, artists and travellers flocking to visit him. They came to ask for his advice and help, and to pick his brains. His great reputation as President of the Royal Society, his integrity and his enormous wealth, enabled him to advance enterprising schemes, or to help any serious student, who would be encouraged to use his library and collections for research; they all received the warmest of welcomes and his Thursday morning breakfast parties were legendary.

BANKS, THE ELIGIBLE BACHELOR

As a young man Banks must have been much sought after socially. There are various accounts of his love affair with a Miss Blosset, who was seen with him at the opera the night before he sailed to the South Seas, and there was even talk of their being engaged. Miss Blosset is supposed to have knitted him a variety of waist-coats while he was away, but on his return *'he took no sort of notice of Miss Blosset'*. Quoting from another contemporary source *'the Blosset family are rumoured to have withdrawn with a substantial sum of money from Banks to console her for all the knitted waistcoats with which she had sought to enmesh him'*.

Banks was a responsible 35 when he married Dorothea Huguesson, an heiress from Kent – and his sister, Sarah Sophia of whom he was very fond, came to live with them, always in the greatest of harmony, and they both helped him with his work during their lives. There were no children.

Banks was always a shadowy figure in the background of Government, refusing any paid position, and preferring to keep his independence and remain his own man. Yet he seems to have been the moving force in much of the progress in scientific knowledge of the day, as you might expect of the President of the Royal Society. His name and evidence of his influence keep appearing in almost every chapter.

He published very little, but the diaries of his few expeditions, and above all his voluminous correspondence, bring him to life. There are between 50,000 and 100,000 copies of these waiting to be published under various subject headings at the Banks Archive at the Natural History Museum in London, where his library and herbarium are now to be found.

Banks corresponded with many people from everywhere with whom he came in contact, through his scientific interests; Carol von Linnhe the younger, Dr Benjamin Franklin, Sir William Hamilton, William Pitt the younger, Josiah Wedgwood, Admiral Horatio Nelson, Captain William Bligh, Empress Josephine to mention a few, nearly always writing in English, but occasionally in French or Latin. Many of his letters were also to the plant collectors, that he hand-picked, trained and then despatched, instructing them where to go, what to look for and how to conduct themselves, always keeping in touch and helping with their problems. No ship ever left or returned to England without letters (and probably plants also) from and to Banks; indeed he used the Navy almost as a private mail service. Many of the Captains were personal friends, and his collectors often hitchhiked along.

THE RETURN OF LIVE SPECIMENS

Joseph Banks' experience as a plant collector on his voyage with Captain Cook had taught him that because of the nature of the voyage, it was very difficult to bring back live specimens; up until then, he relied on the limited ability and goodwill of friends, sailors, embassies and travellers, none of them skilled in plant care.

What was needed was to equip and finance a suitable professional person to go to a specific area, and collect living plants, bulbs, roots and seed and bring them back with all possible protection and the least delay.

His position as unofficial Director of Kew Gardens, and his royal friendship, enabled him to persuade the King of the value of such a plan. Banks had regretted not being able to spend more time in South Africa on his return from New South Wales, and chose Cape Town as the starting place for this first venture.

He found Francis Masson working at the Botanic Gardens at Kew and decided he would be an ideal candidate for the post of the King's first official plant collector. Here was a tough, resourceful, intelligent young man, with a keen eye for a good plant and the skills of a first-rate gardener. He was born and brought up in Aberdeen, where after a basic formal education he was apprenticed as a garden boy. Later he found his way to Kew, and at the same time taught himself botany and learned to become a good botanic draughtsman. Masson was to be paid £100 a year and £200 expenses.

He sailed with Captain Cook in *HMS Resolution* at the start of Cook's second great world voyage, and landed in Cape Town in 1772. He had no experience of travel, and it took him some time to realise what a harsh and dangerous world he was to endure.

He met and made friends with another botanist, Dr Carl Peter Thunberg, a Swede who had been another of Linnaeus' pupils at Uppsala in Sweden. Thunberg had been invited by wealthy merchants of Leiden in Holland to go to Japan to collect rare plants.

'As no nation' he says, *'except the Dutch is suffered to go into Japan, it was necessary for me to understand Dutch and speak it; to obtain this I requested to be permitted previously to pass a couple of years at the Cape of Good Hope and to be taken into the service of the Dutch East India Company'.*

Thus it was that he stopped at the Cape on his way to Japan, eventually returning to Uppsala, and as a Professor, publishing several books – among them *Flora Capensis* and *Flora Japonica*.

Thunberg and Masson decided to travel together; the latter, with his expenses, was able to provide transport; a bullock cart with eight bullocks and a Hottentot driver, and horses for them both to ride, as Thunberg was temporarily financially embarrassed.

They were ideal companions – Thunberg providing the scientific expertise and Masson the horticultural skills. They made several journeys together, but the first was the most successful, when they climbed over the Winterhock mountains, then through the Little Karoo and back to CapeTown. Masson says in his *Account of Three Journeys at the Cape of Good Hope 1772–1775:* '*The whole country affords a fine field for botany, being enamelled with the greatest number of flowers ... the Hottentots are a savage people, very thievous.'*

I managed to buy this little book by telephoning South Africa – thinking this very dashing behaviour – and was impressed by the salesman there who told me to ring again in five minutes to confirm that they had it. They did, although the postage eventually cost more than the book.

Thunberg and Masson's journey was full of adventure as well as discoveries; forcing their horses through the Gouritz river in full flood, the waters reaching their saddles, then through contrasting red rocky soil, burning dry and almost too hot to touch; crossing the Van Staadens river and riding across green plains, dangerous with African buffalo.

For over four months they trekked over semi-desert and vast grasslands, alternately soaked or parched, but found what they wanted – superb plants.

On their return to Cape Town, Masson spent weeks sorting and preparing the plants for shipment. By 1775, when he had returned to England he had added more than 500 new species to the King's Garden at Kew, and a special Cape House was built to accommodate his South African bulbs.

He will always be remembered for the *Strelitzia reginae,* which Joseph Banks himself named after Queen Charlotte, who had been a Princess of Mecklenburg Strelitz before she married the King. One can imagine the excitement when this stunning Bird of Paradise flower emerged slowly from its most exotic bud, after the several years it took to grow from seed. It bloomed just in time to be the 'pièce de résistance' in a collection of plants sent by King George III to Catherine the Great, Empress of Russia.

This diplomatic present was in reply to a request from *'The Grand Duchess of all the Russias for a selection of plants from His Majesty's exotic collections at Kew,'* with which she wished to adorn her new Palace of Pavlovsk, being built for her son and heir, the Grand Duke Paul, near St Petersburg.

The King sent her over 300 plants, only three of which had ever been seen in Russia before. Catherine was a follower of the Enlightenment and a keen gardener – an admitted plantaholic.

STRELITZIA, NOW NOT SO STARTLING

Somehow, this so sensational flower in 1773 has lost its impact, now that we see it in bunches of cut flowers all over the world, and even in the most mundane backgrounds of supermarkets and garages. However, it joined my greenhouse museum collection after a visit to the Canary Islands, and I have cared for it and its progeny for several years in pots. It flowers obediently, but I think it regrets our excessively wet climate, and cannot forget the sunshine it left behind.

I made an interesting sortie to St Petersburg to see if I could find any trace of the Diplomatic Present to Catherine the Great, but sadly what had remained of it was destroyed by the Germans during the siege of the city in 1941/42.

Nevertheless, there was Catherine's garden, made for her by the great Scottish architect Charles Cameron, where she walked her beloved greyhounds, and where Cameron also built her a mausoleum for her precious pets with their names engraved – naturally they all had titles. She loved her dogs dearly, and apparently used to take them not only to bed with her, but to the theatre as well.

During my visit to St Petersburg, I stayed with a delightful Russian family and we made friends for life, using a peculiar mixture of Russian, French and English, with the teenage son's English teacher also joining in. I was concerned after a few days about the discomfort I was causing my hosts in their very small flat, and moved to an amazing apartment in a palace, which was being renovated and which had belonged to Tchaikovsky.

I was assured that it had en suite facilities – by no means the norm in Russia to say the least – but my hopes were dashed when I found in the very middle of my bedroom, and alongside a floor level wooden bed, a large cluster of sanitary ware, including a huge bath, bidet, taps and U bends, all totally unconnected to anything.

BELLADONNA, ALSO A PRIMADONNA

Among Masson's bulbs which are of interest to me is the exquisite *Amaryllis belladonna,* named by the Greeks after a beautiful shepherdess, and which was irresistible to poets of the 16th and 17th centuries. The juice of the tiny black seeds contains a deadly poison, used by ladies to give brilliance to their eyes, hence the name *belladonna*. It is found in rocky places and in gullies beside streams, and in its native country is called March Lily. Here, in Cornwall, it takes all summer long to warm up sufficiently to send up, almost overnight, its long plum-coloured naked stems, crowned with the heavenly scented, majestic blooms.

It is something of a primadonna as well as a belladonna and refuses to perform if deprived of the hot sunshine it needs during its dormant period. Furthermore it does not like wet feet, or tiresome neighbours who shade it from the sun.

Several of its bulbs from Madeira, planted along my wall, grew leaves but no flowers – perhaps a sort of protest. I have now moved them all together in case they are socially inclined, and shall watch closely to make sure they are satisfied with their new accommodation.

THE ECHIUM PERENNIAL

The Canary Islands are the home of my prize possession, the red *echium,* and you may be as surprised as I was to know that more than 80 varieties of this species were catalogued in the Kew *'Index Plantarum'* 1902.

Most of them behave as I described earlier, being biennials and seeding themselves wherever conditions suit them, but there is one blue variety which is a perennial and quite small,

Above: Amaryllis belladonna, the Jersey lily, painted by Sydenham Edwards, Curtis's Bot. Mag. 1862. Below: the same plant growing in my garden.

the *Echium webbii*. I spotted it growing at Greenway, Agatha Christie's garden in Devon. The garden has been a nursery for many years and her son-in-law, a most knowledgeable gardener, was often to be found among his sensational collection of rare plants, and willing and able to advise on the best variety to choose, or how to grow them; there were small discreet plants in pots with almost indigo blue flowers and pale, silvery-green, foliar rosettes. This echium has behaved brilliantly for several years in my greenhouse, flowering about Christmas.

35

I noticed that during its summer holidays, when it revelled in being out on the terrace, it would show by a sudden droop in its leaves that it was displeased. Perhaps it had not had quite enough water, but what really upset it was, when I was transferring it back into the greenhouse, one of its roots which had come through the pot broke off, and it sulked for several days before cheering up again. It has grown too big for the greenhouse now, and had to be found an outside bed with serious tenting to get it through the winter. In its new position it flowered again, quite out of season to show its pleasure. It was finding a space and making more light for this favourite plant that triggered my assault on the conker tree.

There is another very dark red *echium* which I have never seen in flower called *E. russicum*. This is very compact, with neat spikes of rich crimson red florets throughout the summer and only 24 inches tall, but it is not very long lived. I have acquired small plants of it, and placed it near *E. wildpretii*. We shall see.

A white one *E. simplex,* produces a single stem from 8 to 12 feet long, tipped by a great inflorescence of white flowers, which must be a striking sight on the coast of Madeira.

THE RAVISHING AGAPANTHUS

I am greatly in debt to Masson for another of his lilies, the stately *Agapanthus,* belonging to the Liliaceae family. Literally translated from the Greek, it means 'the flower of love'. This I discovered in a marvellous reference book by William T Stearn called *'Stearn's Dictionary of Plant Names for Gardeners',* which reveals many interesting facts about the origins of plant names.

Agapanthus is another valuable late summer ornament, making a ravishing display when the plants are massed together. They inhabit a bed on the edge of my terrace, out of which climb three different honey-suckles up their larch poles. The agapanthus like to be divided up from time to time, and if not indulged may refuse to flower at all. It is thrilling to see those wonderful thick stems, with the fat, flat buds, shooting up from the happy-looking foliage; their flowers, great umbels of blue blossoms, each petal etched in white, take a long time to come out fully and choose very different angles at which to grow, though some at least are perfectly perpendicular.

The deepest blue are the best; they look as if they enjoy being blown by a gale with never the slightest danger of breaking off, their stout powerful stems are ready for anything. The blooms are very slow to fade, and even when they have completed their performance, their dying skeletons continue to grace the garden. Hybridisation occurs so freely that, according to the *RHS Dictionary,* all garden forms may be hybrids and it could be that there is only one very variable species.

Another very essential little pet

Schizostylus coccinea – Kaffir Lily

from the same continent, which flowers late, is *Schizostylus coccinea;* these are pink and white mini lilies, but the red is the best. It looks well against the wall by my garage, mixed up with *Salvia uliginosa,* a pale blue favourite of mine, and *Clematis x Huldine* simply covered in white flowers and buds, fluttering above them both.

BANKS' SATISFACTION WITH MASSON

Banks relates Masson's achievements during the years 1772-1782 in a memorandum, in his capacity as President of the Royal Society: *'Mr Masson collected and sent home a profusion of plants, unknown till that time to the Botanical Gardens in Europe ... By means of these Kew Garden has in great measure attained to that acknowledged superiority which it now holds over every similar establishment in Europe; some of which as Trianon, Paris, Uppsala etc till lately vied with each other for pre-eminence without admitting even a competition from any English garden…..as far as I am able to judge His Majesty's appointment of Mr Masson is to be accounted among the few Royal bounties which have not been in any degree misapplied.'*

A genus was named after him, *Massonia,* described by a journalist as *'one of the humblest and least beautiful members of the Cape lily family',* but Professor Mac Owen, Director of the Botanic Garden, Cape Town, says : *'as was only fitting Masson's name is commemorated in a curious endemic Cape genus of Liliaceae, whose fragrant hyacinthoid flowers, rising in a sessile cluster in the crevice between two broad prostrate leaves, attracts the dullest eye by their very singularity.'*

Even so, I am not convinced. It was his friend Carl Thunberg who wanted to call this genus after him; Masson would not accept the honour *'from any other authority than the great Linnaeus',* writing a real Uriah Heap letter to beg his consent. To his great delight, Linnaeus approved the name *Massonia* being given to the new genus.

THE AMAZING CYCAD

Another plant I owe to Masson is the cycad. In 1775, Masson introduced to Kew a species of cycad named *Encephalartos longifolius,* which in 200 odd years grew from ground level to 3.4 metres. It is treasured in the Palm House at Kew as the oldest living greenhouse plant. Perhaps this is a good moment to describe the amazing behaviour of cycads. According to L Stewart's *Palms and Cycads of the World,* some can be subterranean in their habit: a seedling will produce one tap-root, which has small branching fibrous sideroots ; it grows new leaves continuously for the first few years, after which they come seasonally; leaf bases build up to cover the crown and the taproot contracts, pulling the plant down further into the ground; these contractile stems can be recognised by the wrinkled appearance. Some of them produce annual flushes of contractile roots, which swell and push the soil back, then contract and draw the plant down into the place thus provided. If a bushfire were to destroy all its foliage, the fresh flush of new, bright green leaves on top of the charred trunks might be the first sign of plant recovery. Cycads are an incredibly 'antique' family of plants, unique in that they produce motile sperm cells, a primitive feature, while relying on insects to achieve pollination, which is an advanced characteristic. Darwin said that no insect could pierce the hard case of the seed bearing cone. He did not know that the weevil *Tranes lyseriodes* is attracted to the ripe pollen, when once a year and only for five hours, the cone heats up to 17C, causing the woody scales to soften and at the same time to exhale a very particular scent. The insect is coated in pollen and flies to the female plant that is also exuding scent and heating up its cone. I learned this interesting phenomenon from Lady Walton –

Susana Walton of Ischia holding the spindle-shaped bract of the Queen Palm, Syagrus romanzoffiana

another plantaholic if ever there was one – whose stunning garden I visited recently in Ischia, Italy.

Russell Page designed gardens are compulsive viewing for me, and this one, brilliantly created in a quarry by Susana and her husband, the composer Sir William Walton, is of particular charm. It must be one of the few places in Europe where the sensational Amazon lily, *Victoria amazonica,* not only has her own unique house, where she seems to flower all year round, but also flourishes outside in a sheltered pool high up in the rocky part of the quarry garden. Although I cannot possibly grow it, I feel obliged to tell of nature's amazing arrangements which satisfy this exotic creature, rivalling the cycad in its heating process – and as Susana, who comes from the Argentine, relates (in an email in reply to my request to repeat what she had said when I visited her), it changes colour from purest white to deepest pink overnight: *'The Victoria is still flowering in her splendid pool! Her first night flower – that with us (in Italy) opens at 9.30 pm but in the Amazon would be 6.30 pm. The temperature inside the flower rises 11C causing a strong pineapple fragrance that attracts a beetle, which feeds on the spongy appendages that line the interior of the flower, rich in starch and sugars; the flower closes next morning imprisoning the beetle, which pollinates the female organs (ovary and pistils) – the second day the flower has changed sex and pigmentation in only 24 hours.'*

My small plant of *Cycad revoluta,* said to be the most hardy variety, is attributed to Carl Thunberg from his sojourn in Japan. I am concerned for the difficulties it may experience if it feels the urge to be subterranean in its terracotta pot. *Cycad medea* or *circinalis* was also found by Robert Brown, who went as naturalist on the first voyage of circumnavigation of Australia in *HMS Investigator,* commanded by Matthew Flinders. Peter Good, who went as gardener assistant to Brown, kept an excellent diary until he died

of dysentery, still out in Australia, and describes how they found *'the Cycas palm in great perfection and the fruit being both pleasant to the taste and sight; I eat some, as also Mr Brown and Mr Bawer; on coming on board Mr Bawer and I were taken with a violent reaching with sickness which continued with short intervals the rest of the night.'* Captain Cook relates a similar instance which occurred to his crew, *'and on giving the fruit to the hogs they swelled and died.'* Ferdinand Bauer nevertheless made a wonderful painting of it, showing all parts of it in great detail.

MICHELIA, COUSIN TO THE MAGNOLIA

Anton Pantaleon Hove, a Polish gardener from Kew who later qualified as a doctor, was sent to India by Joseph Banks to find as many useful and ornamental plants as possible – and found a michelia which he thought was a magnolia, to which it is related. Michelias are evergreen shrubs or trees, their flowers being borne in the axils of the leaves unlike the magnolia. They are only suitable for the milder lime–free areas, but in Cornwall I can exult in living in such an area, however much I have to suffer during the downside of this climate, which is a good deal of mist and damp, and not nearly enough sun for me.

I am unable to grow the king of michelias, *M. doltsopa,* which grows as big as an oak, but which has exquisitely scented, multi-petalled flowers like huge, white tulips and

Michelia figo

comes from W Yunnan or Tibet. However, I have two, *M. yunnanensis* and *M. fuscata,* which are small and exotic and divine, but temperamental like all primadonnas – and especially the latter, which is almost impossible to please.

It has to be either completely underneath some other plant (where you can hardly see it) or in a pot in the greenhouse, where it gets too big. For the last two years, it seems content to be between two big camellias, which grow towards each other above it, and are the last two twelve foot plants in my best hedge; it has the most unusual flowers, a kind of yellowy–mauve, quite small, but with a sensational smell of bananas and cream.

M. yunnanensis was given to me by Tom Hudson, a friend and neighbour who brought it back from China. I found the perfect place for it, just beyond the myrtle hedge, and it showed extreme satisfaction by covering its bare branches with hundreds of closely-packed, tiny, furry, gingery buds, which developed by the minute almost, and eventually burst into glorious scented, white blooms. But as it grew, I realised, to my horror,

that it was too close to my very beloved and equally valuable hoheria. Moving it with every morsel of root carefully extracted was very nearly fatal, but daily exhortation and paramedical treatment (which included taking off every one of its little incipient buds and not allowing it to waste any energy in flowers) saved the day and it soon began to send out new shoots; it is not completely back to health, and I still speak to it anxiously every time I pass. Next year, with any luck, it will again produce its myriads of closely-packed flowers.

Dr Hove was also instructed by Banks to study the cultivation and preparation of cotton while on his visit to India, and to obtain seed and plants of the best varieties for introduction to the West Indies. On his arrival in Bombay in July 1787 he worked as physician for the head surgeon for two months, then joined a party to visit a hot water cascade on the Mahratta continent. He wrote of his experiences in *Tours for Scientific and Economical Research, made in Guzerat, Kattlewar and the Conkuns in 1787–1788,* in which he says: '*I found a tree full of yellow blossoms which I took by*

41

its fructification and thread hanging seeds for a Magnolia. It grows to about 50 feet, I have not the least doubt it will do well in England; on our return they would not let me pass my little Magnolia trees, which I dug up, but on giving them a bottle of spirits which they took instead of medicine, nothing was said further about it.' It turned out to be *Michelia champaca,* another variety which I have so far never seen. Dr Hove had a very adventurous time in India, taking with him a soldier he had made friends with, Captain Torin. On presenting their letters of introduction to a young Rajah, they were welcomed with betel, a sort of edible, red nut, and ordered provisions, a storehouse being cleared for their abode. Hove tells us that: *'As he (The Rajah) never saw a European before he was so delighted with our persons that he sent for all his relations to come and look at us ... at midnight we took our leave of them and proceeded to our allotted habitation which swarmed with rats of an enormous size. However we had had no rest for three nights and fatigued with the journey we slept very sound, but Captain Torin who paid the Rajah a visit in full dress, had the misfortune of finding all his hair eat up wherever there was an ointment of pomade, that he was under the necessity of cutting it close to his head; after this we erected our tents in the yard where we felt less both by inundation (of rain) and the rats which destroyed everything that came their way.'*

In spite of all these excitements Hove managed to study the entire cotton industry, from seed sowing to the weaving of the cloth, collecting not only seeds and samples but spinning and weaving utensils and plants used in dyeing, always of particular interest to Joseph Banks. Hove had a hard time, always short of money, with all his clothes and medical instruments being stolen, but at last obtained a passage home. En route, he stopped at the Cape, where he met Francis Masson and saw his garden, taking some of his seed home. We get an interesting glimpse of the First Fleet of convicts in a letter Masson wrote to Banks from Cape Town in November 1787: *'I was honoured with your obliging letter of 11th April by the hand of Governor Phillips (on his way out to New South Wales with the first Fleet); I need not tell you that it gave me great satisfaction for I was almost out of hopes of hearing from my friends any more. We had heard some months ago the news of this extraordinary expedition to the Antarctic regions, but I always doubted the truth of it. The Fleet left us yesterday all in good health. Besides cattle and stock of all sorts, they have taken trees, plants and seed of every sorts which the season would admit. Indeed G. Phillips',* (in command of the fleet), *cabin was like a small greenhouse with plants from Brazil, among which was some rare plants, viz Ipecacuana, Jalapa, and Cactus Tuna with its Cocus cochinilifera,* (the cocchineal insect), *breeding on it.'*

LADY BANKS' ROSE

Lady Banks' rose, *Rosa banksiae,* is one of the few plants which brings Banks' name into everyday gardens. This came back from China, sent by his

Rosa banksiae – Lady Banks' Rose, climbing up my house

chosen plant collector William Kerr, and Banks was the first to see its small, double, violet-scented, white flowers in his own garden at Spring Grove near Kew. Touchingly, he named it after his wife. Although it grows brilliantly almost anywhere else I have seen it, I have had great difficulty in settling it happily. For a long time I couldn't get the white one, and every year I would have a letter from the rose grower asking if I would like my 7/6 or whatever back, as I would have to wait another year for it. The yellow one, *Rosa banksiae lutea,* I planted down by the garage on my south facing wall, where the *Trachelospermum asiaticum* flourishes – but they got too mixed up so I cut the rose back, under the impression that it would not mind, and moved it to a large stone pot against the house. It *did* mind and was not a success, so I moved it back to the original wall, but further down, hoping to encourage it to grow over the top of the garage. It has not quite grasped the idea yet, but at last the white one has arrived and seemed quite content in its large stone pot, happily climbing up the house. It is flowering especially well this year, no doubt celebrating dicing with death when in its desperate efforts to escape from its pot it nearly committed suicide, getting its fat little root jammed in the drainage hole when an ill timed Cornish deluge filled the pot with water. With great difficulty Bill and I struggled to release the root without damage and save the plant from drowning; my heart sank at the prospect of tearing

round Cornwall to find a bigger stone pot to match that of the *Jasminum mesnyi* planted in juxtaposition, but I was determined to save my precious rose's life, and about eight nurseries later I found the exact stone pot; it was an easy task to replant it in its chosen mixture with all rose treats. A little well rotted horse manure was the icing on the cake.

BANKS SENDS KERR TO CHINA

William Kerr was another example of a plant collector chosen by Banks for the King's garden at Kew in 1803. Banks had known Kerr for some years as a *'considerate and well behaved man'* and his letter of instructions to him is delightfully verbose, in the 18th century style, never using one word where ten will do. Banks begins by telling Kerr that *'His Majesty,' (King George III),* '*has been graciously pleased to select you from your fellow gardeners and appoint you to the very desirable office of collecting the plants of foreign countries for the use of the Royal Gardens, thereby holding out to you a prospect, in case you are diligent, attentive and frugal by raising yourself to a better station in life than your former prospects permitted you to expect.'* Banks never did go in for excess punctuation. He writes that Kerr is to go '*wholly under the protection and entirely under the command of David Lance Esq, chief supercargo of the English Factory in China; and the more so as the jealous and suspicious character of the Chinese Nation renders great precaution absolutely necessary in conducting the commonest offices of life, to prevent them from taking umbrage even at the most innocent and well intended actions.'*

Sadly, I do not have a copy of the book of drawings which Banks gave to Mr Lance, of the plants he wanted Kerr to collect, but he was particularly anxious to hear how the Chinese, *'render their plants Dwarf, especially the Bamboo',* if he could discover how the *'flat peach might be made to bear fruit in England'*, whether he could investigate the plant from which the Chinese are said to make *'the best white rope in the world'* and every detail of how *'they meliorate and ripen their manure'.*

Kerr arrived in China up the Canton River and off Canton. The sight of the floating city consisting of thousands of boathouses of all shapes and sizes must have amazed him. Canals and waterways divided the land, beyond which was the factory compound of the East India Company where he was to live. No foreigner was allowed to move outside the compound without permission and he was not able to travel or explore the countryside; the fact that he was plant hunting for King George meant nothing to these people. However, he obtained permission to visit the famous Fa Tee gardens, where he admired the astonishing colour and variety of plants. He worked hard to collect as many of the plants he was instructed to find, and many of them were credited to Lance or the Court of Directors, of the East India Company, while the Kerria was named to immortalise Kerr.

Banks was never a front player in all that he achieved, although he was for many years the undisputed expert on botanic and horticultural subjects and the dominating figure in the world of science both at home and abroad. It is only possible to learn of this by reading his innumerable letters, only a few of which are so far published.

BANKS – EMINENT ROYAL SOCIETY PRESIDENT

Someone who spent a lifetime burying his light under a bushel is quite difficult to vivify, but there are some aspects of Banks' activities which truly animate his personality and I take every opportunity of trying to do so. I particularly like one of his curious habits which exemplifies his hospitable nature and sense of humour. When you arrived to dine at the Banks establishment in London your weight would invariably be recorded; at the South Kensington Museum there is *'a stout leather-bound volume, battered and decayed by much use and the lapse of time,'* which lists innumerable weighings of his friends, set out in alphabetical order in his own hand. Banks himself was over six feet tall and at the age of thirty eight weighed 15 stone; five years later was up to 16 stone; later 17 stone 2 lb is registered, but an incredulous question mark follows this entry. Miss Banks, his sister Sarah Sophia, went from 11 stone 8 to 14 stone 3 in sixteen years, and Lady Banks from 9 to 13 stone by the same date. Fortunately, their dog, Mab kept to a more modest 10 lb.

Dining with the Banks in

Lincolnshire was quite another experience: much of his time was taken up with parish and county business, but he always made time for fishing parties which would take place on the river Witham.

The boat would have an awning, and at the end of the day sometimes as many as thirty friends would sit down to dinner; one year, seventeen hundredweight of fish was caught in five days, mostly pike, perch and eels.

Writing on October 20th 1783 from Revesby Abbey, his home in Lincolnshire, he notes:

'This is the day of our fair when according to immemorial custom I am to feed and make drunk everyone who chooses to come, which will cost me in beef and ale near twenty pounds and I am sure there is no quiet in the house all day'.

COURTING OBLIVION

Banks seems to have done everything possible to phase himself out. Indeed, he has been accused of courting oblivion; certainly he hated the public eye.

In his will he asked to be buried *'in the most private manner in the Church or Churchyard of the Parish in which I happen to die. I entreat my dear relatives to spare themselves the affliction of attending the ceremony and I earnestly request that they will not erect any monument to my Memory.'*

The parish in which he happened to die was that of Heston and Spring Grove where he lived, and according to his wish he was buried in Heston Church with nothing to show even the place of his grave, though in 1867 (forty seven years later), the then vicar set up a tablet saying that he lay there.

The Royal Society gave him a very handsome 250th birthday present when they planned what they called a *Global Perspective,* the purpose of which was to select a theme which drew together the many threads of his wide-ranging interests, and to invite speakers to present papers reflecting his world-wide influence.

Fourteen such papers were read at the Conference, held at the Royal Society on 22nd and 23rd April 1993, which was attended by three hundred delegates. A fitting way to say Happy Birthday.

'For decades the undisputed expert on botanical and horticultural subjects, and the dominating figure in the world of science both at home and abroad, Sir Joseph Banks was President of the Royal Society for an amazing 42 years.'

The Royal Society portrait by Thomas Phillips, 1822

PLANTS I OWE LINNAEUS ——AND HIS APOSTLES —— AND CONTEMPORARIES

'The field lectures of the great Linnaeus were attended by bands of trumpets and French horns, to call students together when he wished to discourse on a subject.'

To remind me of Linnaeus (1707–1778), the immemorial paterfamilias of plants, I grow a very special plant called *Commelina dianthifolia,* also known as Widow's Tears or Dayflower. There is a garden in Devon called Coleton Fishacre, which was created in the 1920s by the D'Oyly Carte family, in a spectacular valley sloping gently down to the sea. A few years ago when I was visiting, the Head Gardener was planting some commelina tubers – he offered me some and told me they had small, vivid blue flowers in summer. This they did, but I had not realised how

Commelina dianthifolia, a painting by Pierre Joseph Redouté, from 'Les Liliaceés', in 1813

delicate they were and they did not survive the winter.

By now dedicated to them and finding it impossible to buy them in a nursery, I grew some from seed the next year, and have been richly rewarded by the intense blue of their tiny three petalled flowers, which brighten a rather dull corner in late July. They now share the space and the expensive tunnel with my illustrious *Echium wildpretii.*

Linnaeus named the Commelina after a family of three Dutch botanists, Jan Commelin, his nephew Caspar and a third Caspar who died young. In Linnaeus' words, he explains why he called this little tropical flower after them: *'Commelina has flowers,*

49

Commelina dianthifolia in my garden, known as Widow's Tears or Dayflower

with three petals, two of which are showy, while the third is not conspicuous, from the two botanists called Commelin, for the third died before accomplishing anything in botany.'

Caspar (1667–1731) was the most distinguished, and probably knew Linnaeus when he was at the Hortus at Amsterdam. Many exotic plants were brought there by the Dutch East India Company, to which Caspar was appointed physician. Commelinas have a curious habit of flowering brilliantly until about lunchtime and then firmly going in; 'morningflower' would have been a more accurate name.

Linnaeus' name was revered in the 18th century, not only in his native Sweden but worldwide. Among his many books were his *Systema Naturae* (1735), a seminal treatise on his nomenclature theory, and *Genera Plantarum* (1737), which contains brief descriptions of all 935 genera then known. He was a gifted teacher and seen as such through his many pupil's eyes. He encouraged his *'Apostles'* (as he called his best students) to travel and gather interesting plants for him in far off countries. Daniel Solander, a great favourite, rather blotted his copybook when he came to England. Linnaeus had found for him a professorship of botany at St Petersburg, and expected him not only to succeed him in due course at Uppsala, but also to marry his eldest daughter; Solander's decision to settle permanently in England and the fading of his love for the girl, dented their relationship and they never met again.

Solander was to become immersed in botanical work as Librarian at the British Museum in London, and travelled with Banks on his world voyage with Cook, and subsequently on another tour to Iceland – taking Linnaeus' books among the many that accompanied them on these voyages. Solander became fully occupied in Banks' world, a member of the Royal

Society and Banks' closest colleague and friend.

HERBORIZING LECTURES

Linnaeus' teaching often included what he called *'herborizing lectures',* while he walked through lanes and fields with two or three hundred students. These became social events at Uppsala, and he was always attended by bands of trumpets and French horns, which called everyone together when he wished to discourse on a particular subject.

His colourful language caused him to be somewhat mocked by his opponents, for example, when he described what he called *'floral nuptials'* and spoke of the petals of flowers as *'bridal beds, which the creator has so gloriously arranged, adorned with such noble bed-curtains, and perfumed with so many sweet scents, that the bridegroom may celebrate his nuptials with his bride, with all the greater solemnity'.*

His home life seems to have been full of incident, with a domineering wife, several large, plain daughters and mother-in-law troubles as well. It is perhaps not surprising that he did quite a bit of travelling in his early days, exploring Sweden, his own country, and the unattractive sounding Lapland; here he travelled 4,000 miles on a scientific journey, finding many new plants and wittily naming one of them after himself, Linnea, describing it as *'a plant of Lapland, lowly, insignificant, disregarded, flowering but for a brief*

space – from Linnaeus who resembles it.'

After a visit to Holland, he set out to visit England. His first call was on Sir Hans Sloane, who had bought the Manor of Chelsea and presented the freehold of the site to the Society of Apothecaries, which was how the Chelsea Physic Garden began. In return, Sloane asked that each year the Royal Society should receive fifty different species of plant until the number reached 2,000. These were housed in his incomparable Museum, which he showed Linnaeus, who reported on his visit, rather disrespectfully, that it was in a state of chaos: *'When I went to see Miller,'* (Head Gardener at the Physick Garden), *'which was the main object of my journey, he showed me the Chelsea Garden and named the plants, using the nomenclature then current, for example: Symphytum consolida major, flore luteo (Comfrey or great Consound with a yellow flower), I remained silent with the result that he said next day: 'This botanist doesn't know a single plant'. This came to my ears and when he again began using these names, I said 'Don't use such names;' we have shorter and surer ones',* and he explained his binomial system to Miller. *'He grew angry and scowled at me. He came back in the evening and his ill temper had gone.'*

Linnaeus decided that Phillip Miller's *Gardener's Dictionary* was for botanists, not gardeners, and it was not until the 8th and last edition in 1768 that Miller adopted the by then fashionable Linnaean system of nomenclature.

Illicium floridanum

JACK SCHEPER

THE AROMATIC STARFISH

Illicium floridanum is not very often seen but is highly desirable; it is a small, evergreen tree or shrub, related to the magnolia and found wild in South East Asia and the south eastern United States of America. The name means 'allurement', from the enticing, aromatic scent. It has enchanting little dark red flowers like starfish, and I quite fell in love with it. I was surprised to find a plant without much difficulty, and it settled happily among some of my camellias opposite the house, where I could keep an eye on it.

This exotic species was introduced by the noted botanist John Ellis FRS (1705–1776), an almost exact contemporary of Linnaeus, who describes the yellow variety *Illicium anisatum,* the star anise, in a letter to Lord Hillborough dated November 16th 1769: *'I have sent your lordship in a glaz'd frame a small specimen of Illicium anisatum of Linnaeus, commonly called the Starry Aniseed, the ripe seeds which I presented to your Lordship were collected last August near Pensacola (Florida US), I am in hopes with the help of an intelligent gardener they may be raised here and become an adornment to our gardens, for from what I can collect of the history of this tree it will stand a severe frost.'*

This decorative shrub is highly esteemed in China and the East for its aromatic smell, and used for medical purposes. The Japanese and Chinese admire it as a sacred tree; they offer it before their idols, and burn the bark as incense on their altars. Here in Cornwall, my plant of this yellow variety looks well against the myrtle hedge, where it has to fight its corner against some very enthusiastic

Illicium anisatum – the Starry Aniseed

underplants trying to nestle up to it.

John Ellis' scientific interests date back to his visit to Cornwall to a Mr William Borlase of Ludgvan, who fired his intellect with a gift of fossils. He studied corallines, convinced they were animals, but after further research, had to abandon the notion that zoophytes were the intermediate link between plants and animals. His book on the subject and his modified 'aquatic' microscope had been of much interest to Joseph Banks, and both were taken on the voyage of discovery in *HMS Endeavour* in 1768. John Ellis refers to this when he wrote to Linnaeus at that time: *'No people ever went to sea better fitted out for the purpose of Natural History nor more elegantly. They have got a fine Library of Natural History; they have all sorts of machines for catching and preserving insects; all kinds of nets, trawls, drags and hooks for coral fishing; they have even a curious contrivance of a telescope by which, put into the water, you can see the bottom, to a great depth, where it is clear. They have many cases of bottles with ground stoppers of several sizes to preserve animals in spirits. They have several sorts of salts to surround the seeds; and wax, both beeswax and that of the Myrica'.*

Linnaeus pointed out in 1760 that Ellis' success in his seed preservation ventures *'would enrich gardens all over the Earth and put the whole world in debt to Ellis'.*

THE MAGNOLIA RELATIONS

Magnolias seem to have quite a lot of rather splendid relations, some of which I have mentioned already such as the michelia and the illicium. And magnolias themselves are surely among the most admirable of flowering trees; alas so many of them take up too much room for my patch. However, *Magnolia grandiflora,* a native of North America, which can become immense, grows up a wall beside my office and can be topped from time to time to keep it in order. It flowers in a desultory fashion, on and off during spring and summer, and I sometimes pick one bud and bring it into the house to have the benefit of the huge, lotus–like flower and its delicious lemony scent at every stage.

I also grow the more restrained *M. stellata*, in a corner, formed by the north end of the myrtle hedge and my pergola. It has grown slowly into a small tree, whose branches are studded during the winter with fur coated flower buds; these fur coats disappear when the late flowers come out. It is thought to be a diminutive and multi–petalled form of *M. kobus,* and comes from Japan where it has been propagated for years, both as a pot plant for indoors and for outdoors in the ground.

Several collectors appear to have introduced it and it has become a favourite, being easy to grow, quite small and delightfully fragrant. Like many magnolias, it is very wind resistant, and seems impervious to frost provided it is not in full bloom, when the flowers instantly turn brown. In spite of its promise to remain small, I have had to be ruthless and take a hatchet to it, chopping off two of its lower limbs, which had made a beautiful leafy skirt to the ground, but which were taking up more than their share of garden. This has opened up a most enticing new shady area to be filled with several varieties of plant I have recently come across. For instance, the *Deinanthe* (of which *caerulea* seems to be the choice). This is a sort of herbaceous hydrangea, its name coming from the Greek 'deinos' (wondrous), and 'anthe' (flower). Introduced from China by the Irishman Augustine Henry, it is known for making slowly spreading mats of handsome foliage with clear slate blue flowers. Here in my garden it will be surrounded by delectable native orchids with spotted leaves, and lots of corydalis, sprinkled with early bulbs.

'MAGNOLIA', NAMED AFTER MAGNOL

The magnolia was originally named for Pierre Magnol (1638–1713), Director of the Botanic Garden at Montpelier in France, and Linnaeus confirmed that the 125 species should immortalise him.

Magnolias are known to be among the most ancient flowering plants, their fossil remains having been found dating back to one hundred million years. Because there is no real difference between the petals and sepals of their saucer-like flowers, these floral leaves are named 'tepals', and are arranged in whorls of three. They are pollinated by beetles which have been plentiful long before bees, wasps, moths and butterflies evolved.

Magnolias have the largest individual flowers of any tree or shrub, capable of outdoor cultivation in temperate regions, and often flower precociously on bare stems, well in advance of leaf growth.

HENRY COMPTON

One of the great gardeners of his day was Henry Compton, Bishop of London (1632–1713), who began his career as an officer in the Life Guards, and as Bishop of London was suspended by King James II for his strongly expressed Protestant religious beliefs.

Compton was also one of the aristocrats who invited William of Orange to invade England. Indeed, he girded on sword and pistols, and personally escorted Princess Anne, (later to be Queen), in his own coach.

Happily, he still had time to build up an unrivalled collection of foreign plants at Fulham Palace, many of which originated in the outermost reaches of his enormous diocese – the American colonies. It was one of the Bishop's responsibilities to appoint Chaplains to the 'Plantations', as they were known, and he chose to send clergy who reflected his own plantaholic nature to North America, instructing them to send back specimens and seed.

JOHN BANISTER AND THE FIRST MAGNOLIA

John Banister (1654–1692) was one of those chosen by Compton, sent first to the West Indies and then to Virginia, where he became one of the Bishop's most enthusiastic collectors. Among the important seeds and plants he sent home were *Magnolia virginiana* and *Dodecatheon meadia*.

Sadly, Banister was killed on one of his excursions by a fearful accident, when he was climbing forty or fifty miles above the falls of the James River – tragically at only thirty eight years old. The Bishop received the magnolia seed almost a year after he had consecrated St Anne's Church in Fulham, from which the first immigrant magnolia was raised.

Three hundred years later it was an inspired gesture of the International Dendrology Society (IDS) to plant another *Magnolia virginiana* 'Milton', the nearest variety available, in the very same spot to commemorate the Bishop, who had been a pioneer dendrologist and patron of botany, planting for interest and amenity rather than for economic reasons. The little tree had to be specially propagated at the Arnold Arboretum, and was personally carried by an IDS member, Mrs Vi Lort Phillips of Jersey, to its formal planting, at which I was present. A plaque has since been placed beside it saying, *'Planted on the 19th May 1992 by the International Dendrology Society to commemorate Bishop Henry Compton, founder of St Anne's, pastor, statesman* and botanist, who raised the first magnolia grown in Europe.'

According to *Curtis Botanical Magazine,* the first Asian magnolia – the Chinese Yulan or Lily tree, *Magnolia denudata* – was introduced by Sir Joseph Banks in 1780. This was grown widely in China to decorate temples and gardens, and one of its early names was *M. conspicua;* what could be more suitable? A French report compared it to *'a naked Walnut Tree with a Lily at the end of every branch.'*

There was once a tree of spectacular size at Tregrehan, Cornwall, planted against the outside of the walled garden. It would burst into flower in early March and appear as if by magic in a vast, white halo, spreading perhaps fifty feet along the top of a fifteen foot wall. If it had one flower it had ten thousand; you would catch your breath at the sight. A careless gardener removed the prop, which gave it necessary support in its old age, and an ill-timed gust of eighty miles an hour felled it to the ground.

JOHN LOUDON

In China the Yulan had been cultivated since the 7th century, both out of doors in the vicinity of temples and palaces, and dwarfed in pots or boxes for a succession of indoor blooms.

According to John Claudius Loudon (1783-1843), the landscape gardener and horticultural writer who founded and edited the *Gardener's Magazine* and other journals, this magnolia was so

highly valued *'that a plant in flower, presented to the Emperor, is thought a handsome present even from the governor of a province.'* It was not universally admired in this country for some years, and Loudon deprecated the fact that *'it flowers before the leaves appear, and is therefore far less agreeable than M. grandiflora.'*

The latter grows wild all over the south of north America, but never very far from the sea. It was introduced into England not later than 1728, and was mentioned in Phillip Miller's *Gardener's Dictionary;* its common name was then 'the Laurel leav'd Tulip tree.' Miller says, *'this sort is propagated by layers as the seeds do never come up if sown in England; the layers should remain undisturbed two years, by which time they will take root and may be taken off in the spring.'*

THE EVERGREEN MAGNOLIA

A remarkable garden called Callaway, about seventy miles south of Atlanta, USA. has perfected the use of the evergreen magnolia. There is rather a romantic story of a real American philanthropist, Cason Callaway – of Cornish descent – who made his fortune and spent a lifetime spending it, on making a gargantuan garden. He still hadn't finished when he had 3,000 acres of garden, with 40,000 acres surrounding it, thirteen lakes, golf courses, woodlands, gardens and still more gardens. An example of his typical American big thinking was when he was newly married; his wife told him she was homesick for her native evergreen magnolias, so he bought her 5,000 *Magnolia grandiflora*, and one of the first signs you see of Callaway Garden when you drive down the highway towards it is the wonderful avenue of these trees, which are used almost as hedges throughout the estate.

One of the original specimens was grown in Christopher Grey's nursery in Fulham, London, where it reached twenty feet high and as much wide, and whose fragrance when in bloom perfumed the whole neighbourhood. By 1822 it was dead, but its trunk, which had been preserved, measured four feet ten inches across. This seems to be about as big as it grows in this country, but in America it reaches ninety feet in height. It is said that the Indians would not sleep under such a tree when in flower, because of the overpowering scent, a single bloom of which, if kept indoors, could kill. Several other collectors appear to have introduced it and it has become a favourite, being easy to grow and delightfully fragrant. For example, Veitch had it growing in his nurseries near Exeter in 1878. Like many magnolias, it is extremely wind resistant and seems impervious to frost.

THE MECCA OF MAGNOLIA DEVOTEES

Cornwall seems to suit magnolias and although this is fortuitous, there are other parts of the British Isles, warmed by the Gulf Stream, which are just as favourable. What has made Cornwall the Mecca of magnolia devotees is the brilliance of its plantsmen. The best gardens are always what I call *'owner driven'*, and Nigel Holman's Chyverton is especially so. His father created it, and he has grown up with it and planted it with the best forms of the most interesting, decorative and desirable trees and shrubs from all over the world. However, his collection of magnolias, which are his passion, is unique. Luckily, he is a fan of my garden and often gives me plants for it.

THE GREAT CATESBY

A beautiful illustration of *Magnolia virginiana* was painted by Mark Catesby (1682-1749), and shows a blue grosbeak opening its beak to receive a ripe seed in a magnolia tree, with flowers as well as fruits. Catesby wrote from observation: *'these red seeds, when discharged from their cells, fall not to the ground, but are supported by small white threads of about two inches long.'* The painting is owned by Her Majesty The Queen, and is hanging for all to see in her new Queen's Gallery, behind Buckingham Palace, part of her Jubilee Exhibition.

Some of Catesby's introductions immortalise his name and are to be found as herbarium specimens in Oxford; among those that interest me are *Trillium catesbyi* and *Lilium catesbyi*.

The trillium, which I have just acquired, is described in Paul Christian's *'Rare Plants'* catalogue as, *'rarely available, this mid sized species has superb reflexed, nodding pale pink, (rarely white) flowers over plain leaves'.*

I planted it where I wanted a nice clump beside my camellia *'Contessa Lavinia Maggi',* which I had just cut back to the bone, a treatment often required by so many of my plants. The first year there was no sign of life from the rhizomes, then some beautiful lettuce green leaves came up; perhaps next year my impatience will be rewarded by the pale pink iris–like flowers, for which it is admired.

Catesby's lily, which he painted brilliantly, sounds more difficult; he found *'this red lily growing on open moist Savannahs.'* In Derek Fox's book *Growing Lilies,* he says, *'of all the lilies on the American continent this appears to be the most unique.'* It has a single upright large flower, appearing from June to October; the tepals recurving at the ends are about 10 centimetres long, deep yellow with scarlet towards the tips, heavily spotted, dark maroon at the base ... *'those who have cultivated this lily have not done so for very long',* Fox adds discouragingly.

Catesby, who came from Suffolk, was both a naturalist and artist. When he was thirty in 1712, he went to Virginia in America to stay with his sister Elizabeth who had emigrated with her doctor husband, and lived with them in Williamsburg. Here, he met a circle of people interested in horticulture and science.

During the next seven years he explored the countryside and made more than seventy collections of seed and plants, half of them unknown to science. He then returned to England to raise sponsorship for another expedition, and his drawings and specimens came to the notice of eminent scientists, among them Sir Hans Sloane, who contributed to a subscription raised to defray his expenses.

Catesby duly travelled back to America and spent a further four years with *'the professed design of describing, delineating and painting the more curious objects of nature',* visiting Carolina, Georgia and Florida, and enjoyed a prolonged stay in the Bahamas on the way home.

He was to settle in Fulham and start on what was to be the very first attempt to catalogue North American plants, to show keen plantsmen what might be grown in Britain. His *'Natural History of Carolina, Florida and the Bahamas Islands'* was the most comprehensive study of the flora and fauna of the British Colonies of North America, and both occupied and supported him for the rest of his life.

Catesby could not afford a professional engraver in Paris or Amsterdam, and took lessons in etching and prepared the plates himself so his book could be illustrated with his own paintings. These were made from specimens, *'fresh and just gathered,'* and often included birds, insects and even fish on the same plates as the plants. They were published in sets of twenty, at two guineas a set; the plants and animals were thought to be *'incomparably well represented ... so that no one can say they are not living, where*

Dodecatheon meadia, the Shooting Star

they stand with their natural colours upon the paper.'

Catesby first described another interesting plant in 1743, the *Dodecatheon,* under the name of *Meadia,* to commemorate the physician Dr Richard Mead, who was *'a generous encourager of every useful branch of science.'*

Linnaeus renamed it in 1751, as Dodecatheon, making use of a name originally given by Pliny – the latter believing it to be under the special protection of the twelve principal gods. It is also called the Shooting Star or Mosquito Bill and the flowers were reputedly used by the Thompson Indians of British Colombia as a charm *'to obtain wealth and make people give presents'* and also as a love potion used by women *'to obtain the love of men and help them control men.'*

The leaves and roasted roots were also eaten by some Indian tribes as survival foods. Indeed, with such qualifications, the *dodecatheon* should surely be de rigueur in everyone's garden. What is more, they have the prettiest cyclamen-like flowers, from deep pink to white, sometimes in umbels or singly; these are fragrant and are pollinated by wild bees. However, they are very easy to overlook, disappearing completely after their short little show off. I have put them near my lewisias, in a sloping, rocky bed at the foot of a wall, where I hope they will all enjoy their environment and the right sort of bees will find them.

THE BONUS OF SUPERB SOIL

Physically planting anything in my Cornish soil is enormously satisfying. Sometimes on gardening programmes, or indeed in other people's gardens, you see the most horrible, lumpy congealed stuff that looks impossible to work. I always dig a much deeper hole than is needed and put all sorts of goodies at the bottom; some grit for drainage and some cow manure, which is always cold, unlike other manures which can burn delicate roots.

Then I usually add some peat, to make it easy for the roots to spread, before I water the hole profusely,

59

making it possible to puddle the plant in. Covering it is the most enjoyable part, when I can filter the deliciously, friable topsoil through my fingers, and settle my plant to just the right depth and consistency. Most shrubs one adjusts to the level of their container, but camellias and other such surface rooting plants simply hate being buried even a fraction below the root level, and may refuse to flower at all.

Potting up is another sensuous occupation in which I revel, always insinuating each tiny, delicate rootlet into the perfect tilth of its chosen recipe.

Fortunately, in such a small garden it is possible to control the watering of every inhabitant; newly planted varieties have to be regularly watered for several months or even a year, one soon gets to know who wants what. Only when I go away does Bill take charge, rushing over twice a day (two or three miles), to check watering requirements, burglars and mealibug, and to make sure I have locked up properly.

COLLINSON

There is a plant I owe to another passionate gardener of the 17th century, Peter Collinson, who was a Quaker: *Cornus canadensis.* Its little cornus leaves are followed by small white bracts, and red berries complete its show off. It fills in many different places, and for no obvious reason is much more successful in some of them than others. I have seen it growing wild in woodland areas, in Maine, North America, like a fitted carpet, and wish it would do the same for me.

PEDR KALM

Kalmia latifolia, known as the Calico Bush, is a most unusual plant. Its flowers are umbels of hundreds of tiny pink upside down umbrellas, but it must have full sun or it will sulk. Although mine has sun and the right kind of acid soil, it does not do me credit, so I have moved it to an inconspicuous place until it can do better.

Another Apostle of Linnaeus, Pedr Kalm (1715–1759), after whom it was named, was sent collecting in North America and Canada. He spent six months in London on his way and wrote an account of his visit, describing Collinson's garden in glowing terms: *'as full of all kinds of the rarest plants, especially American ones, which can endure the English climate and stand out the whole winter. However neat and small this garden was, there was nevertheless scarce a garden in England, in which there were as many kinds of trees and plants, especially the rarest as this.'*

THOMAS COULTER

Romneya coulteri, which seems to grow extremely well in many normal gardens, shooting its beautiful grey foliage in natural clumps and covering itself with stunning white poppy flowers with handsome yellow centres, refused to grow in the many different places I chose for it. Various

Romneya coulteri – the Californian Bush Poppy

people gave me root suckers and I bought very healthy-looking (and expensive) plants, but it would not take off. At last it appeared to approve a position, sheltered by a very occupied, south facing wall, with *Trachelospermum asiaticum* behind and above, and *Clematis x* Huldine clambering about in whatever space it could find, next door to a congestion of toad lilies. Once it decided to settle it did so with a vengeance, trying to invade the toad lilies, diving under the wall and coming up the other side, where I doubt it will be appreciated.

Romneya coulteri, the Matilija Poppy or Californian Bush Poppy, was discovered by an Irish botanist Thomas Coulter (1793–1843). After taking his medical degree in Dublin, he studied botany in Geneva for seventeen months under the famous Swiss taxonomist Augustin de Candolle. Coulter then went to Mexico in 1824 as physician to a mining company, and spent ten years exploring – visiting California and Arizona – and returning to Ireland with such a huge number of herbarium specimens that he was unable to complete the classification of them all before he died in 1843.

It was his successor at Trinity College Dublin, Professor W H Harvey, who found and described, among Coulter's specimens, *'this fine papaveraceous plant, which I soon ascertained to be distinct from any hitherto recorded from that country ... closer examination proved it to belong to a new and curious genus.'*

After some taxonomic problems, it was decided to call it by the second name of Coulter's great friend and compatriot Dr T Romney Robinson, who after a brilliant academic career, was appointed astronomer-in-charge at Armagh Observatory. It happened that the astronomer's father was a portrait painter, and named his son after his master George Romney. There cannot be many plants called after astronomers, and this exceptionally beautiful glistening white poppy would surely have delighted Romney.

Flourishing close to the Romneya against the same wall is another favourite, *Salvia uliginosa*. Some years it does not even bother to come up, but when it does, it produces stately spikes of exquisite pale blue flowers, splendidly late in the season and long flowering.

The Latin name salvia (for sage), was first used by Pliny, and is derived from the verb 'salvere' to heal. The use of foliage in compresses for the treatment of wounds and injuries is recorded by a number of writers in ancient Greece and Rome, and their authority was widely respected by practitioners of medicine in Europe and the Middle East, right up to the 19th century.

Salvia was originally brought to Britain by the Romans, and was known and valued in Anglo Saxon times. In the early 19th century, *Salvia uliginosa* – which means 'of swamps and marshes' – was found in southern Brazil, Uruguay and Argentinia, described and named by the distinguished English botanist George

Bentham.

Its stems are deeply grooved and its lance-shaped leaves are yellow-green and serrated, while its bright sky blue flowers have a white beeline in the throat to guide insects to pollen and nectar. Another salvia I much admire is the tall growing *Salvia guarantica,* which also comes from South America and Mexico. It has almost navy blue, anise scented flowers, and is prone to - absent-minded appearances like its pale blue cousin, though when it bothers to bloom it does so long into the autumn.

'Linnaeus' colourful language caused him to be somewhat mocked
by his opponents, for example, when he described
what he called 'floral nuptials' and spoke of
the petals of flowers as 'bridal beds, which
the creator has so gloriously arranged, adorned
with such noble bed-curtains, and perfumed with so many sweet
scents, that the bridegroom may celebrate
his nuptials with his bride, with all the greater solemnity'.

ORCHIDMANIA
AND TULIPOMANIA

'During the third half of the 19th century, although orchids poured into London in ever increasing numbers, prices continued to rise. It was not uncommon for several hundred guineas to be paid for one rare plant. The tulip has been described as a flower that has made men mad.'

Another scarlet pampered pet that adds a special dimension to my Living Plant Museum is an orchid. Flower Shows are often sad affairs, with beheaded blooms in plastic cups, not at all in their element; but the first year that Hampton Court burst into this orbit it felt imperative for me to go because the Palace is so superb, with the river Thames showing it off to perfection.

Having admired these utterly exquisite, rarefied and desirable orchid plants from afar, knowing that they are quite beyond my scope, requiring a properly heated greenhouse to themselves and demanding to be the centre of undivided attention twenty four hours a day with exactly the right conditions, how could one cope?

But at Hampton Court on that first day, I spotted the brilliant red *Disa uniflora* and picked it up in its pot to examine its three elegant flowers and to ask about its requirements. The two ladies next to me, who were also admiring it, hissed *'It's gone'*, but knowing that possession is nine points of the law, I tightened my grip. I had not known its name of course, nor that it did not need heat, but on discovering that its only requirement was to be grown sitting in water, it was not to be resisted.

It is called 'The Pride of Table Mountain' from South Africa, and is

Disa uniflora, 'The Pride of Table Mountain'

found on peaty banks of mountain pools and streams, among reeds and grasses at about 4,000 feet, and for this reason might be quite happy in a cold greenhouse. It is described by many authorities as the most beautiful of all terrestrial orchids, and is called Disa after the mythical Queen Disa of Sweden, who was commanded to come before the King of the Sveas, neither naked nor clothed. Thus she came wrapped in a fishing net, a fact reflected in a faintly netted appearance of the upper lip of the flower. In an article from *Curtis Botanical Magazine* of 1844, its habitat is described as *'where the temperature is occasionally as low as 31 degrees and also as high as 96 degrees. They live on the margin of pools of standing water, the drainage of boggy slopes of the mountain, where the roots are immersed.'* It seems they are used to a large allowance of strong sunshine and violent currents of wind; it would be interesting to compete with the climate of the Cape, where *'the stems of individual Disa orchids are two and a half feet high and the flowers five inches and a half from tip to tip of the expanded petals.'*

Luckily, as I had never let go of it, I paid for it and swept it away under the noses of my envious rivals. Its journey home in my car presented some problems, but after buying it a suitable receptacle in which it could safely travel in several inches of water – a soufflé dish as it happens, acquired in a Harrods sale – I zigzagged my way home to Cornwall. Then, making some enquiries, I found a disa enthusiast about 30 miles away and immediately made a date, rushing over to spend a day investigating his methods of cultivation.

He was persuaded to part with a

Disa watsonii, a bright pink variety

few of his disa babies, and they all live up to their waists in water. Not just any old tap water will do because of the chemicals added; it must be very pure rain water, (so of course I had to acquire a rain water butt), with an occasional drop of Maxicrop, the liquid manure which contains seaweed, to a gallon of water.

The disas sit in two round trays with water halfway up the pots, and like to be cocooned in sphagnum moss packed quite loosely round them. They were all repotted with loving care, in a special kind of plastic pot which looks like terracotta (unfortunately they dislike the real thing). Two years on, all have now flowered; one named *Disa tridior* is an orangey yellow; another, *Disa watsonii,* is a rather startling bright pink. They require very little attention growing in their moss, which can be bought dried and is very easy to deal with. Playing it by ear they get repotted when their bedding looks less than fresh, and handling their delicate pure white roots – some spindly thin, others fat and squat, but always shiny and healthy – is pure pleasure, and removing the occasional daring and deadly slug pure sadism.

THE BUTTERFLY 'TABLE MOUNTAIN BEAUTY'

The first description of the disa was by the Swedish physician and botanist Petrus Bergius in 1767, who found a specimen with only one flower, hence the misleading species name *uniflora.* It is, however, quite usual for them to have several flowers on one stem, and they produce the largest flowers of any disa species.

In its native habitat it is pollinated by a butterfly called 'Table Mountain Beauty', which is only attracted to flowers with red or pink pigmentation. There are many fires in this mountain area, which have a profound effect on the vegetation, but where the disa grows the plants benefit as the fires sweep over them, clearing away the shade-producing overgrowth. The orchids are only momentarily affected as there is always water protecting their tubers, and the following year will bloom with even bigger flowers, helped by the increased sunlight and nutrients.

FREDERICH WELWITSCH

Disa orchids were later discovered by a dedicated botanist, Frederich Welwitsch, who was born in Austria in 1806. His father wanted him to be a lawyer, but in spite of having his allowance withdrawn he managed to become a doctor, and to continue his passionate pursuit of botany.

Welwitsch was employed to collect plants in the Azores and Cape Verde

Islands, but somehow was diverted on his way and stayed in Portugal for some years. Here he scoured the country for plants, and eventually built up a herbarium of 9,000 specimens. In 1850 the Portuguese Government, under Queen Donna Maria, sent him on a scientific expedition to its West African possessions, where he spent seven years assiduously investigating and collecting plants – including about sixty new varieties of orchid, as well as the Disa.

ORCHIDMANIA

Orchidmania must be the worst kind of epidemic in the botanic world, worst for the plants anyway. Gathering strength through the early part of the 19th century from the demanding private collectors, a number of commercial nurseries found it profitable to send professional orchid hunters to South America, India, Burma, Madagascar, New Guinea and the Straits Settlements. Terrible slaughter was carried out in some areas, where thousands of trees were slashed and denuded of their epiphytic orchids.

These orchids, needing support, grow on other plants but without drawing nourishment from them. Certain areas of Central and South America have had no naturalised orchids since. So little was understood about the needs of these precious plants that very few survived the journey home or their treatment on arrival. The growers treated then exactly as the terrestrial orchids, in airless stove houses, plunging them into tanners' bark or sawdust, with the result that they died in their thousands.

It was Sir Joseph Banks, who in 1817 first devised a method which suited them, in his use of wicker baskets and moss. Mr William Cattley of Barnet, who was a botanist and friend of Banks, was intrigued by the packing material used to protect some of his other tropical plants; he planted it and was rewarded when eventually orchid flowers of unimaginable beauty appeared, quite unlike anything seen before. The orchid was named after him, *Cattleya labiata,* and became the most attractive orchid so far cultivated.

Eighteen years later its habitat was discovered near Rio de Janeiro, and just twelve plants were collected before the whole area was destroyed for coffee plantations and the production of charcoal. A landmark in orchid history was made when it was rediscovered again, fifty years later in Pernambuco. *Cattleya vera,* the true cattleya, is also attributed to Allan Cunningham and James Bowie when Banks sent them off to South America.

RECORD OF A PASSION

Arthur Swinson wrote about one of the most serious cases of orchidmania, calling his book *Frederick Sander, The Orchid King, Record of a Passion.* Queen Victoria

Dactylorhiza - a wild orchid - see page 149

had appointed Frederick Sander as the Royal Orchid Grower; the Romanoffs created him Baron of the Holy Roman Empire; the Royal Horticultural Society awarded him the coveted Victorian Medal of Honour, and most of the crowned heads of Europe were his customers, but it was the editor of Punch who named him *'The Orchid King'*.

Sander was born in 1847 in Bremen in north Germany, but at the age of sixteen he came to England, arriving with half a crown in his pocket; his total wealth. He met Benedict Roezl, the traveller,

naturalist and plant hunter, who introduced him to the orchid, and that was the moment he decided that orchids were to be his life's work; a true plantaholic.

He fell on his feet from his first job as nurseryman in a village in Kent, which bordered a wealthy estate; here he met and married the owner's daughter which was a most happy union, and Elizabeth Fearnley's father settled a large sum of money on her.

SANDER'S ORCHID NURSERY

In due course Sander moved to St

Albans and started his Orchid Nursery. His progress is recorded by a horticultural journalist in 1891, one Frederick Boyle, who visited what he calls *'this orchid farm, for here alone in Europe, as far as I know are three acres of ground occupied by orchids exclusively.'* He says: *'Our road passes beneath a high glazed arch. Some thirty feet beyond, it is stopped by a wall of tufa and stalactite which rises to the lofty roof and compels the traveller to turn left or right. Water pours down it and falls trickling into a narrow pool beneath. Its rough front is studded with orchids from crest to base. There are Cymbidiums, arching long sprays of green and chocolate; thickets of Dendrobes set with flowers beyond counting, ivory and rose, purple and orange; scarlet Anthuriums; huge clumps of Phaius and evergreen Calanthe with a score of spikes rising from their broad leaves; Cypripediums of quaint form and striking half tones of colour; Oncidiums which droop their slender garlands a yard long, golden yellow and spotted, purple and white a hundred tints ... over all climbing up the spandrils of the roof in full blaze of sunshine, is Vanda teres which will drape those bare iron rods presently with crimson and pink and gold.'*

You can tell Boyce was mightily impressed, and that was only a minute corner of Sander's great establishment. He now found himself in a corridor some 400 feet long, *'ceilinged with baskets of Mexican orchids; to the right lay workshops to the left glasshouses, while beyond, workmen were building a magnificent glass structure into which visitors will step* *direct from the train. Cases were received into the Importing Room by fifties and hundreds from every quarter of the orchid world ... they hang in dense bunches from the roof, they lie a foot thick on every board, and two feet below orchids everywhere.'*

Boyle asked the origin of a particular load of orchids and was told that eighty cases had come in from Burma, and at that moment a boy came in to announce that fifty cases from Mexico would arrive at Waterloo at 2.30pm. Sander insisted that all orchids must be met on arrival by someone of experience; bad handling could result in the loss of a whole consignment, and the wrath of Frederick Sander on such occasions was terrible to behold.

The unpacking was equally important, with each layer of moss and shavings being carefully lifted; the packing material was occasionally valuable in itself, (as with the cattleya), and sometimes – not so welcome – emerging from the packaging would be ships' rats, scorpions, centipedes, stinging ants, spiders, giant cockroaches and even snakes.

Boyle was further astonished to find twelve glasshouses 180 feet long, filled with *Odontoglossum crispum* in no less than 22,000 pots. But there was more: *'a magnificent structure, 300 feet long, 26 feet wide and eighteen high to exhibit the warm species of orchid in bloom.'*

Sander's passion was fully indulged in his orchid establishment, and Boyle's enthusiastic contemporary description is graphic enough. Many more letters are quoted in Swinson's book, and he gives a vivid picture of the frightful behaviour of orchid collectors, egged on by their scheming employers to obtain the best and the most, very often hunting in the same area as each other, paying spies, and lying and cheating to out-do their rivals.

SEVERAL HUNDRED GUINEAS FOR A RARITY

No wonder that prices went through the roof; during the third half of the 19th century, athough orchids poured into London in ever increasing numbers, prices continued to rise and especially for novelties; it was not uncommon for several hundred guineas to be paid for just one rare plant.

An article in the *Gardener's Chronicle* stated that *'collectors in all quarters are ransacking the forests to send home plants'* and the Director of the Botanic Gardens in Zurich wrote: *'Not satisfied with taking 300 or 500 specimens of a fine orchid, they must scour the whole country and leave nothing for many miles around – the environs of Quito and Cuenca have been perfectly plundered and no collector henceforth will find any Odontoglossums there.'*

The largest orchid ever discovered came from Malaysia, *Gramatophyllum speciosum*. Sander had heard of it, and was determined to have it on his stand at the Colombian

Exhibition in Chicago. When it was collected from the jungles of Penang, it weighed one ton; it was divided into two, one half being donated to the Singapore Botanical Gardens, where it was reputed to have produced 3,000 flowers simultaneously.

His own portion created an enormous sensation at the show and later he presented it to Kew, where it was said to be, (and I believe still is), the largest orchid in Europe.

Orchidmania continued into the new century, but slowly declined. However, Sander adored displaying his collections at shows, Chelsea being his favourite. In 1912 his group occupied 700 square feet; brilliant varieties of perfect blooms ranged bank upon bank, rivalling his greatest efforts of the past; he was on hand to be greeted by the King and Queen, to demonstrate his linguistic powers to ambassadors, to receive a Large Gold Medal and a Special Silver Cup, and to move again in the splendid international scene that so delighted him.

He was still the Orchid King gaining new awards in the face of tremendous foreign competition and lists his achievements in a publication which came out for the International Show: *'At the first Temple Show held in London in 1888, we were awarded a silver cup, which was then and for several following years, the premier award. At every Temple Show since, including the last one in 1911, we showed large groups, for which we received in the 24 years, 12 Silver*

Tulipa saxatilis, the Candia Tulip

Cups and 13 Gold Medals, and in addition were awarded in 1905 the Veitchian Cup for the finest group in the Exhibition.'

TULIPOMANIA

When it comes to tulipomania there are just so many tulips of such beauty and interest, it is hard to know where to begin. Small numbers of different varieties grown in pots are a great adornment here in early summer. There are granite crocks near the house which I fill with miniature tulips, chosen from the mouthwatering descriptions in Paul Christian's *Rare Plants* catalogue; here are interesting species such as *Tulipa wilsoniana,* which he says are *'of dwarf stature*

with prostrate wavy, waxy bluish leaves and vivid currant-red flowers in May. Easy. Garden. Our stock turns out to be wild source material, collected by Paul Sintenis almost 100 years ago from Turkmenistan, and only 50 pence each.'

Of *T maximowiczii (linifolia)* he says *'a slender and dwarf species with flowers of brilliant vermillion red; this is a dazzling colour in full sun when the flowers open widely to their full 6cm diameter and show their large jet-black centre. The leaves lie prostrate, or nearly so, on the soil surface and are glaucous with a red-lined, undulated margin.'*

A very special tulip is called *Tulipa saxatilis,* which means found among rocks. This comes from Crete and is sometimes confused with *T. bakeri,* which is considered by some authorities to be a cultivar, arising from the very similar *T. saxatilis.* The

Tulipa 'White Triumphator'

scented globe-shaped flowers are pinkish mauve, the outer petals flushed with green and the inner with only a thin green rib. Grown in a stone trough, it is quite a spectacle.

On my terrace, two large, square, stone pots are filled with the long-flowering *Tulipa 'White Triumphator'*; lily-flowered tulips are quite the most elegant and seem to die more gracefully than any others. They are decorative until the last petal falls. An assembly of these stately tulips, ramrod straight and immensely tall, are incomparable – they flower with a totally confident air of holding the stage unrivalled. They are the best, and they know it.

ACCEPTING THE INEVITABLE

The downside of tulips is that you can never get them to repeat their performance two years running. It seems that they are processed to do it once magnificently, and after that

72

no matter how much you feed them as they slowly and sadly die down, they will only be second best. You must accept the inevitable and buy new stock every year.

ANNA PAVORD

The tulip was the ultimate status symbol among botanists in the 16th century. It provided enough history for Anna Pavord to write a whole book, *The Tulip* full of fascinating information about its origins and record. As she says on her book, *'It is the story of a flower that has made men mad. Greed, desire, anguish, devotion have all played their part in the development of the tulip from a wild flower of the Asian steppes to the world wide phenomenon it is today.'* Indeed, she describes what sound remarkably like the first plantaholics.

What made the tulip irresistible was the totally unpredictable trick it had of changing its colour. It may have started out as a plain coloured red tulip, and might emerge the following spring with its petals feathered and flamed in intricate patterns of white and deep red. These *'broken flowers',* as they were known, were madly desirable and commanded incredible prices, but out of a batch of a hundred tulips only one or two might break – in spite of every one of those bulbs receiving exactly the same treatment.

Anna Pavord tells us the story of the tulip's behaviour in her book *The Tulip*. This was a mystery which obsessed tulip growers and caused the wildest of Tulipomania for several hundred years. Every possible theory was applied but any success remained impossible to explain. It wasn't until 1920 after years and years of research, that it was discovered that a humble virus was responsible, and that the even more mundane aphid busily spread it about.

THE FIRST APPEARANCE

Tulips first appeared in Turkey in the 16th century, growing along a corridor either side of the line of Latitude 40N. European travellers brought back news of the *'Lils rouges,'* so prized by the Turks; these were not lilies but tulips, and belonged to the *Liliaceae* family.

The tulip was probably brought to Europe by Ogier Ghiselin de Busbecq, Ambassador of the Holy Roman Empire to Suleiman the Magnificent, who saw them at Adrianople in 1554. Carolus Clusius, the much travelled botanist and Professor at the University of Leiden had seed from Busbecq, and possibly sent tulips to England from Vienna.

Protestant Huguenots from Flanders also brought us tulips, in the second half of the 16th century. Conrad Gesner described some tulips he had seen growing in Augsburg, in 1559: *'the tulip had sprung from a seed which had come from Constantinople or as others say from Cappadocia.'*

Tulipa 'White Triumphator'

'At the height of tulipomania in 1635, a single tulip bulb was sold for the following items: 4 tons of wheat, 8 tons of rye, 1 bed, 4 oxen, 8 pigs, 12 sheep, 1 suit of clothes, 2 casks of wine, 4 tons of beer, 2 tons of butter, 1,000 pounds of cheese and 1 silver drinking cup.'

6

—MOSTLY CLIMBERS—

'Because my garden is so small, vertical plants are extra valuable, so I will begin with the king of climbers which has to be the lapageria – named after Napoleon's Empress Josephine – for her maiden name of Lapagerie.'

I t was in 1802 that Hippolyto Ruiz and Josepho Pavon, Spanish plant collectors in South America, published their *Flora Peruviana et Chilensis.* Describing *Lapageria rosea* they say: *'There is no question whatever that the copihue* (its local name), *is considered the most beautiful flower in our Flora. The intense red of its hanging flowers sparkle amid the dark leaves of the forests, making a proud adornment to our woods; it is for this reason it has been given the honour of being our national flower. In the hot houses of Europe the lapageria has been known since the last century, without ever having reached any significant importance in those countries.*

An elite member of the Liliaceae family, the genus of one species only, was named after Napoleon's Empress Josephine, for her maiden name of Lapagerie, in compliment to her for her

many services to botany; she greatly encouraged the cultivation of exotic plants by growing them herself in her garden at Malmaison, near Paris.'

John Smith, Curator of the Royal Gardens at Kew wrote in *Curtis Botanical Magazine 'that not until 1847 were they favoured with a plant from Concepción (Chile), through the kindness of Rd Wheelwright Esq, an American gentleman, who has been instrumental in establishing steam navigation in the Pacific, and who thus enjoyed superior means for the transport to England.*

The following year, Messrs Veitch and Sons were no less fortunate in importing it through their Cornish plant collector Mr Thomas Lobb, but though extremely flourishing it still had not flowered in 1849.' (sic)

I cannot improve upon the detailed description given by Ruiz et Pavon, translated for me from the

Spanish by a friend: *'Deep in the earth a rhizome extends horizontally with knots and small roots; from the knots grow the aerial shoots, the thickness of a feather quill, at first tender like asparagus, but which harden later. Specifically it is a terrestrial plant, but its search for the sun has enabled it to evolve into a climber, which saves it from extinction in the darkness of the impenetrable rain forests; the shoot grows vertically at first, with no difference from non climbing plants, but during its growth it inclines laterally, taking a horizontal position; the free extreme end is arched and makes circular movements in a clockwise direction, looking for a support; this circular movement originates from the accelerated growth of the cells on the outer side of the shoot, while those on the inner side are retarded.*

This phenomenal growth is the cause of the twisting, which allows the shoot to attach itself to any suitable support and thus continue ever upwards from left to right towards the sun, preventing vertical growth and facilitating its novel method of climbing and attaching itself.

The flowers of the Copihue, also known as the Chilean Bellflower and Chile Bells, appear singly in summer but in the autumn will often bloom in clusters from the axils of the upper leaves; the tiny bud shows little promise of its future splendour but, little by little the red colour develops, while the outer bracts retain some of their green colour; the carmine-red waxy bells conceal the nectar sacs, which are finally penetrated by birds with long pointed beaks, which thus pollinates the flower.' If only.

PLANT IQ

Ruiz and Pavon's saga of this remarkable plant behaviour, written in Spanish nearly two hundred years ago, inspires one greatly to admire the lapageria's one-track mind – one has to say almost its thought process – which has outwitted nature's thoughtlessness, careless for its survival. If there is such a thing in the plant world as IQ , (and I have long suspected it), the lapageria must rate very highly. This readiness to accommodate its ways has enabled it to choose where to settle; fortunate indeed are its fervent admirers if they have chosen an agreeable and fitting site for this capricious, but wholly desirable plant.

LAPAGERIA DIET

It is a challenge to accommodate such a determined climber. I have researched its requirements to the merest whim to make it feel at home. As if in a rain forest I water its leaves, using the hose like a fierce and frequent storm. It likes acid soil so I give it very tactile, friable, ericaceous mix with sharp sand and crumbled cow manure, with plenty of fragmented charcoal for extra drainage. In the spring it is topped up with trace elements, cow manure mulch and a sprinkling of dried blood. The lapageria's response to this is often to send up its 'asparagus' shoots, almost before the heavy rain shower is over. Unfortunately, they are the slug's 3 star gourmet choice.

THE MEALY BUG

This was all before the very hot summer when the dreaded mealy bug moved in. This devilish pest is a scale insect which seals itself on to the backs of the leaves and sucks the delicious juices out.

The only successful method of dealing with it (now that the Volke/tobacco mixture, which used to be effective, is banned by the EC) is to wash each leaf with soapy water – an activity which might take you the rest of your life. I had, at that time, several lapageria plants, not only the ordinary red but the exquisite white, which can have greeny sepals or faintly flushed pink – mine was the latter. There was also the pale, flesh pink – and best of all, a unique and ravishing picotee, which is white edged with scarlet. In spite of all my efforts, it died.

I doubt I will ever find another.

LAPAGERIA – FROM SEED

However, plantaholics are never daunted for long – and I told my sad tale to Noel Gieleghem of Napa, California – a specialist lapageria grower – with whom I sometimes communicate on the internet, who told me that the only way I was likely to replace it was to grow one from seed. He described many varieties of which I had never heard, such as those with streaks and spots, and other pale-flowered forms stippled with violet, striped with green or – wait for it – picoteed with red.

'Would I like some seeds?' he asked. *'Yes, please!'* Thus, about two years ago this valuable little registered packet arrived filled with them. I bought fifty pots and Bill and I took half each with two seeds to a pot. (Never mind if I might have to move house).

Noel said they could take weeks or months to germinate (if they ever did) and between three to five years to flower. Although I was disappointed, I was also relieved that they did not all survive, and that now we only had ten little potential picotee seedlings.

They would require a great deal of attention and space, indeed they needed a whole wall, already occupied by my other precious pets. There was only one remedy that I could see – I would have to build a new glasshouse for them.

The only possible place for this was on the south-facing side of the garage, opposite where my plants sometimes convalesced. The compost heap was here as well and the site of occasional bonfires. It had been a sort of glory hole, like an In Tray labelled *'TOO DIFFICULT'.* But no longer.

This last bastion of my garden, that you might call the bottom of it, (but certainly no fairies here), this furthest away or easterly section by the garage, had never been secured, and this was the moment to erect the barricades, up drawbridges, and cocoon my garden with more, dark green fencing and evergreen creepers. This would muffle a particularly vocal household of periodic yells and shrieks, which occasionally assaults my ears from the all too close council estate. It will be a major upheaval, including demolishing a huge and hideous old elder which excluded the light, and which I had long wanted to be rid of. With the compost resited and hedges planted on the perimeter, there would then be a sheltered and salubrious dwelling for the young lapagerias to grace. It was a race against time as the little seedlings had already put up some climbing tendrils, and they would not be allowed to attach themselves too tightly to anything – until I was ready for them.

It was a several day job for Bill, who directed his team of Patrick and Andrew. In no time the elder tree was safely down, and cut up into manageable pieces for disposal in Bill's trailer or the bonfire. New fencing was put up and painted, and a new site gouged out of the bank on my border to rehouse the compost. There was also time to trim some more untidy old elders behind the garage (the previous owners of my territory must have had elder as well as thrift mania).

I planted more Banksia roses to climb up the neatly trimmed stumps and cover the garage – growing towards the one already there, approaching from the adjacent wall; how delightful to have the whole structure covered.

In spite of numerous setbacks (such as Bill having to go into hospital, the greenhouse man getting appendicitis and the weather taking a sharp downturn) the new greenhouse was eventually in place, the potential picotee parents installed, and Bill had recovered.

JOSEPHINE LAPAGERIE

The lapageria, being named after Josephine Bonaparte (her maiden name of Lapagerie), brings her frequently to mind when I am admiring its exquisite, late summer festoons and garlands of flowers, almost too beautiful to be real. Her particularity as a botanist or plantswoman are rarely described, except for her renowned collection and love of roses.

Josephine had to have at least one plant of all the varieties of rose then known, (about 250). She was more famous, perhaps, for her extravagance and habit of buying 36 hats at a time, yet she had almost a botanical garden at Malmaison with many unusual plants housed in a huge 'serre' (or conservatory) she had built for them.

THE IMPORTANCE OF LETTERS

It is difficult to imagine life without modern means of communication, but in Joseph Banks' day it was all done in handwriting. Among his copious collection of letters was just one which linked him directly with Empress Josephine. It was written in French on 20th April 1803, by her botanist Etienne Pierre Ventenat, to thank Sir Joseph for all he had done to enrich her garden and hoping that she could count on his help in the future. Josephine sent with this the first part of *Le Jardin de Malmaison* promising others to follow, and offering the first five fasciculi of Redouté's *Les Liliacées*.

Visiting Malmaison the other day to investigate what remained of this historic old garden, I took a copy of Josephine's letter to Banks for the Curator of Malmaison, who had no knowledge of any such correspondence, which was very disappointing.

There was only a small piece of the rose garden left. However, there was the recently-restored round summer house where Napoleon had worked, and the Marengo cedar of Lebanon planted by Josephine herself when she had news of Napoleon's victory.

The Chateau of Malmaison has now been made into a museum, with a great deal of the original furniture returned, and filled with nostalgic memories of their short time there together.

JAMES LEE

James Lee, a brilliant botanist and scholar, was the leading nurseryman of England in Josephine's time, and a great friend of Banks. His Vineyard Nursery, at Hammersmith in London, stood where the Olympia building stands today. Lee was the first to translate Carl Linnaeus' *Philosophia Botanica*, which he called *Introduction to Botany*.

Among the letters which Lee wrote to Linnaeus he remarks, *'The passion for plants in this country increases every day and I have the pleasure to tell you that your sexual system is more and more admired and by none more than your affectionate friend and obedient humble servant James Lee.'*

He adds that *'Mr Banks' Herbarium is certainly the greatest and I believe the best that was ever collected; it is the daily labour of many servants to paste them on paper, and Banks and Solander spend four or five hours every day in describing and arranging them.'*

This gives us (and Linnaeus) an interesting insight into Banks' occupations.

James Lee corresponded with people worldwide, who would send him seed from which he grew new and exotic plants, and established a reputation for supplying all the great gardens of Europe.

The Vineyard Nursery was the first to receive seed from Botany Bay in 1788, and the saw-leaved Banksia – *Banksia serrata* – was the first plant to be raised from it. Sadly, this is a plant I have tried and failed with, but on my pilgrimage visit to Australia I could not resist buying a large collection of dried banksias (how could I add to my luggage at the last moment this awkward and unwieldy package?) and I have them in my house in an old Chinese jug, surrounded with dried eucalyptus from my own tree to make them feel at home.

JOSEPHINE'S EXTRAVAGANCE

The Vineyard Nursery supplied Josephine with £2,600 worth of plants in 1803 and £700 worth in 1811, just two examples of her amazing extravagance.

An Admiralty Order went out to all officers of the Fleet *'that should any enemy prize captured on the high seas contain plants or seed addressed to the Empress, their safe and speedy passage was to be assured.'* It is possible that Banks had something to do with this order, the wars seem to have been very gentlemanly in those days.

Another snippet of information was to be found in William Paul's *The Rose Garden: 'The late Mr Kennedy of Lee and Kennedy's Vineyard Nurseries, Hammersmith, was provided with passports to go and come during the war, in order that he might superintend the formation of the garden'* (at Malmaison).

It is tantalising not to find any more revealing letters. Josephine clearly associated with all these men of science, in touch with each other and Banks. The voyages of the 18th century, by many European botanists as well as English, resulted in the discovery of unusual species of interest to them all and welcome homes were found for the introductions at Le Jardin des Plantes in Paris as well as The Royal Gardens at Kew.

One of these plants, brought back to Josephine from the scientific expedition sent by Napoleon to explore Australia in 1800, was named *Kennedya rubicunda* after John Kennedy of the Vineyard Nurseries, who helped her create the gardens at Malmaison.

It was during this expedition (described in the later chapter on Australia) that Nicholas Baudin, in command, met Mathew Flinders of HMS *Investigator* at Encounter Bay, south of Adelaide.

I found a large plant of the *kennedya* displayed as a stock plant, and had considerable difficulty in persuading the nursery to part with it. It grows up a south-facing wall just below my office and requires a great deal of attention, wrapping up with fleece in the winter, slug prevention and so on. I admire it for its historic interest but have never warmed to it, perhaps because regrettably, it rather resembles a runner bean.

Another letter which links Sir Joseph directly with the Bonapartes is dated 8th May 1802, and further indicates the spheres of Banks' activities. It is from Sir Charles Blagden, Secretary to the Royal Society (of which Banks was President) who writes *'without delay'* to recount an important conversation he had with Napoleon, chiefly about Banks.

Blagden had been invited to dine with the First Consul (as Napoleon then was). At the reception Napoleon came up to him and enquired after Banks' health, and when the former was coming to Paris. Sir Charles explained about

Passiflora x exoniensis, the Banana Passion Fruit

Banks' severe attacks of gout, but said he was much better. Napoleon then asked what age Banks was, and when told he was in his 60th year replied *'That is not old'*, in a tone which implied that Banks should overcome all difficulties and make him a visit.

THE PASSIONFLOWER

Perhaps the next most exotic climber is the passionflower. The name was given by early Spanish missionaries in South America, who likened the corona filaments to Christ's crown of thorns – the five anthers to his five wounds, the three styles to the nails – and who saw the sepal, petals and leaves as all representing some part of the passion.

P. caerulea came into Europe in 1699, and is accredited with the Passion legend. It is very hardy, but although the blue and white flowers are beautiful, it grows in such an untidy way it is not an adornment.

One of its cultivars – bred in Exeter, England, and growing in my greenhouse – is called 'Constance Elliott'. She is most unusual with green flowers, white filaments and green stamens with purple stigma and makes an arresting sight.

A STROKE OF LUCK

As usual, the most interesting plants are the least obtainable. However, visiting Cambridge Botanic Garden one very hot day, what should be flowering away in the conservatory but the most brilliant scarlet *P. vitifolia* which has fragrant flowers from May to September and is said to be the best of all the scarlet passionflowers.

My luck was in, as the head gardener actually had a small plant he could sell me. In fact I was their first customer – as the edict allowing sales had only just been issued.

Another most unusual dark red passionflower is *P. alata,* which grows wild in Brazil and has edible fruits. Besides having ovate leaves – quite unlike a normal passionflower, its multiple corona filaments are striped obliquely, in purple and white reminding one of a Venetian gondola, too exotic for words.

Another very elegant variety which grows away happily in my greenhouse is *P. citrina,* covered in quite small, bright yellow flowers which spring from tube-like buds reminiscent of those short, press-button umbrellas. It has only recently

Passiflora citrina

been discovered in West Honduras and East Guatamala and is one of the very few yellow passionflowers.

THE BANANA PASSION FLOWER

P. sanguinolenta, from the mountains of Equador, is a further small but very free-flowering variety. A larger, pale pink flower, similar in form to *P. citrina,* it also produces the most elegant fruits, shaped like pink-bordered Chinese lanterns. It grows rather wildly (in my greenhouse, all mixed up with *Clematis florida and C. florida* Sieboldii*)* and was introduced by Maxwell Tylden Masters (1833–1907) during his travels in South America.

Far the best is *P. x exoniensis,* which has very large pink flowers. This is known as the Banana Passion Flower and is a cross between *P antioquiensis x mollissima* raised in 1870 by Veitch, both of which are more readily available at nurseries. It is supposed to set fruit (banana-shaped) in mild counties of England, but it has yet to do so with me.

83

The Banana Passion Flower was one of many plants to be seen in Agatha Christie's garden at Greenway in Devon, recently presented to the National Trust, where it grows up the front of her house, outside. It must be the largest passionflower. Its magical, vivid salmon-pink blooms remind one of Chinese waxy paper parasol. It flowers at the north and darker end of my greenhouse from May, and even now the following April it still has an occasional brilliant blossom.

Sometimes its leaves go very pale and I realise with foreboding that it must be repotted – a mammoth task requiring considerable dexterity, as the plant has to remain suspended by its many climbing stems. Bill usually manages to wrestle it out while I hold the pot on its side; then a new and even bigger pot must be filled with all of its favourite mixture of John Innes, lots of grit, some of my special compost and soil and extra trace elements, fish blood and bone and anything else I can think of. I wasn't at all pleased with the result, and wished we had been able to tease its roots out better. Bill looked at me and said he knew I would worry about it all night if we did not redo it all over again, so we did.

Passionflowers are another of the dreaded mealy bug or scale insect's favourite hosts. When Bill arrives for work, his first action is to peer into and behind every leaf of both lapagerias and passionflowers and seek out the brutes. We use a very

soft toothbrush and soapy water and I often spray with some vicious insecticide which I have left over from earlier days. Anything to outwit them.

BONPLANT AND VON HUMBOLDT

P. vitifolia was introduced by the French botanist Aime Bonplant, who collected plants for Empress Josephine. He made friends with Alexander Baron von Humboldt, a German naturalist and traveller, who invited him to join his expedition to South America as botanist.

Von Humboldt was a remarkable young man of aristocratic birth who, like Joseph Banks, paid for his travels out of his personal fortune. He was inspired by Captain James Cook's travels, and passionately wanted to visit a country where he would see *'a grand and wild nature.'* He also wanted to study the laws that brought order to the natural world; to analyse and measure electricity, magnetism, barometric pressure; and to investigate the interaction of all the forces of nature. And above all he wanted to collect plants and animals.

The two arrived in Venezuela in 1799, and spent the next four years in great hardship exploring the Orinoco jungle, the Amazon, the Andes and Mexico. Their reward was a collection of around 6,000 new plant species, more than half of them new to science.

Von Humboldt and Bonplant were

helped by Jose Celastino Mutis (1732-1809), a physician of Cadiz, who went to South America in 1760 and settled in Bogota, from where he sent plant specimens to Linnaeus and his son.

'This great botanist', he is decribed by von Humboldt *'whose gifts impose upon us an eternal gratitude.'* Mutisia *grandiflora,* a climber of the Compositae family which *'rises above the trees like the smilax and bauhinia'* and some species of bignonia was named after him. This is a scrambler more than a climber and I tried it out after seeing it at Greenway, but it needs a whole plant to itself to lean on and has rather boring daisy-like flowers. I found I could live without it.

SUPREME ACHIEVEMENT

Von Humboldt's observations resulted in what is considered to be the most significant scientific survey of South America ever undertaken. 200 years before anyone had invented the word 'ecology', he found that the felling of trees and disruption of forests by the native population guaranteed a shortage of water and fuel.

He further discovered that as you climbed high into the Andes (or whenever the climate altered) plants changed their characters in a vertical progression. Von Humboldt also made wonderful maps, illustrating the changing zones of plants and the basic principles of plant geography.

His description of the distribution of plants and animals was very closely connected with the origin of the species, and Charles Darwin was much influenced and inspired by his conclusions.

Von Humboldt writes with warmth and enthusiasm of what he owes Aime Bonplant, and their friendship shines through his words: *'The plants have been gathered by us two, in spite of astounding labour, my geology researches have been made possible by Bonplant's devoted work, often at the expense of sleep, he alone has prepared and dried almost 60,000 specimens of plants.'*

He describes how they were often enclosed for whole months suffering the burning climate of these regions, the multitudes of venomous insects, the damp air and endless rain and the lack of drying paper. All these contributed to the frightful conditions, and the enormous difficulties in arranging the transport of their collections thousands of miles – especially as they were not backed by Governments, but dependent on their own resources. Von Humboldt writes:

'If this work is one day considered to have contributed to the advancement of botany it should be attributed to the 'zele actif' of M Bonplant'.

Before returning to France in 1805, von Humboldt and Aime Bonplant travelled north to Washington to visit Thomas Jefferson, to present their respects and express their admiration for the liberalism of his ideas in setting up the first free republic of America.

They were invited to Montecello, and the visit coincided with the departure of Lewis and Clark on their westward exploration of the Missouri River towards the Pacific Ocean.

On his return, Bonplant was appointed Botanist to Empress Josephine and given charge of her collections at Malmaison and Navarre. Sadly, my plant of *P. vitifolia* – the beautiful scarlet passionflower which Bonplant introduced – died eventually, after a great struggle, from lack of light in the winter months.

FUCHSIAS

Also attributed to Bonplant is another plant to which I am much addicted, and grow in several places in my garden. It is *Fuchsia microphylla,* a minute bright pink bloom with tiny leaves, which never seems to stop flowering. It is the only fuchsia that I really like. Even when it is cut down by frost, it pauses for a few weeks and then triumphantly recovers.

Fuchsias were first mentioned in the 14th century, when plants were of most value for food, and it is known that the Incas cultivated them for their edible berries. The first recorded fuchsia was discovered by the botanist Father Carole Plumier (1646-1704), a French Catholic Priest from the Order of Minims. He found a plant, now called *Fuchsia triphylla,* drawings of which appeared in *Nova Plantarum Americanum Genera (1703),* although the actual specimens were lost in a shipwreck.

Plumier named his discovery after a famous German Doctor of Medicine, Leonhart Fuchs, and the first plant given to The Royal Botanic Gardens at Kew was credited to a Captain Firth in 1788.

THE MARMALADE BUSH

The Cambridge Botanic Garden first introduced me to the *Streptosolen jamesonii,* the marmalade bush, a beautiful scrambler and very much a match with Mr Frank Cooper's best – having small, bright orange, tubular flowers in great profusion and belonging to the potato family *Solonaceae.*

It is a very well-behaved plant which requires practically no attention. At the moment my marmalade bush must be amazed to find hundreds of little pink *Passiflora sanguinolenta* flowers from its neighbour masquerading among its foliage. There will be something of a clash when its own flowers appear.

It was found by John Miers in South America in the early 19th century, and introduced by William Lobb in the 1840's.

JULIEN DE LA BILLARDIERE

Finding suitable climbers to cover my pergola was quite a challenge. *Billardiera longiflora* did well until its light was dimmed by *Stauntonia hexaphylla,* an evergreen twiner of

Syd.ᵐ Edwards Del.   Pub. by S. Curtis Walworth Nov.ʳ 1.1812.   F. Sansom Sc.

Billardiera longiflora by Sydenham Edwards - Curtis's Bot. Mag. 1812

Billardiera longiflora or Blueberry as seen in my garden

great enthusiasm.

The Billardiera is grown especially for its fine purple fruits which cover the plant in late summer, and before this it has little yellow flowers among the lance-shaped leaves which are evergreen.

It was found in Tasmania and named for the French botanist Jacques Julien de La Billardiere, who wrote a book on the flora of Australia in 1804. He visited Banks in London in 1785 at the request of the French, who were mounting an expedition under the command of the navigator La Perouse.

Perouse and his fleet disappeared, and in 1791 the French sent a second, ill-fated expedition to search for them. La Billardiere went as naturalist, taking advice from Banks on how best to preserve and record his findings. The expedition disintegrated with the politics of the Revolution, and when La Billardiere returned, his collections had been lost – although they turned up later in the hands of the British.

Banks used his formidable powers of tact and persuasion to get the collections returned intact to the young French botanist, which at one time had been presented to and accepted by Queen Charlotte.

The *stauntonia* (which several paragraphs ago was suffocating my billardieras) has quite leathery leaves and attractive racemes of scented flowers, charming in their greeny white, violet-tinted colouring.

Once it gets going it climbs at a furious speed, and covers its allotted wall in leaps and bounds making a huge mound of greenery topped with new shoots which have nowhere left to go. Bill spends hours on his ladder trimming its enthusiasm, but it teasingly produces

new tendrils almost at once, waving cheerfully from the top of the wall.

It is very similar to (and often sold as), *Holboelia latifolia,* and after a really sunny summer it produces a huge sausage-shaped fruit, which from its early pale green develops deep purple as it ripens.

Its name comes from Sir George Staunton, who accompanied Lord Macartney on the Embassy expedition to China in 1791.

Staunton was a friend of Banks, and as an amateur botanist was eager to collect plants to bring home. Banks wrote him some helpful instructions on how to go about this, but could not conceal his disappointment at what came back when he found that the specimens had been *'indifferently selected, and as ill managed in drying,'* and that there were no botanical notes on the structure of the plants.

Schisandra grandiflora var. rubriflora is a very rewarding climber, clambering over the pergola; there

Holboellia latifolia or Stauntonia

Schisandra grandiflora var. rubriflora, cousin to the Magnolia

have to be two plants, male and female, to get the delightful spike of red berries in the autumn. It is deciduous unfortunately, but has pretty red petioles and flowers. It looks particularly attractive with the tiny evergreen leaves of the billardiera growing through it.

It was very difficult to get different sex plants, discussing at length with the nurseryman which was which. It has decided, entirely its own idea, to scramble up its cousin, the now leafy magnolia, and gazing up from under the tree you see the whole canopy dotted in bright red stars.

It is to be found in West China and was named by Alfred Rehder, a German botanist, who worked at the Arnold Arboretum, Boston, USA.

A relation of the *schisandra* is the *Kadsura japonica* belonging to the same family; this was growing up one of the supports in the temperate house at Kew, labelled *coccinea* but with pale green–yellow flowers and leaves; it seemed possible that the label belonged to the next door plant.

It was unknown to me but it looked extremely promising as a new evergreen climber. It was finally tracked down, and two plants of it with luscious red foliage (labelled as above, but with *suromi* added) were very much more coccinea (scarlet), than the one at Kew.

It comes from Japan and instead of red spikes it has fruits which Von Siebold describes as *'viscid tasteless and uneatable,'* and it is used by

Japanese ladies to cleanse their hair of the pomatum they so largely employ. It will suit me very well.

At the feet of these climbers grows *Convolvulus sabatius,* valuable in many ways as an excellent ground creeper, and particularly because it does not get massacred by slugs. According to *Curtis Botanical Magazine,* it is *'a very pretty and little known species of convolvulus detected in the interior of northern Africa, near Constantine'.* It flowers away all summer, sometimes following the other climbers up the trellis, then dies down over winter but appears again – well multiplied the next season. *Convolvulus cneorum* is also useful here with its beautiful silvery foliage covered with delicate white, tinted pink blooms; it is a native of Spain and the Levant and cultivated in the Botanic Garden in Chelsea in 1739.

Seed of *Clematis montana* was first brought back to England by Lady Amherst in 1828. Lord Amherst was Governor General and he made an official tour of the Northern Provinces of India, taking his wife and daughter, both keen botanists. The Right Rev Reginald Heber, Bishop of Calcutta, made a delightful sketch of Lady Amherst on her elephant, and he describes the scene in his *Narrative of a Journey through the Upper Province of India from Calcutta to Bombay,* to be found among the rare books at the new British Library:

Heber says *'The country is now splendidly beautiful. The tall trees which delighted us with their shade and verdure when we landed are now many of them covered in flowers literally hothouse shrubs 30– 40' high; the fragrance of a drive through the park at Barrackpoor is answerable to the dimensions of this Brobdingnag parterre; some of the trees and those large ones too, lose their leaves entirely at this season throwing out large crimson and yellow flowers in their place.'*

He concludes his letter with the sketch he made of *'part of the park at Barrackpoor with Lady Amherst, mounted on an elephant, for her morning airing. The large tree in the centre is a peepul, sacred to Siva and with an evil spirit, as the Hindus believe, dwelling under every leaf. In the distance between that and the bamboo is a banyan and in the foreground an aloe and over the elephant the cotton tree, which at certain seasons exchanges its leaves for something like roses.'*

Clematis is an irresistible species, and I can no longer count the number of varieties I grow – to which I am always adding. *C. montana* 'Tetrarose' is quite a large flower and it grows with *C. spooneri,* so similar to *montana,* that it could be taken for a more superior form, which flowers at the same delightfully early spring season, romping away over everything in sight. The deep pink of *C. montana* 'Tetrarose' and superb white flowers of *C. spooneri* are designed to cover the north wall of my house, so when I approach from that direction by car I give myself a lovely surprise.

Another most valuable clematis

Clematis armandii

(and very early flowering), is *C. armandii*, an evergreen species with luxuriant red bronzy new leaves, which smothers all my fence panels in front of the house, and likes to mingle with the camellias. Its tiny pink/white flowers appear as a rosy cloud, and are visible from the opposite direction as I approach. I put in several plants at judicious intervals, which have all joined up with much encouragement from Bill. Patrick also takes a keen interest in its progress, and whenever he comes he makes sure there is time to undo its knots and extend it further, taking his life in his hands to stretch its longest tendril up the conker tree.

Late flowering clematis also make a valuable addition to summer colour, and against the east side of the myrtle hedge climb *C. texensis*

'Gravitye Beauty' and *C. texensis* 'Etoile Rose', which both have small, pink, turks' cap flowers, the former pointing upwards and the latter hanging down; *C. texensis* 'Sir Trevor Lawrence' climbs up a camellia, cheering its flowerless season greatly. *C. x durandii* is the most intense indigo blue, but has no inclination to climb, one of its parents having been *C. integrifolia,* the herbaceous species of clematis. *C.* x 'Huldine', which is pearly white with crimson ribs reflected from the underside, both illuminate the myrtle.

Two more uncommon species of clematis are worthy of mention, *C. viorna* and *C. viticella* 'Mary Rose'. The flowers of the former look like ripe raspberries, and the reflexed sepals tipped with yellow are followed by enormous seed heads. It was named by Linnaeus in 1730 and is found in Eastern North America. The latter is one of the oldest clematis known; Barry Fretwell in his book *Clematis* tells of a *'very good illustration of it which is to be found on the plate titled 'August' in Robert Furber's 'Twelve Months of Flowers' (1730).* In 1629 it is described as *'of a dull or sad bluish purple, which produced no seed.'*

It has small fully double, spiky grey, purple rosettes, with a mass of narrow, recurved, lavender grey sepals, like a reflex chrysanthemum, and it is very free flowering. *C. viorna* climbs the wall by the garage, where it tangles with *Euchryphia milliganii* and *Trachelospermum asiaticum.*

Clematis florida

Clematis florida painted by Henry Andrews Andrews Bot. Repository 1804

Clematis florida 'Alba Plena' and 'Sieboldii' both in the greenhouse

The Viticella mingles with one of my few roses, *R. roulettii* 'Pom Pom de Paris', on the wall by my office, whose small double pink flowers are not unlike the clematis.

C. florida 'Alba Plena', mentioned as entangled in the glasshouse with *Passiflora sanguinolenta*, is a most worthwhile but unpredictable clematis. It came to Japan from China around 1700, and the former was introduced to Europe by Thunberg in 1776 after his sojourn in Japan.

The flowers start as tiny, single, pale green stars, developing in size and grandeur as they come out in succession on the narrow serpentine tendril. They finally reach their ultimate glory of greenish-cream, double flowers with an anemone centre of matching petaloid sepals – or in the case of *C. florida x* 'Sieboldii', the centre petaloid sepals are a dramatic, dark purple and could even be mistaken for those of a passionflower. It was introduced by von Siebold during his first stay in Japan in the 1820s.

For some reason both this and

Alba Plena are reluctant to grow satisfactorily, either inside the greenhouse or against a south facing wall outside – but in spite of losing several of these historically interesting and sensationally beautiful plants, one must keep trying.

Don Elick advises growing several plants of 'Sieboldii' together, because its wispy habit and delicate ways need a concentration of growth to show off its myriad blossoms. His skill and experience are a good example, and it shall be trimmed back to the first pair of strong buds in late winter, as he advises, which will leave alarmingly little of it to struggle through the season.

VON SIEBOLD

Any plant with 'Sieboldii' or 'Sieboldiana' after its name is bound to be of note. Doctor Philipp Franz von Siebold (1796-1866) was one of the few men of the period to study and collect Japanese plants, and he also had a very good eye.

The Japanese were very suspicious of foreigners, and after throwing out some Portuguese traders in 1638, did not allow anyone to linger until, first, Dr Englebert Kaempfer, who acted as doctor from 1690-1692, then Dr Carl Peter Thunberg in 1775-1776, (Masson's friend) and finally, von Siebold, sent by the Dutch East India Company in 1823-1829.

THE THREE DOCTORS

It was through these three young doctors impersonating Dutchmen (who were considered by the Japanese to be more acceptable than other foreigners), that the affairs of Western Europe became known in

Clematis florida 'Alba Plena' in the greenhouse

the mysterious and isolated nation of Japan, and exchanged for the virtually unknown oriental intrigues. All were shrewd, well-educated men, of eager curiosity, high intellectual ability and great medical skill. They were also good observers and diligent recorders, and bequeathed a vast heritage of scholastic achievement in the domain of Japanese botanical research during the Edo period of national isolation.

The doctors were confined (in succession) to the fan-shaped artificial island of Deshima, built in Nagasaki harbour for the Portuguese traders in 1635. Von Siebold came from a brilliant family of doctors (that included an aunt) who practised in Franconia, South Germany.

He quickly learned Japanese, and taught them the latest western surgical techniques, particularly in opthalmic surgery and obstetrics, his two areas of special expertise.

Von Siebold restored the garden on Deshima, neglected by Kaempfer and Thunberg, and won renown for his teaching and medical skills. In 1824 he wrote to his uncle, *'my house is a university in which all science is studied'.*

No women were allowed on the island except prostitutes, so when he fell in love with a beautiful girl of 18, O-Taki-San, she had to register as a prostitute and came to live on the island with him.

O-Taki-San bore him a daughter, O-Ine, who was to become the leading midwife in Nagasaki.

VON SIEBOLD'S ACHIEVEMENTS

Von Siebold was extremely popular, and acquired thousands of plants from his many friends and patients. He employed local artists to paint many of them, but his insatiable thirst for knowledge about Japan was his undoing.

He was asked to demonstrate his medical competence in Tokyo, and on his journey there, when for a part of which he was carried in a palanquin, he was besieged by students asking for the scientific names of specimens they brought. In return for his teaching he was shown wonderful works of art including the great, secret Tadataka map of the Japanese coast, of which he managed to get a copy.

With such success he became too grand and above himself, and made enemies who sought his downfall. He was planning to take his immense collections of plants, including the famous lilies *Lilium longiflorum and L. auratum,* and his paintings and works of art to Europe, and later return to Japan to rejoin his beloved O-Taki-San and daughter, but a terrible typhoon devastated South Japan, both demolishing houses and killing the inhabitants.

Von Siebold escaped but was arrested as a spy, and although he managed to bury his most dangerous possessions, his collections sailed without him and few survived. It was under such conditions that his lilies and *Camellia japonica* first reached Europe.

While he was in prison, his friends and grateful students helped him to such an extent that he was able to collect 12,000 herbarium specimens which he took with him when he was finally banished, as well as 485 of the most remarkable and beautiful Japanese plants, some from the wild and others from Japanese gardens for European cultivation.

In 1855 the Japanese government revoked his lifelong banishment, and he was once more able to visit his daughter who was now 31, and whom he had last seen when she was two. He worked there for two years, when he was again thrown out.

No man had done more to make known to the west the culture of the Japanese and their natural history, or to promote the benefits of western medicine to them. Those plants named Sieboldii are a constant reminder of what we owe to this masterful, arrogant and many-sided but extraordinarily gifted doctor.

Von Siebold was to settle in Leiden, and to dedicate his life to

publishing the most voluminous treatise on Japanology, and several volumes of his *Flora Japonica*, the unique record of beautiful paintings of plants.

His published work was acquired 60 years after his death, in 1866, by C P Maximowicz for the Botanical Institute of St Petersburg available only to Russian scientists, and not until 1991 (due to the opening of the USSR) was it accessible to scholars.

Now that the von Siebold collection has been rediscovered, in the old Russian Imperial Capital St Petersburg, it is being published in Japan, the land so beloved of von Siebold who dreamed of returning there until his very death.

LOUIS DE BOUGAINVILLE

As a ubiquitous climber, I cannot leave out of this chapter the *Bougainvillea spectabilis,* collected in Brazil by Banks and Solander on their voyage with Captain Cook in *HMS Endeavour.* Sydney Parkinson painted it, and it was named after the renowned and amazing Louis Antoine de Bougainville.

Spectabilis really is the word for it; Parkinson's illustration does not do

Bougainvillea

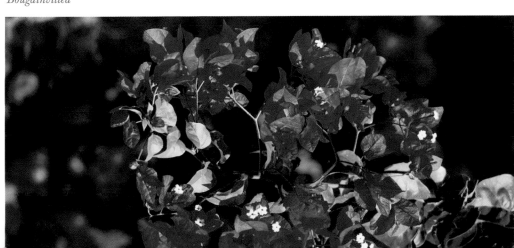

justice to this dramatic climber, vast phalanx of which rampage over the walls and buildings of every country in the world to which it has been exported, shrieking its purple power message to welcome you to every heavenly hot climate.

Besides the puce and purple variety, it comes in various shades of white, pink, red and orange; indeed, a small plant of pinky orange travelled back with me from the south of France one year, but never took off and certainly never looked at home.

Louis de Bougainville (1729-1811), was a mathematical genius. First

Failing in this (trampling the English) de Bougainville abandoned soldiering and took to the sea. His first voyage, to take possession of the Falkland Islands for France, was heartily approved by his King and his Ministers, but the Public Exchequer was, as usual, penniless.

Nothing daunted, de Bougainville floated La Compagnie de St Malo, subscribed to by many of his wealthy shipowner friends and by most of his own large fortune, and set out from St Malo in two ships *L'Aigle* and the *Sphinx* on 15th September 1763.

Without going into great details of

LOUIS ANTOINE DE BOUGAINVILLE
(1729-1811)

A French navigator and scientist, Bougainville was a mathematical genius, first appointed Secretary to the French embassy in London and made a Fellow of the Royal Society when he was just twenty seven. He was to become both a Field Martial and an Admiral.

After the end of the Seven Years War (during which he served with Montcalm in Canada) he joined the Navy and established a French colony in the Falkland Islands. He sailed round the world (1766-1779) and rediscovered the Solomon Islands, one of which is named after him. He served with distinction in the War of American Independence, but then occupied himself entirely with science. De Bougainville was a friend of Diderot and Rousseau, and his membership of the Legion d'honneur was one of several distinctions conferred on him by Napoleon.

---

appointed Secretary to the French Embassy in London and made Fellow of the Royal Society when he was twenty seven, he became both a Field Marshal and a Vice Admiral, and served with distinction as an Aide de Camp to Montcalm at Quebec. He was renowned for singing the warsong, *'Let us trample the English under our feet'*.

this amazing venture, it is essential to mention at least one of the distinguished members of his staff, after whom an interesting plant, *pernettya*, was named.

DOM ANTOINE – JOSEPH PERNETTY

Dom Antoine – Joseph Pernetty –

of the Benedictine Community, was not only an erudite monk, but a naturalist, botanist, Egyptologist and no mean artist. De Bougainville is supposed to have lured this holy man on board against his will, and detained him over dinner, until the ship was well out to sea.

Pernetty wrote an interesting account of this, *'Voyage to the Malouines Islands'*, translated and published in English in 1771. He found the plant near the Straits of Magellan and called it *'Bruyère à feuilles pointues'*, or 'Prickly Heath', and its Latin name *Pernettya mucronata* preserves his meaning, 'mucro' meaning a sharp point.

He describes it : *'It has the delicate and sweet scent of the myrtle; its ligneous branches lie close to the ground creeping like that of the wild thyme, which this plant resembles in its stems and leaves, with this difference only that they are not quite so acute. I never saw it in flower, nor do any of our officers remember to have seen it, but whatever the flower may be, it is succeeded by a fruit, resembling that of a myrtle, only larger when it comes to maturity.'*

It has been cultivated entirely for the sake of its ornamental fruits, which are also eaten as cranberries (ie pernettyas). Here in my garden museum they share the sloping bed made for the lewisias – with the brilliant fat pink berries providing a splash of colour until early winter (as long as you have arranged male plants along side the female).

PHILIBERT COMMERSON

After de Bougainville's return from this expedition, (which took two years), he again set sail in two French ships, the *Boudeuse* and the *Etoile,* which were placed at his disposal by the French Government, and set about circumnavigating the globe. During this voyage a young botanist, Philibert Commerson, went as naturalist.

Commerson was born in 1727 in Chatillon of an impoverished country family. He did everything with fanatical devotion, including his studies of medicine and natural history, and formed a remarkable herbarium with his usual violent energy. He collected species of fish, which he pressed between stout paper as if they were plants. The mere suspicion of an unknown plant was an irresistible attraction; he thought nothing of scaling almost inaccessible mountains, and both risked his life and ruined his health by his exertions.

His career as a brilliant naturalist was interrupted when he fell violently in love, and married, Antoinette Vivante Beauafortune in 1760, and settled down to the rather humdrum existence of a country doctor. However, this was a very happy marriage; *'cette union douce et charmante'* as it is described by his friend.

Commerson was particularly good at diagnosis, and performed some remarkable cures.

Tragically, his beautiful young wife

died three days after giving birth to their son Archambault, and he was prostrated by this evil stroke of fortune and quite inconsolable. In after years, Commerson dedicated a new genus of plants to the memory of his wife which he describes in a letter written to his brother in law: *'A large and fine tree, growing in forests, and easily distinguished at a distance, and which strictly speaking, bears more flowers and consequently fruits, than leaves; the greater number of these last, shaped like hearts, bear flowers (curiously enough), in doublets and triplets on each side; the fruit encloses two kernels united in the shape of two hearts. This tree, I say, is that on which I have engraved two names never to be separated. This new genus will be named Pulcheria commersonia. I will find the drawing of this plant to send to you, but preserve it for me as part of my collection'.* Most unfortunately his brother in law lost it, so one finds no *Pulcheria commersonia* in modern botanical works, it is not even certain which plant he meant to honour.

Philibert Commerson left his son in the care of his brother, and went off with de Bougainville. Arriving in Brazil, he delighted in the exquisite beauty of Rio de Janeiro.

'This country is the loveliest in the world', he writes, perhaps to his brother, *'in the very middle of winter, oranges, bananas, pineapples continually succeed one another, and the trees never lose their greenery; the interior, rich in every sort of game as well as in sugar and in rice, in manioc etc offers without any labour of cultivation, a delicious subsistence to its inhabitants, as well as to thousands of slaves, who have but the trouble of gathering its fruit.*

The mines with which this country abounds are of gold and precious stones; a bay from eleven to fifteen leagues in circuit, whose waters are the richest in fish of any in the world, forms a seaport able to hold a hundred thousand vessels, and is so sheltered from every wind, that one can always go on shore in a canoe.'

He continues, *'You know my mania for observing everything, in spite of a formal prohibition to go outside the town, and even notwithstanding a fearful sore that appeared on my leg, while still at sea, I ventured to go outside twenty times with my servant in a canoe, which was paddled by two blacks, and visited one after another the different shores and islands of the bay.'*

I just love Commerson for his plantaholic behaviour, always doing everything fanatically and violently, whether it is falling in love, or collecting plants, or *'pressing fish specimens between stout paper, as if they were plants.'* He made a rich harvest of fish and plants, and the *Bougainvillea spectabilis* was founded on one of his Brazilian specimens.

BARE (OR BARET)

What makes Commerson – and certainly his servant particularly unusual – is best given in de Bougainville's words: *'There had been a rumour that M. de Commerson's servant (Bare or Baret by name) was a woman. His features, the tone of his voice, his beardless chin, the scrupulous*

100

care which he took never to change his linen before anyone and so on, as well as other indications, seemed to confirm this suspicion.

But how could one believe that this was a woman; the indefatigable Bare, already an expert botanist whom they had seen dutifully following his master on all his expeditions, over the snows and icy mountains of Magellan, carrying even on those laborious excursions his provisions, arms and botanical portfolios, with a courage and strength which had made the naturalist call him 'his beast of burden?'

'A scene which occurred at Tahiti removed all doubt about the matter: M de Commerson had disembarked to botanise: scarcely had Bare set foot on shore with portfolios under his arm than he was surrounded by Tahitians, who cried out that it was a woman, (trust the Tahitians!), and who wished to do her the honours of the island; one of the officers who was on guard on shore was forced to come to her assistance and escort her back to the ship.'

He continues, 'When I was on board the Etoile, Bare confessed to me, her eyes streaming with tears, that she was a woman. She told me that she had deceived her master by presenting herself before him in men's clothes at the very moment when he was about to embark. She said she had already been a lackey in the service of a Genoese in Paris; she was an orphan born in Burgundy and had been rendered utterly destitute by the loss of a lawsuit, so that she had chosen to disguise her sex.

Moreover she knew that it was a case of voyaging round the world and this had aroused her curiosity, for she would be the first of her sex to do this. I must in justice say that she had always conducted herself with the utmost propriety. She is neither ugly nor pretty and is not more than twenty six or twenty seven years of age.'

Commerson's biographer adds rather disappointingly that, 'It is best, after the lapse of a hundred and sixty years or so, to add no comment whatever to this extraordinary story'.

However, Commerson did not forget her hardy faithfulness; he dedicated a plant to her under the name of *Baretia,* but this name had to be dropped because of a prior name, and is now called *Quivisia heterophylla Cav.*

Commerson's Latin dedication to her is gracefully put, and translated for me by a kind friend it reads: *'This plant, which makes such fools of us with its leaf like foliage is here specified by the names of that Amazon of botanists, whom we all once knew – she who, changing into men's clothes but preserving the refined dignity of a woman, dared thus equipped to traverse the whole world by land and sea for the sake of our researches and sometime in my company I remained ignorant of her physical nature. Yes, she it was who, nimble footed, so many times would follow in my footsteps both up among the peaks of the Strait of Magellan or down into the forest depths of the Australian isles. She was a bow and arrow girl like Diana, but like Minerva sensitive and strict in conduct. So she eluded all the many traps set for her by man or beast alike, and emerged safe and sound often*

Tweedia caerulea, also known as Oxypetalum caeruleum

from very great dangers both to life and virtue, doubtless thanks to the influence of some benign spirit.

She was the first of her sex to complete in its entirety, by land and sea, the whole circle of the globe, in the process traversing more than fifteen thousand leagues! To that heroic spirit we owe so many plants recorded for the first time; so many plants diligently nursed and watered; so many insect swarms and oyster beds mapped out that for me and all other devotees of Natural History it would simply be a crime not to repay her memory with the highest honours Flora has to give.'

Commerson settled in Mauritius for a time, and there is a last letter from him describing his illness from which he died there in 1773.

His biographer writes: *'So passed away that ardent indomitable spirit, working up to the last moment and in the very hour of death remembering his boy Archambault, far away in the beautiful hamlet of Toulon-sur-Arroux'.*

Jeanne Bare married a soldier, and eventually returned to live in France.

Our Linnean Society of London has about 1,500 herbarium specimens from Commerson's collections, but the rest are scattered.

TWEEDIA CAERULEA

One other climber which grows alongside the yellow passionflower and must be mentioned is called *Oxypetalum caeruleum;* that is to say when it isn't called *Tweedia caerulea.*

Oxys in Greek means sharp, so sharp petal is its other name after that of James Tweedie (1775-1862) from Scotland and Argentina. It is not very common, but extremely decorative in a shy or unobtrusive way.

It is hardy enough for a greenhouse where its perennial, pale green, lance-shaped leaves, covered with soft down, twine among the passionflowers producing star-shaped forget me not blue flowers which somehow manage to be tinged with pink. Hillier in his *Manual of Trees and Shrubs,* describes the flowers as *'powder blue at first, slightly tinged green, turning to purplish and finally lilac.'*

You get the picture.

They flower very freely and set long twin-horned pods of seed in the autumn, and there is another variety with pink flowers which it may be possible for me to acquire.

James Tweedie decided to emigrate to Argentina when he was fifty, having spent his life so far at several Scottish estates and as Head Gardener at the Royal Botanic Garden at Edinburgh. He was a contemporary of Bonplant, and though they are known to have corresponded, there is no record of them having met.

He collected plants during several long and tedious journeys, but it was the third and most successful trip – from Santa Catalina near Buenos Aires to Tecumen in 1835 into the interior of Argentina – of which he wrote *'A Few Rough Notes of a Journey across the Pampas of Buenas Ayres to Tecumen in 1835'.*

Tweedie had joined a Tropa which consisted of seventeen wagons, each of which together with its cargo was computed *'to weigh about three tons and was pulled by six bullocks; the wagons were 15 feet long with wheels 8 feet in diameter. 'Thus',* he says *'when these unwieldy uncouth looking vehicles are set in motion, you might imagine that a village of Indian huts had suddenly taken a mind to walk, the whole appearance being as curious as can well be imagined.'*

A TROPHY, THE NASTURTIUM

Tropaeolum speciosum is a ravishing climber with which I have so far completely failed.

According to *Stearn's Dictionary of Plant Names for Gardeners,* it is the nasturtium of gardeners, although not of botanists.

Named by Linnaeus from the Greek 'tropaion', a trophy, the plant reminded him of a classical trophy, a sign of victory, originally consisting of a tree trunk set up on the battlefield and hung with captured helmets and shields. Indeed Linnaeus compared its rounded leaves to shields, and the flowers to spears and pierced, blood-stained, gold helmets.

The word *nasturtium* is Latin for a pungent-tasting plant, the true *nasturtium* being, surprisingly, watercress. It is also called the Flame Flower and was introduced from Chile in 1846. I have come to the conclusion that as a plant, it is a great snob, and will only condescend to grow where it considers its background suitable. It is quite happy growing up yew hedges, though it has a mind of its own, and if you put it on one side of the hedge, it will often come up on the other. It is particularly successful in Scotland, where I have also seen it almost smothering camellias.

I have tried it a dozen times without luck; even if it gets away at the start, a slug will demolish it. C. E. Lucas Phillips, in his *Climbing Plants for Walls and Gardens,* says the finest he ever saw was in Galloway, Scotland where it *'threw a scarlet cloak over its host – a climbing hydrangea.'*

I shall buy another immediately and try once more, this time up my *Schizophragma* which is very similar to the hydrangea and could do with a scarlet cloak.

JOSEPH PAXTON

A very different but valuable plant is the *Solanum jasminoides,* a jasmine-like nightshade, probably from South America. Not only is it hardy and evergreen but it flowers late in the season, and keeps going until the weather turns wintery, flourishing wherever you put it.

It was named by no less a person than Sir Joseph Paxton (1803-1865). Paxton's name resounds in many contexts, but he is of particular value to researchers, having started a monthly magazine in 1831 called the *Horticultural Register,* followed by the *Magazine of Botany* and *Register of Flowering Plants.* The latter ceased in 1849 and became the invaluable *Gardener's Chronicle,* which is still going strong and must be one of the most used resources by diverse authors on every possible horticultural subject.

Paxton was perhaps first known for beginning his career as Head Gardener to the 6th Duke of Devonshire, when he was only 23. The Duke found him at the Horticultural Gardens at Chiswick where he was working as gardener, and he so impressed the Duke that the latter employed him on the spot and, confident in his choice, left England for a long journey in India.

Paxton's account of how he took up his employment at Chatsworth in his employer's absence is typical of the man: *'I left London by the Comet Coach for Chesterfield and arrived at Chatsworth at 4.30 am 9th May 1846. As no person was to be seen at that early hour I got over the greenhouse gate by the old covered way, explored the pleasure grounds and looked round the outside of the house. I then went down to the kitchen gardens, scaled the outside wall and saw the whole of the place, set the men to work there at six o'clock; returned to Chatsworth, got Thomas Weedon to play the waterworks, went to breakfast with Mrs Gregory (the housekeeper) and her niece. The latter fell in love with me and I with her, and thus completed my first morning's work at Chatsworth before 9 o'clock.'*

Paxton was unable to discover any certain information about the solanum's native country or introduction into Britain, but he first saw it at Messrs Young's Epsom Nursery in November 1839. It had been obtained from the Glasgow Botanic Garden and was considered a South American plant. It was grown in a pot in the camellia house and trained round a small circular trellis. He says, *'the blossoms were borne liberally in copious clusters, each having from eight to twelve opened at the same time and exhaling a delightful fragrance.'* Messrs Young planted it outside during the next years, and it flowered enthusiastically until frosted in late November.

'The generic name', says Paxton, *'was given by Pliny but on what it is founded it is impossible now to do more than conjecture the greenness of the young shoots, and the size, form and surface of the leaves, give it the aspect of some form of Jasminum, on which account the specific appellation has been bestowed'.*

'One would not wish to presume a comparison with Empress Josephine except in the sphere of her extravagance, where I had always thought I would never justify myself. Her purchases from the Vineyard Nurseries, £2,600 in 1803 and another £700 in 1811, amount to about £154,000 in today's money. However reckless I am, there is considerable leeway before I catch her up.'

7

CAMELLIAS AND CHINA

'La Dame aux Camellias and La Traviata lend a romantic background to this fabled family of plants. It is impossible to imagine that such an exotic would condescend to flourish in any but the most pampered featherbed. Nevertheless there are nearly a hundred (which I sometimes count in my mind when I can't sleep), nearly all different varieties, lending something of an aura to my Living Plant Museum.'

The camellia or tea plant has been subject to many changes in botanical classification. In 1712 it was placed in a separate genus, Thea, but after Linnaeus named it camellia it became *Camellia sinensis*. He called it after Father George Josef Kamel, a Moravian Jesuit priest who spent a lifetime in the Philipines investigating species of orange, and on his return is reputed to have called at a Chinese port and brought plants, thought to be the tea plant of China, to Europe. Linnaeus then established the name camellia in his honour.

ANCIENT CAMELLIA PLANTS

The earliest trading outpost on the mainland of China was established by the Portuguese in 1557. There is no record yet found of camellias brought back to Europe at such an early date, but there are very old camellia plants in Portugal and Spain whose history has never been satisfactorily explained. Stirling Macoboy in his *The Colour Dictionary of Camellias* describes two camellia trees which have a combined spread of 140 square yards in the Condo de Campo Bello Garden, near Oporto, which were planted in the early sixteenth century.

The ornamental varieties of camellia, mostly *Camellia japonica*, quickly became popular in England, and enterprising nurserymen took them on to New York, from where they soon spread all over America. In 1860 there were 623 varieties named and illustrated in the Belgian Verschaffelt's *Iconographie des Camellias*. Although named *japonica*, the species is equally found in the provinces of south west China; Verschaffelt did well to include 623 from the conservative estimate of 20,000 varieties now known. They account for more than three quarters of all camellia cultivars, grown everywhere in the world.

One camellia which still eludes me is Lady Banks's Camellia, a form of *Camellia sasanqua* (the autumn flowering species). According to The Botanical Register of 1815 *'It is of recent introduction into Europe, having been first received from China (to which it belongs as well as Japan) in 1811, by the Court of Directors of the East India Company in the Cuffnels, Captain Wellbank. We believe it first flowered in the conservatory of Sir Joseph Banks, after whose Lady it has been named in the late edition of Hortus Kewensis'*. It will be a worthy exhibit to find.

In Japan, *Camellia sasanqua* is known as 'The Mountain Tea Flower'. It is a Japanese endemic and seems to have been overlooked as an ornamental until the 17th century. There are no noteworthy records of named garden varieties before the 1695 book *Kadan Jikinsho,* in which about fifty kinds are described. *C. sasanqua* 'Narumigata' is my first choice. It was introduced in 1898, and its flower – produced in October-November and often still blooming at Christmas – comes from a deep pink bud, turning white but edged with pink. It opens wide and flat, has a musty fragrance and lasts well. It grows against the back wall under the pergola, next to another *C. sasanqua;* this is a favourite which has large, shell-pink double flowers, and is called 'Jean May'. Sad to say she has no illustrious forbears, no pedigree, but was bred by an American in Florida, from unknown seed parents.

The Japanese sasanqua camellia was traded abroad, especially to China, not for its beautiful flowers but for its seed, which secreted a special oil famed for its properties of almost magical powers of healing. In Japan itself it was valued more as a cosmetic, especially for dressing the hair, and as a cooking oil. The use of these shrubs, with their exceptionally fine, shiny, evergreen foliage as hedges is very notable in Japan, where trimmed low and narrow, they mark paths through parks and gardens. Cut at conventional heights they make flowering fences and even conceal buildings. Where we in Europe would use hornbeam or beech for the allées of the 18th century grand gardens, they used camellias.

KUNMING

Kunming in Yunnan has long been the centre of camellia growing in China, and it is from this province that the *Camellia reticulata* originated. Yunnan has more and larger gardens, temples and monasteries decorated with these shrubs than other any part of China, and in Guan Kaiyun's book, *Yunnan Camellias of China,* he describes the oldest living plants. The most ancient tree is supposed to have been planted in the Yuan Dynasty, in 1347. It has a height of 10 metres and is still vigorous and flowering. A photograph in his book shows another venerable example, said to be 500 years old, and though propped up here and there with what might be taken for walking sticks for an old gentleman, it is a mass of scarlet flowers. This memorable plant was still to be seen on my recent visit to Kunming, and photographs from many angles confirm its magical flowering

Camellia reticulata at Kunming

capacity. Kunming was one of the places where I managed to get left behind by the sight-seeing guide, who failed to tell me we were leaving an hour early. Luckily all Chinese are glued to their mobiles, so armed with my destination – written in Chinese by the hotel porter and the guide's mobile number (I had no idea where I was being taken or indeed the name of the hotel I had come from) I pursued them in a taxi, for which I made the company pay. Being unable to communicate with my driver I was shocked when she suddenly seemed to lose her nerve and muttering to herself in Chinese did a U turn and returned us to her family home where some heated Chinese discussion took place and I began to wonder whether I would ever be seen again. Having no idea where I was going all I could do was wave the mobile number under their noses. At last, a braver relation appeared and invited me into his taxi and we eventually overtook my group who had been waiting crossly in a layby en route.

THE GORGES OF THE YANGZTE KIANG

Having decided to go to China to join in the International Camellia Congress at Jinhua, (near Shanghai), I could not let pass the opportunity to visit the doomed Gorges of the Yangzte Kiang, due to be flooded in a few months time. Travelling alone and by air to Beijing, Shanghai,

Chongqing and other places but only with the briefest of itineraries from the travel agent, I was handed from one Chinese guide to another like a parcel never trusted with a ticket until practically in the plane.

For some reason the river was not deep enough at Chongqing to accommodate the five star boat, so a dilapidated, no star and no shock absorber bus was arranged to take me to Feng Du, down river, where the boat awaited.

LOCAL DELICACIES

The Chinese were ingenious at filling any spare waiting time with profitable visits; in this case it was to a silk factory with restaurant attached. I had not given a great deal of thought to food in China, having expected optimistically to find prawns in sweet and sour sauce, delicious duck and so on. I did remember hearing a story from an old friend, now an Admiral, who had served on the China station, about his experience at a Chinese banquet, where he had been given live baby mice, dipped in treacle as an hors d'oeuvre; but I was not expecting to go to any banquets, so when I sat down to my totally unidentifiable lunch at the Silk Factory restaurant, my mind was more on the book I had just read by Colin Thubron who described Steamed Cat, Braised Guinea Pig (whole), Python Soup, Bear's Paws, as being local favourites, and it took me a minute or two to recognise what was on my plate. But of course – having been shown the entire process of silk-making from the mulberry to the silk duvet – I should have guessed that there must be a future for the OAP silk worm. What could be more sensible than to make your foreign tourist pay for it and eat it?

INTREPID TRACKERS

The Three Gorges were sensational, and we raced through all three of them in the day. I occupied myself

Wu Gorge

Towpath

Modern day trackers

Shen Long River

trying to photograph the narrow towpath cut in the sheer, perpendicular rocks, about 200 metres above the surface of the water. The fast flowing river varied between fifty and a hundred feet wide between the massive gorges, hundreds of feet high. As Robert Fortune described, (we come to him shortly), these pathways were used by the trackers, whose job it was to haul the boats upstream against the ferocious currents. There might be as many as two hundred trackers, dragging the boats with arm-thick, plaited bamboo ropes tied to the mast.

Plainly visible, and parallel with these narrow tracks, was another pathway higher up the vertical mountain, along which the imperial court officials and rich merchants would travel, carried in bulky sedan chairs by coolies. This was the only road-path connecting the counties of

Fengjie and Daxi and these ancient pathways – anything from 0.4 – 1.5 metres wide – were built during the Qing Dynasty (1644–1911), all with such tools as hammers, chisels and awls. It is impossible to imagine how the coolies kept their footing while travelling at the required speed. All these will vanish when the river is flooded.

Best of all, at the entrance to the third Gorge we disembarked into small wooden boats and were towed by modern-day trackers who punted, pushed, hauled and kedged us up the Shenlong river (a tributary of the Yangstze), with eight or so young men to a boat with fifteen passengers in each.

They urged each other on with a powerful, melodious, age-old shanty or war song known as the Wei Hi chorus, which must have been passed down from their ancestors.

MY CAMELLIAS

My chosen camellias represent many aspects of their story. *C. japonica* 'Adolphe Audusson' is my oldest and largest plant, sheltered by the conker tree; this variety originated in the Guichard Nursery of Nantes, in France in 1877. It is a large semi double, dark blood red, always covered in flowers during its long blooming season. Somehow the Guichard nursery managed to produce some of our most valued varieties, competing easily with anything produced over the next century or so.

My 'Adolphe Andusson' grew so large I had to give it a tremendous prune to prevent the smaller plants under it from complete blackout.

C. japonica 'Contessa Lavinia Maggi' is another historic variety which was bred in Italy by Conte Onofrio Maggi. It keeps to no rules, but sends out flowers closely though irregularly striped in deep red and white; every now and then a whole branch will have no white at all, and then again an odd flower or two will have sections wholly red. I admire its independence. No doubt the very grandness and exquisite form of these flowers necessitated a title, so it is not surprising that so many of the early ones were named after the nearest nobility.

C. japonica, 'Lady Clare', is another most beautiful, large, semi double, deep pink with particularly elegant, dark, pointed leaves. Who she was named for remains a mystery, but *C. japonica* 'Lady Hume's Blush' was imported from China in 1806 and named for Lady Amelia Hume, the daughter of an EIC Director. It is the palest pink and imbricated to perfection; unfortunately it is one of the many desirable varieties not so far located.

Another favourite is *C japonica* 'Adelina Patti' – tiny single cupshaped pink, edged with white – too elegant for words.

C. reticulata 'Lasca Beauty', which has the largest flowers of any in my collection is of particular note; it was bred in America by Dr Clifford

Camellia japonica 'Adelina Patti'

Parkes of Arcadia, California, as recently as 1973 and is much sought after, for its very grand, semi-double, shell pink flowers, with heavy textured petals and exceptionally big, dark, green leaves. There are a great many large American cultivars, some of which are quite blousey, and of an undistinguished pink; not so 'Lasca Beauty', which unlike many reticulatas grows away enthusiastically.

My tiniest camellia flower is produced by *C. transnokoensis,* a species from Taiwan. Too delicate to grow outside in winter, it has to live in a pot. Its small leaves are dark green above and pale below, turning red towards the end of each branch, and it flowers very early; masses of neat little white flowers tipped with red. It is a delight to have around about Christmas time, and continues flowering until March.

Two new hybrids have recently joined the greenhouse, *C.* 'Scentuous' and *C.* 'Quintessence', both bred from another tender species called *C. lutchuensis,* whose chief claim to fame is its wonderful fragrance. So far 'Quintessence' is the favourite, covered with white, shading to pink flowers and quite strongly scented.

CAMELLIAS LOVE CORNWALL

Camellias revel in their luck finding themselves living in Cornwall; the endless rain or misty damp days are just what the doctor ordered. The flowering capacity of each plant is

Camellia transnokoensis

astonishing, simply covered in buds and flowers for weeks, followed by the delectable new shoots, so that in no time at all the plant seems to double its size. I am rather brutal in trimming them back – Bill says they tremble when they see me approach with my secateurs. His father had a theory that a flock of birds should be able to fly through a shrub, which bears out my idea that pruning should begin in the middle of the plant. To cheer them up they get extra rations of trace elements and cow manure.

The Camellia Nursery in America, Nuccio Nurseries, Altadina, California has a habit of pollinating a great many promising varieties, in the hope of making new cultivars, with enormous success. One such is described as 'black red' and named 'Bob Hope', (to be found in my biggest bed). Two of the most beautiful are called 'Nuccio's Jewel' and 'Nuccio's Pearl'; the former has ruffled white petals edged pink, while the latter is the same colouring but a formal double. Both of these flower near camellia 'Adophe Audusson'.

To come from Nuccios must be provenance enough: Guilio Nuccio was the grandfather of Julius who owns the nursery now. He gave me a conducted tour on my Californian visit and introduced me personally to almost every plant, telling me that 'Guilio Nuccio', their first and best japonica cross, raised and named by his grandfather, was wrongly spelt, (it should have been 'Giulio'), when it was registered and has had to remain so. It was a chance seedling of the fishtail camellia 'Mermaid'. My large plant of it is almost facing the front door and has particularly attractive leaves, occasionally showing its inherited fishtail. Because camellias flower so early in the year it has been seen festooned with snow, but covered in huge, double, coral red flowers, quite undaunted.

SPORTING

Camellias have an agreeable habit of 'sporting', that is, producing a shoot bearing quite different flowers to their usual. Indeed *Camellia japonica* 'Elegans' is a champion of thirteen new varieties. It was grown by Alfred Chandler, a nurseryman of Vauxhall, London in 1826, from a seed of 'Waratah', itself a seedling of the old Chinese variety 'Anemoniflora'. The flower is described in his catalogue of that date as, *'a delicate rose 3-4 inches in diameter'*. It sported in eight different

gardens in America in 1936, thus being given eight different names, and ended up as 'CM Wilson'. In spite of this unthrilling name, it is a stunning camellia. Its spreading habit of growth neatly fills a niche in the garden below my office. It has large, silvery pink blooms with very dark leaves.

HYBRIDS AND HISTORY

Hybridisation of camellias took a great leap forward when George Forrest (1873–1932) introduced three of the most important species from the frontiers of Burma and China. *C. saluenensis,* named for the river Saluen, *C. cuspidata,* and the wild form of *C. reticulata*. The former, crossed with *C. japonica* by J C Williams of Caerhays Castle in Cornwall, was a remarkable breakthrough, and the *C. x williamsii* hybrids, as they were called, proved more cold hardy than either of their parents. They are vigorous plants, which flower earlier, longer and have many more blooms. Unsurprisingly, they caught the imagination of the gardening public, and sprang into fashion. Other hybridists soon followed, and an enormous number of new varieties appeared.

Half the camellias in my garden are hybrids, some of whose birth pangs, as one might say, I witnessed. These were the Carlyon collection of Tregrehan, Cornwall, one of which was a cross between *C. cuspidata* and *C. japonica* 'Rosea Simplex', resulting in *C.* 'Cornish Spring' which takes pride of place in my major piece of garden between the palm trees *C. cuspidata* has tiny inconspicuous white flowers with pretty bronzy leaves, and it was a pleasure to see the latter trait successfully inherited by its progeny, which is covered in miniature, pale pink, single blossoms. I have all the best of these hybrids, sharing the task of hedging round my garden. Among them is the very late flowering *C.* 'Gwavas', a deep pink, formal double, and one of my absolute favourites, with the emerging flower more beautiful at

every stage. *C.* 'ETR Carlyon', is also very late with large, double white, almost begonia form blooms. *C.* 'Tregrehan' is a baby pink double, whose fat round buds open half at a time.

MINIATURES

There are miniature camellias as well; one particularly exotic is *C. japonica* 'Bokuhan', which is mentioned in Japanese literature as early as 1719. Only just under two inches across, it is a single flower with vivid red petals, which opens flat to reveal an anemone centre of white petaloids.

   Stirling Macoboy describes two lost miniatures, only known from an exquisitely painted 17th century screen by Ogata Korin, which shows the red centred variety 'Asahi Yama', the exact negative reverse of 'Bokuhan', with red centred petaloids against white petals. What a coup it would be to display them both together.

A PROFITABLE CARGO

Early introductions of camellias from the Far East to Europe came in ships of the East India Company, including *Camellia sinensis,* the tea plant, grown indigenously in China. The EIC found it a most profitable cargo, and built special ships for the trade called clippers, because they clipped the time usually taken by the regular packet ships. Speed was of the essence, as all the glory, plus 10/- a

Camellia x Gwavas

114

ton premium, went to the first ship home with the new spring picking.

In China, tea was grown by smallholders, and at harvest time the whole family was involved – from the youngest child who could just stand to the oldest member who could still stand. Only two leaves and a bud were taken off each shoot, which made it very laborious to pick, but very high in quality. It went down by river to the nearest agent, to be processed, graded and packed in tea chests, and then sent on down to the big rivers such as the Min, to the port of Foochow, where the clippers lay waiting to load.

It was from Foochow that the legendary clipper races began, between the Americans, who raced the British, and the British who raced each other. It was a long haul of 16,000 miles, nonstop, round the Cape of Good Hope to London. In 1866 the most famous race was between five clippers.

The first three beat up the Channel neck and neck, with only ten minutes between the first and second, and the third just half an hour behind. People used to watch all along the south coast of England; it was as good as Derby Day.

TEA, AN EXPENSIVE TASTE

Tea cost 60/- a pound in those days and with such an expensive commodity there was a mad rush to bring live plants back to England, propagate them and then re-export to our own colonies of India and America to grow them on, hoping to cut out the Chinese entirely. Needless to say, the Chinese knew exactly what we were up to, and would often craftily substitute the ornamental kind of camellia for the tea plant, thus introducing new varieties to Europe.

ROBERT FORTUNE

Robert Fortune, (1813-1880), was employed to go to China, both by the Horticultural Society and the East India Company. He was a Scot from Berwickshire and learned his skills at the Botanic Garden in Edinburgh. From there he went to the Horticultural Society of London as Superintendent of its hothouse department, then at Chiswick. Fortune so impressed the Society with his ability and industry, both as botanist and gardener, that he was sent

Robert Fortune, from Journal of Horticulture & Cottage Gardener 1890

to China to search for the many desirable plants known to exist there. He was given a long list of plants to find, among them such items as the Pekin peach, grown in the Emperor's garden, said to weigh 2lb apiece. Others included double yellow roses, other than the *Rosa banksiae* which was already in cultivation, blue paeonies, yellow camellias, (*'if such exist'*), enkianthus in the wild (the plant used for making rice paper), varieties of illicium and the true Mandarin oranges. The list is very reminiscent of that of William Kerr fifty years before, though not couched in such graphic language.

Robert Fortune agreed with Sir Joseph Banks, and *'the most attentive botanists'* (Banks' words), that the green and black teas, grown all over China and varying greatly in appearance, all came from the same species. Fortune says: *'the tea plant is multiplied by seed, and it is perfectly impossible that the produce can be identical in every respect with the parent';* there would also always be slight differences due to soil and climate. I never reached the Bohea hills of China where tea grows indigenously, but I was taken to several tea factories, where the plantations rolled away into the distance. Tea plants just a foot high were thirty years old, and had been harvested annually for all that time.

Robert Fortune's life just overlapped that of Sir Joseph Banks; he would have been seven when Banks died in 1820. However, there is a tenuous link. In 1780, Lt Colonel Robert Kyd (1746-1793) of the Bengal Engineers, a much respected employee of the East India Company, conceived the idea of making a botanic garden in Calcutta where they could grow black pepper, cinnamon, cotton, tobacco, coffee and tea. The Directors of the EIC warmly welcomed the idea and gave him the go ahead, but wrote to Sir Joseph Banks for his advice, particularly with regard to the cultivation of tea. In 1788, a letter Banks wrote to the Deputy Chairman of the EIC begins: *'In obedience to your wishes I readily undertake to give my opinion relative to the possibility of tea becoming an object of cultivation and manufacture in the possessions of the East India Company and the probable means of effecting that very desirable object'.*

THE INFANT ADVENTURE

The Chinese had always been very secretive about how to cultivate and process the tea plant. Tea had been enjoyed by the Chinese for at least three thousand years before it was heard of in the west; Japanese priests had brought it back to Japan and used it as a sacred remedy; but no one had ever been allowed to learn from the Chinese how it was grown or processed.

Sir Joseph Banks recommended that Chinese tea manufacturers from Canton should be *'induced by the offer of liberal terms … to embark with their tea shrubs and tools of manufacture, and migrate with them to Calcutta, where they will find the Botanic Gardens ready to receive them, 20 acres of which is already prepared, and lying under very nearly the same latitude as Canton, could not fail to suit in every particular this infant adventure.'* He warned them not to involve the supercargoes, or foremen, as it was not in their interest; perhaps they ignored this part of his advice because, sadly, the infant adventure did fail.

HOW TO GROW TEA

Banks recommended that tea should be grown in northern Indian provinces, almost exactly where it was found growing indigenously in Assam in about 1830. This was just the moment when the monopoly of the tea trade, held by the East India Company until then, ran out.

It was not until 1848, nearly 30 years after Banks was dead that the EIC sent Robert Fortune on exactly the same mission: he was to obtain the finest variety of tea plants, and persuade native manufacturers to bring their implements for the Government Tea Plantations in the Himalayas. As well the manufacturers, Fortune brought from China 2,000 young tea plants and 17,000 germinated seedlings which gave a flying start to the industry.

It was British pioneer tea planters who eventually discovered how to grow tea, from studying the indigenous plants in Assam. Before that, much time and money was wasted when they could not agree where to grow it, and eventually chose, disastrously, the only place in Assam where it was impossible for tea to thrive, being regularly drowned by the confluence of two huge rivers, a more suitable terrain for rice.

However, within a span of three generations, enduring unspeakable hardships, they made and lost fortunes, but carved tea plantations physically out of the jungles of India, covering two million acres and employing over a million coolies. India at last took possession of the markets monopolised by the Chinese for 200 years.

In 1852 Robert Fortune published his book *'A journey to the Tea Countries',* in which he says that *'all attempts to grow it commercially in such countries (our colonies), will end in failure and disappointment. The tea plant will grow wherever the climate and soil are suitable, but if it is to be cultivated as an object of commercial speculation we must also inquire into the price of labour. Labour is cheap in China. The labourers in the tea countries do not receive more than twopence or threepence a day; can workmen be procured for this small sum in America or Australia? How will the manufacturers in such places compete with the Chinese in the market?'*

MINIATURE GREENHOUSES

On Fortune's first visit to China, for the Horticultural Society, he took

CLEMATIS LANUGINOSA *Lindl.*

with him European seed and plants in some of the new *'Wardian'* cases, invented by Nathaniel Ward in 1831. Fortune also used these for bringing the tea plants from China to India. These cases were the greatest boon to the plant collector, providing an almost foolproof way for plants to travel safely. They were the natural development of the plant cabins Banks had built on all ships carrying plants for him.

They were miniature, portable greenhouses, a simple but brilliant idea; you planted your seed and plants directly in the glazed case, watered them well and closed the case. Provided the case was kept in full daylight, photosynthesis would

bringing back *Clematis lanuginosa,* which was the first large-flowered clematis to reach us, and which he found in Eastern China in 1850. (The name means woolly, referring to the leaves and the flower stalks). This species is an example of the original introduction being no longer easily obtainable and being replaced by excellent hybrids. Many of the large-flowered varieties were bred from it, and among the best is *C.* 'Marie Boissolet' which displays its large, white flowers on the wall below my office and sometimes climbs daringly and decoratively into the lantern tree.

Several more valuable climbers

Trachelospermum asiaticum on the wall

take place, and the water vapour thus released would be recycled and the plants kept damp for months at a time. In this way the plants would not have to be disturbed until they reached their final destination. This revolutionised plant travel from that date until air freight began.

Fortune must be thanked for

are owed to Fortune. For example, in 1844 in Shanghai he found the delightful smelling *Trachelospermum asiaticum* and *T. jasminoides,* both of which adorn my walls. The former by the garage, has the most intense scent, many more flowers and is the hardier of the two, and the latter by the terrace has slightly larger silver variegated leaves. They both have clusters of small ivory white flowers late in the summer. The plants take a long time to establish but are worth waiting for patiently, with their shiny, evergreen leaves which turn brilliant, bronzy-red, during the autumn and winter months.

ELICK AND BOOTH

One learns of the latter's behaviour from reading Don Elick's description of how he grew it in his garden in Japan. He paints with words what Raymond Booth depicts with colour, in their *Japonica Magnifica,* published in 1992. The trachelospermum has apparently no means of clasping or twining, only producing aerial roots in times of high humidity which clamp onto its host. Elick calls it

Akebia quinata

a climber with a strong will of its own, not climbing until the spirit moves it. He managed to grow it into a huge circular ball on top of his gatepost, with great *'determination and rigorous pruning'.* It will however *'range along the ground for twenty metres or more, disdaining trees, fences and buildings and then decide, as likely as not, to climb something too flimsy to support it.'* Mine luckily have climbed, more or less where they were planted, but *T. jasminoides* had a hard time to start with; for ten

years or so it was nearly smothered by *Solanum crispum* 'Glasnevin', planted absentmindedly in front of it; only when this grew too big and was cut down did one find the long-suffering trachelospermum lurking behind.

AKEBIA QUINATA

I am mad about *Akebia quinata,* another native to China that Fortune found in 1845 on the Island of Chusan near Shanghai. Plants of it grow up each of the four larch poles edging my terrace, and twine their way up to meet over the adjoining arches, making a very untidy but luxuriant, overhead bush. The scent from the small purple flowers in spring pervades half my garden, and in the summer the long tendrils that appear from every shoot seem wildly out of control.

Pruning it is an annual anxiety – however, if it were not pruned it might become too heavy and bring its supporting larch poles down. Some years I tell Bill to give it a short back and sides while I am away, because I cannot bear to watch him doing it. In spite of having to avoid the berberidopsis, all mixed into it and a much sparser plant anyway, he manages to reduce it by at least half, and on my return, my first glance tells me he has safely succeeded again. I am beginning to think we can't kill it.

Although in some parts of China, Fortune found it possible to wander in the wild to search for his plants, in other parts all *'foreign devils'* were forbidden to travel inland, so he had to search in gardens and nurseries. He visited the celebrated Fa–tee Gardens near Canton, where William Kerr had searched, and where plants are cultivated for sale. It was full of flowering camellias, azaleas, tree paeonies and roses, but the plant he mentions which is of particular interest to me was *Michelia fuscata* (another variety of the Michelia found in India by Dr Anton Hove) now known as *michelia figo,* and described earlier.

FOREIGN BARBARIANS

We know Joseph Banks' opinion of the Chinese, but they in their turn were very suspicious of *'foreign barbarians'* as they called any stranger, who at that time was not permitted inland. Fortune travelled extensively all over China, using his considerable nerve and wits to get himself out of trouble. He became as crafty as some of the Chinese who, he says, *'will say anything that suits their purpose, and rarely give themselves any trouble to ascertain whether the information they give be true or false... latterly I made a practice of disbelieving everything they told me, until I had an opportunity of judging for myself.'* He learned enough of their dialects, and

adapted himself to the many unexpected situations he found. When he was robbed of almost everything, he bought native dress, shaved his head and wore a pigtail, which he said came to his ankles, and passed himself off as a Chinaman. In two of the several books he wrote *'Three Years Wanderings in China',* and *'A Journey to the Tea Countries',* he tells of his adventures, making light of the perils he endured. He faced pirates at sea, horrific typhoons and monsoon storms, as well as attacks by bands of robbers who tried to murder him.

NOT SUCH GOOD FORTUNE

Fortune paints a dramatic picture when he tells of his encounter with pirates off the River Min on his way to Ning Po. His junk was one of a convoy of about 170, carrying a cargo of wood. Arms were not permitted to the crews, so the Captain was very pleased when Fortune showed him his double barrelled shotgun and two pistols, warning him that they were certain to be attacked by pirates or *'Jandous'.*

It was not long before the Captain's prediction came true and the 'Jandous' appeared, right ahead, lying in wait for them on the horizon. The convoy scattered into twos and threes; the crews prepared for battle by hiding all their valuables under the cabin floorboards, and changing into ragged clothes so as not to appear worth kidnapping; and baskets of small stones, were distributed round the deck as ammunition – quite useless as the pirates were well armed. Fortune knew he would be killed at once if he were taken, as his presence alone would endanger the pirates. At the first salvo of shot from the *'jandous'* all the men ran below and hid. Fortune ordered the helmsmen at the point of his gun to remain at their post – they had every stitch of sail set and were proceeding at about eight knots. Fortune relates: *'Again the nearest pirate fired on us, this time the shot fell just under our stern. The third broadside came whizzing over our heads, without however wounding the men at the helm or myself. The pirates now seemed quite sure of their prize, and came down upon us hooting and yelling like demons, at the same time loading their guns and evidently determined not to spare their shot. This was a moment of intense interest. The plan which I had formed from the first, was now about to be put to the proof; and if the pirates were not the cowards I took them to be, nothing could save us. Their fearful yells seem to be ringing in my ears, even now, after this lapse of time and when I am on the other side of the globe.'*

Waiting as it were, until he could see the whites of their eyes, and at the critical moment, he continues: *'I raised myself above the high stern of our junk and while the pirates were not more than twenty yards from us, I raked their decks fore and aft with shot and ball, from my double barrelled gun. Had a thunderbolt fallen amongst them, they*

could not have been more surprised – the whole of the crew, not fewer than forty or fifty men, who a moment before crowded the deck, disappeared in a marvellous manner, sheltering behind the bulwarks or lying flat on their faces. They were so completely taken by surprise, that their junk was left without a helmsman, her sails flapped in the wind, and as we were still carrying all sail and keeping on our right course, they were soon left a considerable way astern.' After this Fortune became for the Chinese crew, *'the greatest and best of men in existence; they actually came and knelt before me and expressed their deep and lasting gratitude, which, however'*, he adds, *'did not last long.'*

FLOWERS AND GRAVES

Fortune was always interested in Chinese cemeteries and the use of plants for decoration. He noted that *'no camellias, moutons or the finer ornaments of the garden are chosen for this purpose … when I first discovered the Anemone japonica it was in full flower among the graves of the natives which are found in the ramparts of Shanghai; it blooms in November, when other flowers have gone by, and is a most appropriate ornament to the last resting place of the dead.'*

He introduced it to England and noted it in full bloom at Chiswick in 1846 on his return, *'as luxuriant and beautiful as it ever grew on the graves of the Chinese.'* Luckily it does not need a cemetery to show its charms, and can spread itself round, tactfully filling gaps, here and there, where its

Jasminum mesnyi, the Primrose Jasmine

little, white or pale pink, single flowers look very well, with a background of myrtle.

When Fortune was travelling about three hundred miles west of Shanghai, in one of the best tea districts, he came across a dilapidated old garden where he found *'a very fine evergreen berberis, belonging to the section of mahonias,* and describes it: *'each leaflet of the pinnate leaves was as large as that of an English holly, spiny and of a fine dark shining green colour; the shrub was about eight feet high, much branched and far surpassed in beauty all other known species of mahonia; it had but one fault – it was too large to move and take away.'*

The berberis was much prized in that district, but Fortune, with a certain amount of bribery and corruption, managed to find three good plants to take with him. He named it *Mahonia bealei* after the father and son Thomas Beale, both of whom had splendid gardens. The former lived for fifty years in Macao, and the son, Fortune's great friend, in Shanghai. It has been confused with *Mahonia japonica,* and the huge plant in my garden is probably the latter. Its scented, pale yellow racemes come out just about Christmas, and vie for attention with the *Hamamelis mollis* which frames it. Some of its fine pinnate leaves turn a vivid scarlet in the autumn, greatly adding to the winter decoration.

A riveting story surrounds a very favourite Chinese plant, *Jasminum mesnyi.* It is known as the primrose jasmine, and indeed its semi double primrose-like flowers are very striking. I first saw it in the conservatory at Syon House, just outside London. It is nearly evergreen, and like so many of the marginally tender/hardy species, it likes a sheltered south-facing wall, and with luck will flower from March until May.

My primrose jasmine is climbing experimentally from a large stone pot up my house by the front door, slightly protected by the bay window. It will either dislike being in a pot and refuse to flourish, or more likely from its present behaviour, take off and smother my way into the house.

WILLIAM MESNY

Jasminum mesnyi was found in China by a remarkable young man called William Mesny, and I saw it growing there in many different places, quite commonly. G R Balleine wrote *'A Biographical Dictionary of Jersey'* in 1948 and quotes from *'Mesny's Miscellany; Family Information'* as his source. Mesny was born in Jersey in 1842, the son of a cobbler, but when he was twelve he went to sea, working his way around the world, eventually jumping ship in Hong Kong. Here he quickly learned the language fluently, and made many Chinese friends among the merchants, especially among those with pretty daughters, anxious to secure a British son in law. He fled from this fate to Shanghai, where he found himself embroiled in the civil war between the Tai-ping rebels, who were trying to overthrow the Manchu dynasty. Both sides were recruiting foreign mercenaries, and Mesny tried to raise a company for the Emperor's service. His international band of ruffians was foiled by the intervention of French marines, who arrested him as a naval deserter.

In no time, this brilliant and enterprising young man found ways of exploiting this confused state of affairs. Ordinary commerce was at a standstill, and the Yangtze river – that great highway into China – was

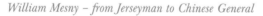

William Mesny – from Jerseyman to Chinese General

the scene of competing merchants, trying to get their cargoes through the danger zone.

Navigation was very dangerous, with fighting on both banks, and both sides seizing any available cargo. Mesny plunged in headfirst, starting with a small sailing boat and progressing to a Chinese junk. He found that bags of salt could be bought for a dollar at Shanghai and sold for thirteen at Hangkow; he also made what he called *'a few very successful speculations in the arms trade'*.

Once his boat was captured by the Imperialists, and twice he was wounded. Then he was taken prisoner by Tai-pings, who fixed his ransom at 100,000 dollars, *'a princely price for a poor Jerseyman'* he wrote in letters home. At first he was cruelly treated, but when his captors discovered he could play Chinese tunes on his four octave flutina, their behaviour completely altered. After six months of not unpleasant captivity, he was rescued by a British gunboat.

Mesny's extraordinary career continued when he became a Lieutenant under General Gordon, who had been lent by the British Government to the Chinese to suppress the Tai-ping Rebellion, and when Gordon returned to England in 1865, Mesny remained in the Chinese army. He saw much active service and was promoted Colonel in 1869 and awarded the 'Hua-ling Plume', followed by the 'Star of China', and in 1873 at 29 he became

Major–General and was created 'Penetrating Knight of the Pa-t'u-lu,' the Chinese equivalent of the Legion d'Honneur. He married a Chinese girl, Han, and had a Chinese family, and about this time took to wearing Chinese dress, grew a magnificent pigtail and was said to be the only European who could speak Chinese without a trace of a foreign accent.

His military duties did not take up too much time, and he became an enthusiastic geographer and explorer, travelling in 1877 for twenty months across Tibet to the Capital of Yunnan, and making another three thousand mile journey from Canton to Turkestan. He penetrated into districts no European had entered before, and sent records of his discoveries to the Royal Geographical Society, of which he became a Fellow.

Mesny was also a keen-eyed botanist, and sent many new plants home to England, among them my very beautiful *Viburnum setigeron*, and *Jasminum mesnyi*, named after him. He never abandoned his British citizenship, and kept closely in touch with his native island of Jersey. In 1895 he began to publish in Shanghai a chatty little magazine called *Mesny's Miscellany*, written by himself and full of information he had gathered about Chinese customs, plants, etiquette, superstitions and secret societies. He died at the age of seventy seven in Hankow in 1919.

What a man.

8

FOCUS ON LEWISIAS —AND— REDWOODS

*'The Lewisia is named after Meriwether Lewis,
of the Lewis and Clark expedition sent by Thomas Jefferson
to open up the North West passage. Their plant collection was
not large, but much of it was new to science – The Lewisia is
Montana's state flower.'*

One has to go to extreme lengths to grow lewisias; I tried planting them into crevices in walls – their reputed favourite position – but mine must be the wrong sort of walls. It is the miraculous perfection of this tiny, pink bloom which makes it so desirable, but its passionate hatred of sitting in the damp and its determination to decide for itself what are suitable conditions (no matter what the planting instructions say) makes it a hard object to satisfy. Drainage is the magic word, and to achieve it walls must be rebuilt, chunks of granite acquired and exactly the right angle of slope prepared for the infinitely fussy model.

Ashwood Nursery specialises in lewisias and has the National Collection, so it seemed a good idea to visit and study the chosen habitat; unfortunately, however, the plants

5395.

3

4

2

Lewisia rediviva by W Fitch – Curtis's Bot. Mag. 1863

were all growing in pots. It had launched its *lewisia cotyledon*, 'Ashwood Strain', nearly twenty years ago, and the new hybrid 'Carousel' was available in late spring. Ten little plants, beautifully packed, duly arrived in late April and were dealt with according to the leaflet: *'For best results'*, it advised, *'potting up in John Innes No 2 (three parts), to one part gravel chippings, until well established and growing freely, then they may be planted out, in a sloping, well drained outdoor rockery, preferably with a northerly aspect to provide a little shade.'*

They clearly liked pot life and flowered very quickly, but I did not want them in pots; I wanted a bed of them, happily flowering outside. There was only one faintly suitable place in a narrow bed at the foot of a wall, which already had holboelia, a honeysuckle and a schizophragma growing up it. Their bed would have to be steeply sloping, and it was prepared with as much grit and granite as possible, with a granite edge to give the illusion that it was a

wall. It was here that Bill, with his mason's training, was in his element – and created this narrow bed at a suitable gradient, enough to give the lewisias the gritty drainage they so crave. We planted them in full flower, and for a while they seemed fooled – but gradually they became smaller and smaller and almost disappeared. However, I need not have gone to all that disappointing trouble because the *Lewisia cotyledon* plants, found in several adjacent nurseries, were three times the size and flowered enthusiastically, just as I wanted them to, obviously approving of their nicely sloping bed. Lewisias always know best.

MERIWETHER LEWIS

The plant was named *Lewisia rediviva* after Meriwether Lewis, who is always now referred to as 'Lewis and Clark,' as if the two were indistinguishable. Thomas Jefferson, the third President of the United States of America, was possessed by his American Dream: to send an

Lewisia cotyledon, the Bitteroot in their sloping bed

expedition by boat from the west of the great Mississippi River, following the equally vast Missouri River from St Louis to explore the unknown territory across the Rocky Mountains and reach the Pacific Ocean, opening up the North West Passage and finding a new trade route to China.

Meriwether Lewis came from a farming, soldiering background and had some experience of the wild country, inhabited by Indians. Jefferson chose him to be his private secretary, and this proved a very rewarding relationship – something like father and son. Jefferson was 61 and without a son; Lewis was 26 and had been left an orphan.

Jefferson began to plan the realisation of his dream, based on Meriwether Lewis as leader of the expedition. He had been spurred on by reading the account of Alexander Mackenzie, (a Scotsman, after whom the river is named), of his journey in 1793 across Canada to the Pacific, in which he hoped to find an all water route from the Atlantic, *'which would give access to the fur trade, fishing of both seas and the markets of the four corners of the globe'*.

The die was cast, and Lewis was to start on his journey as soon as possible. Mackenzie's chronicle was used as a guide, and Lewis planned to take a party of ten or twelve men on a journey estimated to take around eighteen months. They would take river boats, (light enough for portage over the mountains) and many presents for the Indians as

well as all the necessary equipment. Lewis taught himself celestial navigation, and spent a month studying methods of describing and preserving botanical specimens; a medical kit was assembled for him and he was lectured on its uses. He wrote to his friend Captain William Clark, with whom he had served and who knew how to fight and negotiate with Indians, to ask him to join him in this venture, and Clark replied *'my friend, there is no man lives with whom I would prefer to undertake such a trip'.* Clark was six feet tall, red-haired and four years older than Lewis; he was to be of equal seniority, and the two captains would share command. Clark was accompanied by his *'paunchy slave, York, who acted as cook and orderly for the leaders,'* and Lewis brought along a large Newfoundland dog named Seaman.

JEFFERSON'S DETAILED BRIEF

Jefferson wrote page after page of instructions for his pet project, starting with *'Find the North West Passage and the most direct route to the Pacific, draw maps, make detailed observations of the soils, minerals, crops, animals and weather; meet the Indians, record their languages, populations, religions, customs, food, clothing, willingness to trade with Americans.'* He insisted on detailed and multiple records, and Lewis and Clark ordered the sergeants to do the same. Sadly, the one person who fell down on this was Lewis himself, who left long lapses and gaps in his journals; it is a great loss as he was the more articulate of the pair and wrote most accurately and descriptively when he bothered to write at all. Luckily the diaries written by other members seem to fill in most of the gaps.

It was 14th May 1804 when the Corps of Discovery finally set off *'under a gentle breeze'*, having crossed from the east side of the Mississippi upstream from St Louis, opposite the mouth of the Missouri. They had two 'pirogues' or river boats, and a large keel boat – fifty five feet long, ten feet wide and capable of carrying ten tons of provisions. The weather was bad, the mosquitoes appalling, but the huge wide Missouri, *'choked with snags'*, was the worst obstacle; with a favouring wind they could sail the keel boat, but more often it was oars or setting poles, or worse, 'cordelling', with the men wading along muddy banks pulling her with a rope. Fourteen miles was considered a good day.

As they moved slowly up country the landscape changed; trees disappeared, vast grasslands covered the Great Plains, and huge herds of buffalo ranged before them. Lewis collected, pressed and (eventually) returned with 240 plant specimens, which later scientists drew and named. Among them are *Clarkia pulchella* and *Lewisia rediviva* named after the leaders. The latter, a delightful little pink flower that has brought about this whole saga, is also known as the bitterroot and

eaten by the Indians. Lewis described it as *'naucious to my pallate'*, but it is now Montana's state flower and a mountain chain and major river are also named for it.

The collection of seeds and specimens made by Lewis and Clark was a relatively small one, but together with his herbarium, almost everything in it was new to science. Another Lewis discovery that I value highly is the *Philadelphus lewisii*, or 'Mock Orange' as it is known. One of the hybrids grown nowadays is called 'Belle Etoile', which has white, heavenly-scented flowers flushed maroon at the centre, which grows and flowers well in a shady position under the conker tree.

After six months the expedition had travelled only sixteen hundred miles, and there was no sign of the mountains or the source of the river, which they had hoped to reach before winter set in. The Captains therefore decided that with frosts at night and the occasional snow flurry, it would be wise to over winter where they were. They spent the time profitably, making friends with the local Indians, studying every aspect of their lives, and all the wild life of interest. Then, in the spring, they dispatched the big keelboat back down river to Mr Jefferson at Montecello.

NUMEROUS PERILS

Armed with the knowledge from their Indian friends of what lay ahead, they looked forward to seeing the tremendous waterfalls and the great range of *'shining mountains'*, expecting that portaging the canoes round the falls would take half a day, and the mountains two or three days at most to cross. In the event, the portage took nearly a month and the going was terrible; the men wore through a pair of moccasins every two days, blistered their hands and feet on the prickly pear cactus and endured heat stroke and hailstorms, but worst of all were the plagues of mosquitoes.

They had taken warnings of grizzly bear rather lightly, but learned better after one or two near fatal encounters. Lewis met a *'monster'*, weighing an estimated 600 lb, and when wounded, the grizzly chased six men over the twenty foot river bank and plunged into the water behind them. After *'nine shot in him'* he was killed by a tenth to the head. *'His feet were nine inches across the ball and his nails seven inches long.'*

It was 12 August when Lewis and Clark finally reached the source of the mighty Missouri. Over the ridge way ahead was where the two Captains expected to find the land beyond falling away, and the river Columbia flowing down to the Pacific. What they saw instead was *'immense ranges of high mountains still to the west of us, with their tops partially covered with snow.'* The *'half day portage'* had turned out to be a 340 mile overland trek, some 140 of those miles over tremendous mountains often covered in snow. It

was the end of the North West Passage dream.

Somehow they carried on, pulling and pushing their boats on makeshift carts over the Rocky Mountains, to where they could at last continue to boat down the Columbia river, finally to reach the Pacific ocean on November 7th 1805. Clark looked up from his canoe and wrote, *'Ocean in view; O the Joy'*.

On reaching the ocean they had fulfilled one of Jefferson's missions. However, Jefferson had hoped they might have been able to return by sea; another huge miscalculation. Clark wondered how the sea had come by its name *'as I have not seen one Pacific day since my arrival in its vicinity; its waters are foaming and perpetually break with immense waves on the sands and rocky coasts, tempestuous and horrible'*. But the Corps of Discovery took it on the chin, and faced the awful prospect of returning by the way they had come. On 23rd September 1806 they arrived in St Louis after two and a half years travelling; it was a journey which had been over 4,000 miles each way.

Sadly, that was the end of Lewis, who made himself ill with drink and opium, could not bring himself to write up the story of the expedition, and finally shot himself. It was to be one hundred years before his interesting discourse on natural history was published, and the courageous story told.

Before becoming President of the United States of America in 1801

Thomas Jefferson had been Ambassador to France, and would have been imbued with the spirit of the Age of Enlightenment. He probably met and mingled with the great men of the era, and heard how Captain Cook's last attempt to find the North West Passage from the Pacific side had ended in disaster, and how he had died – murdered by Hawaian natives. He would have met Sir Joseph Banks, President of the Royal Society, who spent a lot of time masterminding expeditions from England for the same purpose of discovering the passage. Banks' friend, Sir John Franklin, had made two overland expeditions before being lost at sea in his last attempt to find it from the Atlantic. Jefferson knew it was a race between Americans and the Europeans, and that whoever discovered this valuable short cut from one ocean to the other would control the trade routes of North America.

THE LURE OF THE REDWOODS

I did not feel much like following Lewis and Clark on their uncomfortable and cold explorations, and much regretted not being able to see the lewisia growing wild. But I did want to visit North America and inspect those enormous redwoods. I had even tried to grow one – a strange looking, tall, thin *Sequoiadendron pendulum*. However, it was not very decorative and I soon gave it away. I had always wanted to visit the coastal redwoods ever since I saw, as a child – at the top of the stairs in the Natural History Museum in London – a very large slice of redwood displayed. The legend gave its diameter as 14 feet and its age as 1,300 years. It was cut from a tree in Fresno, California, for Chicago's World Fair in 1892, and was shipped to England from San Francisco in a barque called the Candida for £154.

It was purposely to see the trees that I rashly accepted the offer to visit Woodside, near San Francisco, to give my talk about Sir Joseph Banks, where they had just invested £150,000 in the 723 coloured prints in *Banks' Florilegium*. I had also been asked to address a banquet, and had been trying not to think what this might involve. What I had not anticipated was the legendary hospitality of my host and hostess, who lived appropriately in Redwood City, and seemed to have rearranged their entire lives to show me what I wanted to see.

ALAN MITCHELL

Before I left England I had heard from my friend Alan Mitchell, the well-known tree consultant. He had spent a lifetime measuring trees all over the world, and kindly supplied me with the names and addresses of every redwood over 250 feet in height, with instructions on how to find them, and the numbers of maps and roads to follow. *'Do not waste time on Muir Woods'* (San Francisco) he advised, *'miserable things few over*

Giant Redwood trees

200', all but one circles of sprouts from burned stumps; go to 300' trees of quality and size in fine nearby groves between San Jose and Santa Cruz.'

It was easy to adapt the day planned for my benefit, in order to picnic beside the Pacific Ocean (no one could understand my determination to paddle in this, an ocean I had never seen before) and cover the seventeen mile drive round the Monterey peninsular, visit Carmel, and include a call on 'Giant' (285' x 51'), who was to be found in the Henry Cowell Redwoods State Park. Nearby in Big Basin Redwoods were 'Mother of Forest' (310' x 47'), 'Father of Forest' (260' x 53'), and 'Washington Tree' (276' x 37').

All I can say to try and describe these huge trees is that they are vastly bigger than one could possibly imagine, towering almost beyond one's vision, dramatic in effect because of the darkness they generate and the opaque silence in such a forest is not penetrated by ordinary sounds.

Alan had drawn up a list of trees to occupy me for three weeks, so it was extremely lucky to be able to fit so many into the three available hours. He had told me that Mariposa Grove in Yosemite National Park was an *'absolute must'*, so I tore myself away from my kind American hosts, and after a diversion for some more lectures in Pasadena, the banquet (which turned out to be at lunchtime to my surprise) was not a big deal after all, and I got away with it by just talking them through my slides. Then it was on to another few days of luxurious indulgence and garden sightseeing, and a flight back to San Francisco in time to take a three day bus tour, with California Parler Car Tours to Yosemite.

CHIEF TYPES OF REDWOOD

The two main varieties of redwood, both evergreen and cone-bearing, have much in common, and are the coastal redwood *Sequoia sempervirens,* and the giant redwood *Sequoiadendron giganteum.*

During prehistoric times such redwoods were spread over much of the northern hemisphere, but climatic change has reduced their habitat, and today the *Sequoia sempervirens,* the tallest trees in the world, are found only along a 450 mile corridor stretching from Oregon to the southern limits of the Monterey County, restricted to the moist fog within 30 miles of the sea. The oldest of these is between 1,500 and 2,000 years and the tallest 370 feet.

Both varieties reproduce by seed, but the coastal redwood has the advantage of sending out shoots from the burls, which are large growths at the base of the tree, inside which are a mass of dormant buds. The tree has only surface roots, and these extend 50 feet or so in the upper reaches of the soil. This system, of young trees growing from the root crown sprouts, is their principal method of propagation – often in a circle round the parent tree.

A SOCIAL HABIT

Coastal and giant redwoods have a sociable solution when many seedlings germinate too closely – fusing their roots to hold each other up; or at other times grafting on to another quite high up, where they touch and grow on into one enormous tree.

Both varieties benefit from the reddish, fibrous, spongy bark, sometimes several feet thick, whose tannin content makes it resistant to fire and to attacks by insects and fungi. Fire clears the forest floor so the redwood seed can reach the mineral soil it needs to germinate.

THE WELLINGTONIA

The giant redwood *Sequoiadendron giganteum,* or Wellingtonia, has the distinction of being the largest living thing in the world, past or present.

It has been measured up to 310 feet tall, with a base diameter of 35 feet, the greatest reported age being 4,000 years.

The entire native habitat is now only 250 miles long by 15 miles wide – on the western slopes of the Sierra Nevada – where it is primarily found at elevations of 5,000 feet to 7,000 feet, in distinct groves, which are recognised by name throughout the range.

SAN FRANCISCO TO YOSEMITE

The bus from San Francisco to Yosemite took all morning, driving through vast wind farms, flat, fruit farming land, until the road began to climb into forests of Douglas fir, Oregon maple, Californian Live oak, Ponderosa pine and Californian laurel, with assorted ferns, sorrel, wild ginger and trilliums for ground cover. The remains of terrible forest fires were all too evident from acres and acres of blackened dead trees.

After lunch, an open air bus took two hours to explore the valley, driving slowly with the guide giving details of the massive 4,000 feet cliffs towering above, with their various domed or peaked shapes named El Capitan, Cathedral Spires, Three Brothers and others, and the next day was booked for Mariposa Grove, a six hour marathon, with the driver providing another interesting commentary.

The 'Fallen Monarch' is a dramatic sight; the fir tree leaning over its upper section suggests it fell several hundred years ago and stage-coaches are said to have driven along the trunk. Next you come to the 'Three Graces,' an example of the giant sequoia's capacity to grow to great size in close proximity; these three are probably between 200 and 260 feet tall, their roots fused together for support.

'The Faithful Couple' is two trees which have grown closer together over the years, exhibiting the ability to graft to one another; the combined trunk is 40 feet across at the base and the twin columns 250 feet high.

The 'Grizzly Giant' is the largest and oldest in the grove: only 200 feet tall but its great trunk rises in a straight column; at the base it is 31 feet across tapering to 16 feet at 60 feet above the base, and is still 13 feet across at 120 feet. The first large limb at 95 feet is 6 feet in diameter. The estimated age is 2,500 to 3,000 years. You have to pinch yourself to believe what you are seeing.

My final lectures were in Vancouver Island and at the Van Dusen Botanical Garden, Vancouver. I booked a sleeper on Amtrak's Superliner, the Coast Starlight, from San Francisco to Vancouver Island, via Seattle. Normal Americans travel by air, so those who take the train are a motley crew. You start off by catching a bus at the huge, unsalubrious bus depot, where we were greeted by a mini, comic Cassius Clay, who explained that as the train was four hours late, he would take us for a nice bus trip round San Francisco to pass the time. Meanwhile, he would only let us board the bus if we agreed to kiss him first, which having no alternative we all meekly did. The first class sleeper was on the upper deck of the train and consisted of a long bunk with rock hard pillow, seemingly impregnated with tobacco and alcohol, and opposite this, en suite as it were, was a tall thin door concealing a minuscule shower and loo, in a sort of cupboard. You had to decide which sex you were before entering, as once inside there was no turning round.

The train takes you north through Sacramento, capital of California, and climbs the Cascade Range to about 4,800' at Cascade Summit, passing spectacular peaks up to 14,000 feet. To do this, it does some remarkable hairpin bends, and goes through no less than 22 tunnels climbing 3,600 feet in 44 miles. It continues through Klamath Falls – where the scent of freshly cut wood pervades the air – to Eugene, the lumber capital of the US. Douglas firs cover the lower slopes, and there are many clearings for felling. The whole journey is illuminated in October with the brilliant yellow of the big leaf maple *Acer macrophyllum*. I thought of Lewis and Clark as I crossed their path in the very tolerable comfort of First Class Amtrak, compared to the sufferings they had to endure. The train crosses two arms of the Columbia River and from the steel bridge over the Willamette River at Portland, Mount Hood at 11,235 feet, is visible. The line approaches Seattle along the Puget Sound, (named after Vancouver's Lieutenant), with the Olympic Mountains to the west.

There was just time to see the Van Dusan Botanical Gardens which are comparatively new, but splendid imaginative planting has been done there. My last abiding memory of it will be of a small grove of young *Sequoiadendron giganteum* growing so elegantly in their teenage; perhaps in a few hundred years they will also find it necessary to fuse roots, and hold together like their sociable elderly cousins in California.

There were one or two other plants from this part of the world which I cherish, such as *Menziesia ferruginea* which is a very small, slow growing but neat shrub with lily of the valley-like flowers. It is deciduous, which is a pity, but its terminal clusters of pink, waxy bells make up for it. I have planted it in the bed in front of the house, where everything is low growing, bowing down in front of the camellia hedges behind it.

Arbutus menziesii is very desirable, but its fellow *Arbutus unedo* outshines it – having real-looking strawberries as well as hanging baskets of pink and white panicles, which are its flowers. It is not at all fussy about where it is planted – which in my garden is next to a Pieris – and is an ornament at all times of the year. *Gaultheria procumbens,* or weeping wintergreen, is a splendid ground cover under the palm trees. Each plant promises to cover a square yard – a promise yet to be redeemed; it is aromatic and evergreen with small pink or white flowers, sometimes in racemes, followed by red berries. All these were found by Archibald Menzies, who plant hunted for Joseph Banks several times in North West America.

It was while Thomas Jefferson was sending off Lewis and Clark that Sir Joseph was busily orchestrating another voyage for the same purpose, but also to determine the position and extent of the west side of North America. *HMS Discovery* was chosen for the voyage, to be commanded by Lieutenant George Vancouver, while Archibald Menzies (1754–1842) was to go as naturalist.

Unfortunately, Vancouver was a difficult man to get on with, described in various biographies as, *'ill bred and tyrannical'* and *'irascible',* and there was tension between him and Menzies from the start. Banks did his best to iron out the problems before they sailed – mostly about the management of the plant cabin, any help he might have from the crew, salary, servant's wages and mess arrangements, all rather vital details on a four year voyage and at such close quarters.

Menzies behaved with patience and tact and managed to carry out Banks' instructions, apart from losing all the live plants he had collected through Vancouver's uncooperative behaviour. When Menzies protested, Vancouver flew into a rage, accusing him of insolence and contempt – the final row being over the ownership of Menzies' diary, which the latter insisted was Banks' property. Menzies was to spend the last three months of the voyage under arrest and confined to his cabin, in a ship

that size about the area of a cupboard.

Menzies came from a Perthshire family. An addict to botany, he trained as a gardener at Edinburgh Botanic Garden and also studied to become a doctor at Edinburgh university before joining the Navy for a voyage of commercial discovery to the north west coast of America. Sir Joseph was asked by the Admiralty to give him instructions for the expedition with Vancouver, which he did with his usual enthusiasm.

Menzies was to study the whole of natural history of the countries visited and *'to pay attention to the nature of the soil and in view of the prospect of sending out settlers from England, whether grains and fruits are likely to survive.'* He was to identify all trees, shrubs, plants, grasses, dry as many as possible and collect seed. Any valuable plants that could not be propagated from seed were to be dug up and put in the frame (provided for the purpose); he was to search for ores and metals, note the sort of birds and beasts and fishes, in particular the sea otter and the wild sheep, also where whales and seals were to be found. He was to keep a regular journal and describe the manners, customs, language and religion of the natives, and obtain information about their manufactures, *'especially the art of dyeing.'* Banks also wanted any information about the *'abominable custom of eating human flesh'.* There is, of course, much more which makes good reading.

When I visited Victoria on Vancouver Island during my Californian tour, I found it extremely difficult to find any record of George Vancouver's part in the island's history. However, the island was named after him because he was the first to identify it as an island; previously it was thought to be part of the mainland. A statue of him in the main square, pointed out to me by a lady born and brought up on the island, turned out to be of Captain Cook. He seemed to be eminently forgettable and forgotten but I persevered and eventually found a small section of the Maritime Museum dedicated to him. Here at last was a real memento – the very chronometer he had used on the voyage. On his return, this same chronometer had been given to William Bligh on his journey to Australia, where he was to become its Governor – a period which also ended in disaster for Bligh, with another mutiny and the Rum rebellion. The chronometer then disappeared for two hundred years until it turned up for sale in London, and was bought by the Vancouver Maritime Museum.

During the voyage Vancouver surveyed not only the west coast of Australia on his way out, but the enormous extent of coast from Lower California to Cook Inlet. His meticulous charting put on the map of the world the intricacies of Puget Sound, and the whole of the west coast of mainland Canada up to Alaska, where he and Menzies spent five arduous and dangerous months surveying, in temperatures below 7 degrees F., until ice flows forced them south. Vancouver died shortly after his return to England in October 1795, aged just 40. Of those 40 years, 22 were spent at sea, where he sacrificed his personal life and burned out his health in the performance of his duty. He certainly earned some Brownie points.

NOT A VIP

Bringing myself firmly back to the present century, it was necessary to face a few urgent problems with my own prospects. Lecturing in the States sounds so immensely grand that one immediately thinks of people of either national or notorious calibre, even ex Prime Ministers, invited to air their weighty opinions; professors with brilliant ideas to impart, paid in the region of £20,000 a shot, with Concorde available, or at least first class airfares, and stretch limos provided in all directions. These people are all, obviously, immensely sought after, and have great difficulty fitting in a suitable date three years ahead. I might as well inhabit a different planet with my circumstances, and I kept thinking of 'Lucky Jim', Kingsley Amis' wickedly funny film (of the book) with Ian Carmichael, giving his Professor's lecture with disastrous results, and being reminded of the terrible fate that might await a self-invented lecturer like myself.

I didn't often go into details when I was asked (rather jealously), how I had come to be invited to lecture in the US, leaving rather vague my nefarious methods based on bluff and nerve, but I had often been rather good at organising things I wanted to do. I had one bit of luck when trying to become a member of the Garden Club of America, which you had to apply for – as if for a job – with a CV, photograph and testimonial. I had written to an old friend at Kew, explaining my plan of action and asking him to write me a reference. In the event he wrote such a good one that it sounded as if I were a lecturer already, and of course with such a magic printed heading as *'The Royal Botanic Gardens, Kew'*, I was swept in immediately.

Luckily, the yardstick for lecturing is not something tangible. It is hard to tell if you are a success or not, as Americans are extremely polite and treat you as if you were a film star. I was quite overcome by the deference and respect I generated. Dinner parties were given in my honour, and I was introduced to local celebrities and taken miles to visit the many wonderful gardens within range. Never having been in such a position before, I found it rather jolly. However, I certainly had not made any money – because in America you get paid by the number in your audience and my travel expenses had soon gobbled that up. It occurred to me that the only career move I could make would be to consolidate what I had achieved so far, and try and find an audience in England. After all, I had not been drummed out of America, I was unscathed and had nothing to lose – in fact I might yet earn my garden's living.

As a Naval Officer my husband had been much in demand as a lecturer, but his reward was usually a bottle of gin. I aimed higher than that. My ever kind friends told me of a Society that sounded as if it might suit me: what is more, it paid a reasonable fee, better than any other society in fact, plus all expenses, had branches all over the country, and the committee members who were responsible for looking after you sounded as if they would make sure you could count on a decent drink before dinner. Old naval habits die hard.

Needless to say there were several hoops to go through before I could be accepted; the first condition was to give the date and place of my next three engagements – so they could send an inspector to come and listen – and naturally, I didn't have any. However, something had to be done, so I wrote an amended version of my letter which had been successful in the States, and sent it off to as many local gardening clubs as I could think of, meanwhile having a bit of practice with the Women's Institute, always eager for speakers, and the local Yacht Club.

SO FAR, SO GOOD

I procured exactly the three required engagements, and in due course several rather high-powered, blue rinse ladies came all the way to the Lizard Peninsular to investigate me. You had to have your own equipment – projector, screen, and so on – but all went well, in spite of having to borrow a bedside lamp and large cardboard box to stand it on so I could read my notes, and I was on to the next obstacle. This was an exam in London when I would have to face a quite intimidating board. For some reason I was not in the least nervous, it all seemed totally unreal or even, dare I say it – funny? Anyway, to my amazement I was approved and the final hurdle was to address about 300 chairmen of the Branch Societies, who all meet once a year, and where the new lecturers are put through their paces. You had three minutes – with a stopwatch – to persuade them that your lecture was irresistible, and that they must choose you to address their local group. If lucky, they would come up to you afterwards and engage you.

I did wonder whether I ought to take it all more seriously. I have an actor friend who said I should have breathing lessons so I could project my voice and went for one session somewhere in Hampstead, where I was made to lie on my back for the entire afternoon and charged £70 for the privilege. I decided I'd have to get on without special breathing.

My unexpected career took off and continued for several years, although it was quite hard work to keep updating the lectures, practising with a tape recorder and inventing something new each time, more for my benefit than that of my audience so as not to bore myself to death. At the lectures I found you would take your cue from your audience, every one of which is wildly different.

If my first joke goes down well, you breathe a huge sigh of relief, but if my sense of humour was not appreciated, woe betide. After that, probably as my friend had advised me, no-one was listening anyway, and of course lectures after lunch are guaranteed to send everyone to sleep.

RUMBLED AT LAST

Just as I was beginning to think enough was enough, I had a letter from one of the blue rinse ladies, sending me what I can only describe as the 'black spot'. Was it blind Pugh in *Treasure Island* who received it? Perhaps they were going through the lists and chucking out Old Age Pensioners, or maybe they had rumbled me at last. Anyway it said politely they thought I must find the travelling very tiring, not realising that for me travelling is the best part. I took the hint and decided to write this book instead.

I hate having nothing to do.

Philesia buxifolia by W Fitch, Curtis's Bot. Mag. 1853 - see page 148

—WHAT VEITCH'S— COLLECTORS FOUND

'Faced with the worst that Cornish weather can do from November on, when the clocks have gone back and gloom and anxiety have set in, what can cheer one better than a brilliant display of Vireya rhododendrons? They come in a rainbow range of colours and not knowing the difference between winter and summer, bloom at all times of the year.'

Vireya rhododendrons were named after a French natural historian, Julien Joseph Virey, in 1826, and are indigenous to the tropical regions of Malaysia and Borneo from latitude 10N to 10S, growing at altitudes from sea level to 13,000 feet. The Vireya species differ from all other rhododendrons in having very distinctive scales on their leaves; sometimes they adopt the delightful habit of flowering in the tops of trees in tall forests, displaying their strikingly dramatic colours to perfection.

Vireyas are all sun lovers in need of much moisture; they produce seed in great quantities, and the seed

is unique in having tails at both ends – doubling its chance of landing, windblown on some suitable vantage point. The construction also enables it to fly over the tops of trees, where it germinates high up in moss and lichen, caught in the cleft of branches, (if only it could repeat this behaviour, here in my trees.) It often grows 'epiphytically', taking nothing from its host but support, and the species is usually deliciously scented.

Even though vireyas are used to a luxurious choice of habitat, they still manage to thrive in terracotta pots in my greenhouse, deprived during our sad seasons of the sun, warmth and light they crave, provided they have almost no soil, rather a loose mix of moss, pine bark, coarse sand, charcoal and peat, and plenty of water and free drainage. Perhaps it is because they sense they are among sophisticated international neighbours and are treated to frequent tropical showers. During the summer they sit outside, decorating parts of the garden and busily setting seed.

THOMAS LOBB AND VEITCH

It was Thomas Lobb, the younger of two Cornish brothers, who found these ravishing plants when he was hunting for orchids, his first love. He and his older sibling William were employed by Veitch of Exeter, and sent to the opposite ends of the earth to search for interesting plants for his gardening customers. Hothouse plants were becoming very popular and nurserymen identified a market for supplying these new gardening enthusiasts.

The family of Veitch was one of the most influential in the development of English gardens, responsible during the 19th century for the introduction of hundreds of exotic ferns, stove and greenhouse plants, and particularly orchids. The Veitchs were also famous for the many hybrids they made. The story begins with John Veitch, (1752-1839), a Scot from Jedburgh, who came south to lay out a park for Sir Thomas Acland at Killerton in Devon. Acland suggested that he should start a nursery of his own

nearby, which Veitch duly did, and where he began trading in 1808. He and his son James were particularly successful, and were succeeded by their sons and grandsons and descendants right up until 1969 when the firm was sold, ending the family's connection with the nursery.

HUGH LOW

Although there are now 270 different species of Vireya rhododendrons, Veitch only had seven from which to hybridise in the early days, but his catalogue of 1893 contained fifty hybrids. His first was between *R. jasminiflorum* and *R. javanicum,* both introduced by Thomas Lobb in 1849. This was named 'Princess Royal', and although its parents' flowers were white and orange-yellow respectively, the hybrid bloomed a delicate rose colour.

Among his seven species was *R. brookeanum,* found in Borneo and brought back by a Mr Hugh Low in 1844, who was collecting plants for his father's nursery in Clapton; '*I shall never forget the first discovery of this gorgeous plant,'* says Mr Low, who describes it as, '*epiphytal upon a tree, growing in the waters of a creek; the head of flowers was very large, arranged loosely, of the richest golden yellow, resplendent when in the sun; the habit was graceful, the leaves large, the roots are large and fleshy, not fibrous as those of the terrestrial Rhododendrons; very high and large trees, in damp forests are its favourite haunts'.* While in Borneo

Rhododendron Vireya jasminiflorum

Low met the famous Sir James Brooke, Rajah of Sarawak, after whom he named his exciting discovery.

Hugh Low returned to England in 1847 and published a book called *'Sarawak'* in 1848, which was a comprehensive survey of the natural history and ethnology of the country, quite a coup for a young man of twenty four. Rajah Brooke was also in England at this time, being feted and honoured by Queen Victoria and he invited Sir Hugh Low (as he became) to return to Sarawak as his Colonial Secretary. In that capacity he spent twenty eight years becoming one of its most able administrators. Indeed, it was his discovery of such plants in this area that prompted Veitch to send Thomas Lobb to collect plants for him. *R. brookeanum* was exhibited by Veitch's nursery at the Horticultural show in London in 1855.

Right: Rhododendron Vireya 'Java Light'

GEORGE ARGENT

I have a quite large plant of *R. jasminiflorum* which flowers on and off for most of the year; it is supposed to be white but is flushed pink. 'Java Light' is a spectacular orange. Like all my vireyas they live inside the glasshouse during the winter, waiting for me on clement days to join them with my picnic lunch.

On one of my plant hunting expeditions I visited the Royal Botanic Gardens in Edinburgh and by great luck found Mr George Argent, the great Vireya specialist, actually there; he is normally off

144

searching for more species in Borneo or New Guinea. He gave me a cutting of what must surely be the smallest rhododendron in the world: *R. anagalliflorum,* with tiny pink bells and miniature foliage. Another cutting he gave me was of *R. stenophyllum,* with extremely narrow leaves and open-faced flowers of deep, waxy orange, as unusual as the foliage. I was very lucky to receive also a plant of *R. zoelleri,* quite my favourite species, it has huge open trusses of spectacular, deliciously-scented, yellow to orange-red flowers. The cuttings rooted very easily in clay pots inside polythene bags, plunged in my lapageria bed. I have managed so far to obtain three of Veitchs' original hybrids, created almost a

hundred years ago. One of the best – 'Pink Delight' – flowers through the winter, while 'Ne Plus Ultra' has long lasting flowers of brilliant crimson. 'Princess Alexandra', is slightly scented white, but one I would love is 'Triumphans', one of its grandparents being *R. brookeanum.*

FAVOURITE HYBRIDS

The species are very hard to come by which is sad, but among the better hybrids of modern times is one called 'St Valentine' from *R. lochae x gracilentum,* which has masses of small scarlet bells, inherited from its *lochae* parent, which is scarlet and the only species found in North Australia. Another is 'Flamenco Dancer', about to burst into flower just before Christmas; it comes from

Rhododendron Vireya 'Pink Delight'

two very desirable species, *R. aurigeranum,* and *R. macgregoriae,* both having orange to yellow flowers.

R. macgregoriae is well known in Papua, New Guinea, for its poisonous properties, being used by the natives as rat bait when mixed with sweet potato – perhaps I should try it on slugs. 'Thai Gold' has butter-yellow flowers with a touch of pink, and the dark green leaves are marked with red. I am amazed that these brilliantly coloured, temperamental plants should flourish in such dark winter days with wild, unpleasant weather so threateningly close.

Thomas Lobb is the despair of the gardening researcher, who longs to have some articulacy from the plant hunter giving a glimpse into his plantaholic soul and telling of his first impressions of everything. Alas, Veitch tells us that he was *'a young man of very respectable manners and appearance ... modest and retiring, of few words and that it was difficult to get him to describe a plant.* But if he ventured *'very pretty',* it was quite sufficient to *'induce extra care'.*

WILLIAM LOBB

To William, his brother, I have many reasons to be grateful; if you look out at my garden you can see a miniature Chile with heavenly plants that he introduced. I could not resist an opportunity to follow in his footsteps a year or two ago, and find vicarious pleasure in imagining his delight at what he saw.

My expedition to Chile did not go exactly to plan, as the ship, supposed to pick us up at Tierra del Fuego, was caught in a frightful storm on its way from the Falkland Islands. It was so badly damaged that we had to be marooned there while it was repaired. Noble Caledonia did its best to entertain us with a wide variety of penguins, some very badly-behaved beavers and some interesting seaweed, but most of the trees and shrubs were prostrated by the ever prevailing wind, which gathers speed from Cape Horn.

My worst disappointment was not being able to see the lapagerias growing up the rain forest trees or the monkey puzzles groves; sadly the repairs to the ship had changed the itinerary and I missed my chance. The most prevalent plant to be found everywhere (and not by any means a favourite of mine) was the lupin, which seems to have been a most successful immigrant.

MONKEY PUZZLES AND MANDEVILLA

William Lobb first worked as a gardener to Mr Stephen Davey of Scorrier, near Redruth in Cornwall. Davey encouraged him to join Veitch's, where Thomas was already employed. He was sent out to South America in 1840, and in his first package home were 3,000 *Araucaria araucana* seeds, so we must consider him largely responsible for the

Mandevilla boliviensis

Victorian Monkey Puzzle mania. William also sent some seed to Scorrier, and a plantation of them appeared there.

These trees look spectacular in their native forests or in groups, especially avenues, but rather lonely in small suburban gardens where they became a fashion, planted singly, often as the centre plant in a box bordered parterre. He sent back from this trip also four species of mandevilla, named after HJ Mandeville, British Minister in Buenos Aires, from which many hybrids were bred; the finest of which was exhibited by Veitch in London in 1842; two of these hybrids, lean and climb in my greenhouse, blooming from May, and still on Christmas Day covered in attractive pointed buds, which open into thickly clustered flowers of bright red, funnel-form with yellow throat, or blush pink, opening to white. *Mandevilla boliviensis,* which I first saw climbing up a trellis in Susana Walton's garden in Ischia, graced my glasshouse one winter,

Mandevilla 'Alice du Pont'

but I didn't manage to keep it going until the next season; it has masses of pure white, beautifully scented flowers, and a lovely, long flowering season.

William's second expedition was spent principally in Chile, close to the coast and there he collected the Chilean Firebush, the *Embothrium, Desfontainea spinosa,* and *Crinodendron hookerianum,* the Lantern tree, as well

Philesia buxifolia, photographed in Chile

as *Lapageria rosea,* which is described in my chapter on climbers.

Lobb also introduced *Philesia buxifolia,* a very slow-growing, dwarf member of the Liliaceae family which I saw growing on the island of Chiloe in Chile. Here it straggled over the rocky island almost at sea level, and the bushes were never more than two or three feet tall in that area. Nevertheless it was a delight to see its bright little flowers flourishing so far south, in this cold, wet inhospitable land.

Sailing round the many low-lying islands and much indented coast in a Zodiak rubber dinghy gave me the perfect opportunity of seeing it unexpectedly, and I imagined once more the pleasure and excitement of William when he first found it. It was crossed with lapageria and the result was called *Philageria,* not a noticeable improvement on either. William also introduced *Mitraria coccinea,* which is of value as a spreading sort of mat, or it can be induced to climb up anything to hand. But, some people are allergic to its violent vermillion flowers, which do not blend easily.

Philesia buxifolia – Curtis's Bot. Mag. 1853

148

Embothrium lanceolatum 'Norquinco Valley'

HAROLD COMBER

My *Embothrium lanceolatum,* 'Norquinco Valley', is from a later importation by Harold Comber (1897-1969), who collected his seed on the Argentine side of the Andes mountains at about 5,000 feet. For this reason it is hardier than Lobb's, flowering a month or so later, and also semi deciduous. It also has the most conspicuously coloured flowers of any hardy tree, being fiery-orange scarlet, narrow and tubular in shape, and thickly crowded on the branches in early summer. In my garden it had to be moved from its first position which did not allow for its height (quite a hazardous undertaking), however in its new position with an evergreen background of camellias, it will be reassuringly free of competition.

Besides his *Embothrium lanceolatum* 'Norquinco Valley', Comber found the genus *Lomatia,* also of the *Protaceae* family, which is interesting botanically, as is the *Euchryphia,* for being found in Australasia as well as in South America. *Lomatia ferruginea* is a most elegant, evergreen tree with beautiful, large, fern-like leaves, originally introduced by Lobb.

Hillier, whose *Manual of Trees and Shrubs* I mentioned earlier, describes it as *'a magnificent Chilean foliage plant; a large shrub or small erect tree with large, deep green, much divided, fern like leaves and red brown velvety stems; its flowers are scarlet and fawn coloured, born in short racemes.'* I grew it in the greenhouse for a year or two, but now it is outside, down by the treefern, replacing an old conifer that was recently disposed of. Its near neighbours are the orchid *Dactylorhiza* (given to me as a birthday present by my magnolia friend, Nigel Holman) and also the roscoeas and uvularias – quite a recherché little corner. Every autumn one of my most enjoyable activities is to divide up these wild

Lomatia ferruginea   *Dactylorhiza - a wild orchid*

Jovellana violaceae

orchids and double the number of these distinguished, aristocratic-looking plants. It is a very bending job so Bill helps me, but I have the pleasure of separating their delicate brittle roots by a little shake and a tweak.

Another desirable plant of Comber's introduction, *Asteranthera ovata,* grows fitfully at the base of one of my palm trees and should be galloping up by now; it is an unreliable but delightful little plant with tiny dull leaves, but produces bright scarlet flowers where it feels at home. *Jovellana violaceae* is not attributed to Comber, although he did bring back some seed from its cousins, the *Calceolaria,* which are also found in New Zealand. *Jovellana violaceae* has the palest of tiny, violet flowers with little lips, and grows happily in some sheltered gardens, and in a pot in my greenhouse.

I have always admired the Chilean holly, *Desfontainea spinosa,* though it is not a plant that blends into place. It needs to be on its own to look its best, having very prickly, shiny, small leaves and bright orange-yellow, funnel-shaped flowers which last well. It was growing very well in Chiloe Island, alongside the philesia at sea level, and there was also the miniature *Gunnera magellanica* spread out like fitted carpets all over the coastal region, and covered in little red seeds. *Gunnera magellanica* has bright green kidney-shaped leaves 2-3 inches across with wavy margins, and will make an excellent mat under my tree fern, the dampest place there is for it. It likes a fairly open situation, and where it is not quite damp enough makes little clumps or low mounds. In Chile, where it was growing within a few feet of the sea, it was trampled on by Magellan penguins who must have enjoyed its slippery surface. They are both named after the Portuguese navigator Ferdinand Magellan (1480-1521). *Gunnera manicata,* the giant, umbrella, rhubarb-lookalike plant is a close relation, though you would never think it. The desfontainea in my garden backs on to the myrtle hedge in a border of shrubs. The myrtle itself, *Myrtus luma,* is another native of Chile, again courtesy of William Lobb; its most extraordinary feature is its mature bark, which becomes piebald, a rich cinnamon brown, later flaking away to reveal a cream-coloured, sometimes pink-tinted, young bark.

William also introduced the Lantern Tree, *Crinodendron hookerianum,* which is another most interesting little tree, with evergreen leathery leaves and myriads of scarlet lanterns which start out as

Podocarpus chilensis or salignus

green miniatures, and develop and stay on the tree for a month or more. It also makes a good hedge; there is a white form, *Crinodendron patagua,* which is not so free flowering but beautifully scented and hardier. This flourishes in a corner of the wall by my terrace, from where the embothrium was moved; its white lanterns will bring light to the corner before the brilliant blue clematis of 'HF Young' takes over. My red Lantern Tree grows against the wall on the west of the house, where several clematis climb and involve themselves decorously among the lanterns.

Lobb also discovered and brought home seed of some new conifers, among them *Podocarpus nubigensis,* meaning 'born among the clouds.' This one has eluded me so far but I do grow another variety, (near the euchryphia), *Podocarpus chilensis,* or *salignus*. Grown from a cutting very easily, it is now fifteen or so feet high; the very pretty, feathery foliage is willow-like, (hence *salignus*), although it is a kind of yew and has red winter berries.

My first *Euchryphia cordifolia* from Chile was planted in 1976, just below my office, a year when we had a severe drought. It seemed likely to die, so another was planted alongside; now both are about twenty feet tall and flourishing – but, as usual, they are just too big and keep the light off some precious plants struggling below. It is my choice of euchryphia, not only for its flowers but for the splendid red colour the leaves acquire after their beautiful flowering season is over; I have a crafty plan to invite the electricity people to come and cut out the offending branches – through which the electric cable goes. Bill and Patrick would do it I know, but I find watching them wield the chainsaw with minimal protection very unnerving.

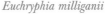

Euchryphia milliganii

I have tried the only pink euchryphia, 'Pink Cloud', a variety of *Euchryphia lucida* from Tasmania, several times, but only my latest new little plant has bothered to flower; its pale pink flowers with crimson centres are worth waiting for. There is *E. milliganii,* also from Tasmania, which flowers earliest and is covered in tiny white scented blooms; it is half the size of the other species but flowers away happily on the garage wall in its miniature way, the flowers being tiny to scale.

In 1849 William Lobb was sent to California, and made excursions to Oregon and the Sierra Nevada. Dr Albert Kellogg, the American pioneer and Californian botanist says tellingly, *'I myself took Mr Lobb to the California Academy of Sciences and showed him the first specimens he ever saw of this marvelous, now world renowned, Washington Cedar, (Washingtonia), which was so named by me before he ever saw the tree'* . Lobb collected a good quantity of seed, herbarium specimens and two living plants by his own account from a recently felled tree which *'measured about 300 feet in length, with a diameter including bark 29 feet 2 inches at 5 feet from the ground.'* Lobb immediately took passage on a ship bound for England, and it is history that on Christmas Eve 1853 Professor John Lindley published the description of *Wellingtonia gigantea* in *Gardener's Chronicle,* naming it *'for the greatest of modern heroes, who stands as high above his contempories as this Californian tree, above all the*

surrounding foresters'. The Duke of Wellington had died the year before, and in crowning a British hero, Lindley unleashed American crossfire that ricocheted for decades to come. In 1862, Piers Patrick acquired Benmore, near Dunoon, in Argyllshire and planted an avenue of giant redwoods which dominates the estate to this day. Naturally having described my mania for this species in the last chapter, you would expect me to make a pilgrimage to view this avenue, which I certainly did; it is a memorable sight.

ALFRED RUSSELL WALLACE

Hunting for clues into the psyche of these dedicated men from their diaries and letters I have been transfixed by their revelations, turning from despair at Thomas Lobb whose only quoted words of description of some ravishing plant he had found was *'very pretty',* to delight with Alfred Russell Wallace (1823-1913) who transformed his journals into *'the most famous of all books on 'The Malay Archipelago 1854-1862'* according to John Bastin who wrote the introduction.

Wallace was on quite a different plane, to the nurserymen or employed plant collectors; he was as much a scientist as a passionate natural historian, and although I cannot be sure I grow any particular plant he introduced, he fits into the background of the 19th century scholars, searching for further enlightenment among the living evidence – and makes one long to stalk him. He writes exquisitely and eloquently about every plant and creature, but it is insects and birds that electrify him.

CHARLES DARWIN

Wallace was a lifelong friend of Charles Darwin and dedicated *The Malay Archipelago* book to him, discussing in many letters as he travels the importance of the origins of species. He finds particular interest in the variety of species – peculiar or common to the huge number of islands in the Indonesian Archipelago – that by their creatures and plants can indicate which territories were once joined before volcanic or earthquake action divided them all into individual lands thousands of years ago. He comes quite independently to the same conclusion as Darwin, and in 1858 – at a meeting of the Linnean Society – Darwin and Wallace were jointly accepted as authors of the theory of evolution by natural selection. But Darwin alone was remembered for this most explosive issue of the day.

Wallace spent eight years travelling through the islands, financing his expedition (apart from the free fare from England granted to him by the Royal Geographic Society) entirely from the duplicate collections in Natural History, which he made and sent back to his agent in London, who sold them to all the museums interested. This accounts for the unseemly way, (in my rather outraged opinion), in which he killed and skinned so many beautiful birds, and pinned and preserved unique and exquisite butterflies and other insects.

There can rarely be such a thrilling written account of his finding a new species of *'bird-winged butterfly'*, or ornithoptera: *'I found this noble insect hovering over a beautiful shrub but it was too quick for me and flew away. The next day I went again to the same shrub and succeeded in catching a female and the day after a fine male. The beauty and brilliancy of this insect are indescribable and none but a naturalist can understand the intense excitement I experienced when I at length captured it; on taking it out of my net and opening the glorious wings, my heart began to beat violently, the blood rushed to my head, and I felt much more like fainting than I have done in apprehension of immediate death. I had a headache the rest of the day, so great was the excitement produced by what will appear to most people as a very inadequate cause.'*

Wallace takes us with him on finding *Ornithoptera Poseidon*, the great bird-winged butterfly: *'I trembled with excitement as I saw it coming majestically toward me, and could hardly believe I had really succeeded in my stroke till I had taken it out of the net and was gazing, lost in admiration at the velvet black and brilliant green of its wings, seven inches across, its golden body and crimson breast ... to capture it oneself, to feel it*

153

struggling between one's fingers and to gaze upon its fresh and living beauty, a bright gem shining out amid the silent gloom of a dark and tangled forest. The village of Dobbo held that evening at least one contented man.'

He also remarks upon his terrible suffering from insects *'who seemed bent upon revenging my long-continued persecution of their race.'* The ants certainly had a good go at him at one of the Aru Islands near New Guinea. He says, *'they immediately took possession of my house, building a large nest in the roof and forming papery tunnels down every post; they swarmed on my table as I was at work setting out my insects, carrying them off under my very nose, and even tearing them from the cards on which they were gummed if I left them for an instant. They crawled continually over my hands and face, got into my hair and roamed at will over my whole body, not producing much inconvenience until they began to bite, which they would do upon meeting any obstruction to their passage and with a sharpness which made me jump again and rush to undress and turn out the offender.'*

His enthusiasm is contagious when he sees these brilliant creatures, and I am grateful to him for his articulate descriptions, as he emerges vividly sensitive – and remarkably long suffering – while recounting what he saw one hundred and fifty years ago as if it were this very moment. His elegant prose is the 19th century equivalent of David Attenborough TV programmes which show us these heavenly creatures in brilliant reality.

On his journey home in 1862 Wallace found two adult live males of the Paradise bird species at Singapore, and bought them for the high price of £100 determined to bring them home.

They fed on rice, bananas and cockroaches, and he spent a week in Bombay to break the journey and lay in a stock of fresh bananas.

Cockroaches were scarce in the P & O steamers, and it was only *'by setting traps in the store rooms and by hunting an hour every night in the forecastle, that I could secure a few dozen of these creatures, scarce enough for a single meal. At Malta where I staid a fortnight I got plenty of cockroaches from a bake house and took with me several biscuit tins full as provision for the voyage home.'*

(One wonders what P & O would have thought in its beautiful cockroach free ship, if they had known what was in Wallace's biscuit tins). The birds arrived in London in good health and spent several years at the Zoological Gardens, *'often displaying their beautiful plumes to the admiration of the spectators'.*

He particularly admires the ferns, bamboos, pitcher plants, and other forest vegetation, among which he finds brilliantly coloured flowers. It is impossible not to be carried away by his sensationally graphic words, which make one wish to quote his whole book verbatim.

Tree Paeony 'Duchess of Marlborough'

TREE PAEONIES

Tree paeonies must be responsible for many plantaholics. No matter what you might have to displace, once you have seen them, there is no going back. The most desirable variety is the legendary species *Paeonia rockii,* but it costs £150 at the time of writing. It would be worth every penny of course, but while saving up, a more affordable hybrid is called 'The Duchess of Marlborough'. Kelways of Langport, Somerset - the unique Paeony nurseries, with the National Collection – describes her as *'one of the finest of all tree paeonies and a garden favourite for over one hundred years.'* She has the most beautiful bronzy foliage and her expectant, fat, pale pink buds have to be visited daily, as they slowly open to reveal crimson flares at the base of the ruffled, curled petals. At present, mine has ten huge, semi-double, saucer-shaped, exquisitely scented flowers and promises a few more every year. I hope that 'Cardinal Vaughan' – a hybrid of Kelways from 1897, with whom she shares her bed just below my office window – appreciates her. He is described as having *'glorious blooms of deep, Episcopal purple, with a richness that does not fade.'* Recently another irresistible paeony called 'Rinpo' has joined them, which is an *'unusual lilac, purple with silvery edges, of ancient cultivation and rarely to be found for sale.'*

The origins of the tree paeony are a mystery; certainly Sir Joseph Banks wanted William Kerr to bring it back when he was sent to China. Perhaps Banks had seen *P. papaveracea* – introduced in 1802 from cultivation in China to the garden of Sir Abraham Hume at Wormleybury, Hertfordshire. The tree paeony was on Fortune's list as well, but the seed

Tree Paeony 'Cardinal Vaughan'

brought back was all collected from garden stock – the only field for plant collecting allowed to *'foreign devils'* at the time.

According to Alice Coates, whose wonderful and brilliantly researched *Quest for Plants* is my faithful guide to plant collectors, there is a 17th century manuscript which describes Mou-tan-Shan, the Paeony mountain, *'where they grow wild and in great profusion, scenting the air.'*

FARRER AND PURDOM

The word *paeony* comes from the classical Greek name said to commemorate Paeon, the physician of the Gods, and the reputed discoverer of its medicinal properties. We still speak of a *'paeon'* of praise, originally a hymn to Apollo. Mou-tan, one of several Chinese names for the flower, means male vermillion. No-one claims to have found the wonderful place of Mou-Tan-Shan in the 17th century document, but Reginald Farrer (1880-1920), who was plant collecting in the Gansu Province in China, did see wild tree-paeonies with large white flowers, marked with dark maroon at the base of the petals, and he pressed and brought home at least one specimen, though he did not manage to collect seed from it. William Purdom (1880-1921), who collected for Veitch for several years, visited the mountain (never before seen by Europeans) and explored it, but no paeonies were to be found. However, he did

find a dark red tree paeony in the wild, considerably west of the region.

The Chinese have always considered wild paeonies to be typically red and that there were two wild varieties of tree-paeony, *Paeonia suffruticosa*, which they called *var. spontanea*, and *var. papaveracea*. They reckoned that all tree-paeony cultivars were derived from one, or perhaps both, of these two wild varieties.

Reginald Farrer financed his own expedition to this tantalising part of North China, near Tibet, in 1914 and was delighted when Purdom agreed to go with him, just for his expenses; he describes Purdom as *'an absolutely perfect friend and helper'.* Farrer was another dedicated, articulate, poetic botanist; in his book *On the Eaves of the World,* he tells of his paeony sighting in his own words, when he was resting after a steep climb. His eye was caught by *'certain white objects ... clearly too big by far to be flowers, yet must certainly be investigated, if only to find out what clots of white wool, or yet whiter paper could be doing in this wild coppice ... probably they had some religious meaning. I would see.'* He rushes off to investigate, *'through the foaming shallows of the copse I plunged and soon was holding my breath with growing excitement as I neared my goal, and it became more and more certain that I was setting eyes on Paeonia Moutan as a wild plant. The event itself justifies enthusiasm, but all considerations of botanical geography* vanish from one's mind in the first contemplation of that amazing flower, the most overpoweringly superb of hardy shrubs. Here in the brushwood it grew up tall and slender and straight, in two or three unbranching shoots, each one of which carried at the top, elegantly balancing, that single enormous blossom, waved and crimped into the boldest grace of line, of absolute pure white, with featherings of deepest maroon, radiating at the base of the petals from the boss of golden fluff at the flower's heart. Above the sere and thorny scrub the snowy beauties poise and hover, and the breath of them went out upon the twilight as sweet as any rose. For a long time I remained in worship, and returned downward at last in the dusk in high contentment.'* Later he adds, *'As for the peony, its home has long been a problem of botanists. Though it has been cultivated for countless ages in all the gardens of the Far East, it was long before it could be traced to its original 'point de depart'. There is, it is true, a certain Chinese mountain called Peony Mountain, and it seems probable that* this was so called because there either were peonies on it or at some time had been. Purdom's earlier research, however had shown that not only was there no present trace of peonies there whatever, but that not even in the memory of the oldest inhabitant was there a hint of peonies ever having being seen there.'* So much for the Paeony Mountain.

Farrer's somewhat over the top style makes his book slightly indigestible, but his ready quotations from Jane Austen are endearing; he mentions in passing what he considers essential equipment on a voyage of two seasons and what is omissible: *'In my own case'* he says, *'I find it reduces itself to the materials of washing and the works of Jane Austen; of the two, at extreme need, it would be the washing materials I would jettison'*. He found many plants useful to me: *Geranium sanguineum,* crane's bill, 'pearly pink' hellebores, many violets and anemones, *Gentiana verna, Lithospermum,* valuable clumps of which make the mats, so necessary in my sort of garden, to take over the bare spaces and suppress the weeds. I have two little stone, oval-shaped baskets on a step below my greyhound, (who lies between the palm trees), which are completely full of brilliant gentian blue flowers from a hybrid, which I have to say is much more successful than the Farrer species *verna* or *sino-ornata* that I usually try. It is called *G x stevenagensis,* and its peak time is the end of October – a most valuable gem.

Gentiana x stevenagensis – hybrid of G. sino-ornata

HELLEBORES AND ACONITES

The hellebores and aconites are the black sheep of the buttercup family, both including species capable of murder; the word from the Greek to kill or destroy speaks a warning. A drastic, cathartis-producing inflammation of the gastric and intestinal mucous membrane with violent vertigo, vomiting, cramps and convulsions, sometimes ends in death. But its controlled use is medicinal and beneficial, and according to legend it was a concoction of helleborus that the Greek soothsayer and physician Melampus cured the divine madness of the daughters of Proteus, the King of Argos, after observing the effect on goats. The plant's reputation as a sovereign remedy in cases of lunacy and manic depression persisted down the ages, and Gerard (of *Gerard's Herball*) recommended *'a purgation of Black Hellbore (or Melampode) for mad or curious men, for melancholike, dull and heavie persons.'*

Two hellebores are rare British natives, and both poisonous, *Helleborus viridis* or green hellebore, and *Helleborus foetidus* or stinking hellebore. The Christmas rose is found in Central and East Europe, and West Asia, while the Lenten rose, *H. orientalis,* is a Levantine introduction into this country in 1839. Most hellebores dislike disturbance, so it is best to plant them and leave them alone. They are absolutely essential and magic in my sort of uncontrolled garden, and with so much shade, where they fill many gaps and flower delightfully at very lean times of year.

JOSEPH ROCK

Joseph Rock (1882-1962) is the Rock of *Paeony suffruticosa* Rock's Variety. He was a contemporary of Farrer and George Forrest, and managed to annoy both these great men by plant hunting in what they considered their own sacred domain of North China, close to the borders of Tibet and Burma. It was there that he found the elusive tree paeony for which he will be remembered, but his finding of the Chaulmoogra tree was of interest as well.

Rock was born in Vienna and escaped from an unhappy childhood by working his passage to America, and eventually Hawaii; he was almost entirely self-taught, and finding he had a gift for languages, he acquired fluency in Chinese and Arabic, English, Hungarian, Italian, French, Latin, Greek and his native German. He managed to get a job in Hawaii, teaching Latin and Natural History in what became the Mid-Pacific Institute, and had to work hard to keep ahead of his students. Somehow he learned enough to be offered his next job – with Hawaii Forestry Service – collecting herbarium material and seeds of rare local shrubs and trees. This was to lead to a Professorship in Botany at the University of Hawaii, and over the next ten years he published over forty works on botany. Eventually he was offered the post with the US Department of Agriculture, to travel to India and the East to search for the Chaulmoogra or Kalaw tree and make a collection of the seed; this seed secreted an oil which was known to be an effective treatment for leprosy, and from this collection he was able to start a plantation of these trees in Hawaii.

The oil from the Chaulmoogra seed has been known for centuries to the natives of Burma and south eastern Asia, and used both internally and externally as palliatives in leprosy and other skin diseases. The National Geographic Society and the Smithsonian Institution were Rock's first sponsors in China. He became known for his meticulous and well-prepared specimens in many duplicate sheets, which enabled the herbaria to trade or distribute the sheets to other institutions. His passion for plant photography illustrating a plant's particular habit and habitat, which supplemented his field notes, made invaluable botanic records.

Travelling in the Sino-Tibetan borderlands, Rock studied the

Clematis heracleifolia 'Davidiana'

lamaseries with great interest and it was in Choni Monastery in Gansu province that he collected his tree paeony. Despite the fact that he had never encountered it in the wild, he thought sufficiently highly of this specimen to photograph it and collect seed, although nobody knew whether it was from a wild species growing in cultivation or a hybrid of some kind. The lamas of Choni lived in a remote part of China, near to Tibet, and were sadly slaughtered with their precious paeony by fierce revolutionaries. This seed is now, according to the contemporary botanist, Stephen G Haw, confirmed as being of wild stock as Rock had always thought. Rock sent the seed to the Arnold Arboretum at Boston and its Director – Professor Charles Sprague Sargent (1841-1927) – distributed it to growers in several countries. Within ten years the lamaserie was rebuilt, and Rock was able to return seed from his paeonies to the restored institute.

HERBACEOUS CLEMATIS

Herbaceous clematis are surprisingly useful in filling spaces where low-growing plants are required. I give them wire hoops to lean on, which they seem to find comfortable; *Clematis heracleifolia* 'Davidiana' has settled in a most unlikely spot, just fitting in between my greenhouse and the wall behind it. This is a most obscure narrow bed, only about eighteen inches wide and almost impossible to get at, but which seemed a pity to waste, so I squeezed in several rather sickly lapagerias and another clematis of the climbing sort, which is covered in late October with tiny pink urn-shaped flowers, about 2 cm long. Called *C versicolor,* it is native to America. The herbaceous clematis is covered in late summer by quite large, strongly-scented, clear lavender blue flowers, which resemble a hyacinth, born on short stalks in circular fashion; its leaves are divided into three, of which the central lobe is wide and ovate and twice the size.

DAVID AND DELAVAY

Père Armand David, (1826-1900), is one of the distinguished, plant-collecting, French 19th century missionaries, who introduced the *heracleifolia davidiana* (which takes his name), followed by Père Jean Marie Delavay (1838-1895), and a medical officer who was also customs inspector, Augustin Henry (1857-1930). Their names alone will forever conjure up visions of their innumerable, magical finds and the epic stories of their journeys.

Père David's most famous find was the unmatched *Davidia involucrata,* the romantic Dove tree, which is too big for me but which leaves me envious of those who can accommodate it. Père Delavay discovered another Chinese treasure, *Osmanthus delavayii,* and two of them make a little hedge behind my greyhound, where I can appreciate the early fragrance. Delavay, a French Jesuit, collected plants from a small area near Canton, and although his range was limited he combed it with great thoroughness, climbing Mt Tsemai Shan sixty times. He called it *'his garden and the Mont Blanc of Yunnan'* maintaining that he had still hardly tapped the resources of the rich alpine flora. It is said that more worthwhile garden plants were discovered by Delavay than any other botanist. He sent seeds of the osmanthus to a firm in France in 1890, and though only one seed germinated, from this all subsequent plants were propagated. The plant was to remain very scarce until George Forrest sent more seed from China early in the 20th century.

Augustin Henry was a very enthusiastic collector, stationed in 1882 at Ichang, a hundred miles up the river Yangtze Kiang; he had become interested in finding the plants used by the Chinese as drugs, to relieve the boredom of his leisure hours. He wrote to the Director of Kew, Dr William Thistleton Dyer, son-in-law of Hooker (of whom more later), sending him specimens for identification, and encouraged by Thistleton Dyer's reply, he started collecting in earnest and continued to do so for many years. Some of his plants find welcome homes with me, of which *Cornus kousa* is a particular favourite; it has to share a small plot by the garage with the embothrium, and is not allowed to become too big. Henry describes the conspicuous white bracts as *'frequently exceeding five inches in diameter.'* It does specially well in full sun, the bracts turning a rosy pink in late summer, and these are followed by fruit exactly like strawberries.

The dried specimens Henry sent to Kew aroused the greatest interest, and when an enquiry was made to him, about sending plants and seeds, he replied *'Don't waste money on postage – send a man'.* Henry reported to Thistleton Dyer how rapidly China was being deforested by the natives, and hoping that a suitable collector could be sent to save the valuable flora, which might disappear within the next fifty years. Sadly Kew had no means of financing this, but Professor Sargent of the Arnold Arboretum, with whom Henry had also corresponded, offered to pay

Styrax japonica 'Pink Chimes'

for an expedition if Henry would lead it. Henry declined, suggesting it was a job for a younger man. Sargent was responsible for helping some of our most important plant collectors, and was a friend of James Henry Veitch (1868-1907), a descendant of the original Veitch who founded the famous firm. They had met when both men were searching for plants in Japan.

RICHARD OLDHAM

Although the Royal Botanic Gardens, (now in Government hands), was crying poverty, they did manage to send the last official collector Richard Oldham (1838-1864) to Japan, where among many other valuable plants he found *Styrax japonica*. I have long gazed green-eyed at this rare and desirable tree, knowing it to be too large for me, but when circulating my local Duchy Nurseries of Cornwall, I spotted what must be a hybrid, *Styrax japonica* 'Pink Chimes.' I recognised at once it was another 'must have'; although it cost £50, it was definitely worth a few lectures. It promised to grow no higher than three metres and was covered in tiny buds. I planted it in front of my largest camellia hedge, to replace a *Cornus capitata,* which had, as usual, outgrown its position and gone to another garden.

It is a good idea to plant the styrax where you can look up to it, as its delicious little pale pink, bell-

L. auratum by W Fitch, Curtis's Bot. Mag. 1862

been consistently unkind. His best introductions were anticipated by collectors a few months earlier in the field; his best botanical discoveries were overlooked and accredited to later travellers. Hooker seems to have treated him with quite unmerited severity. Inexperienced, underpaid, and as it turned out, not constitutionally robust, he was pitchforked into the Orient at the age of twenty three, and died there three years later'. In addition to seeds and plants, Oldham sent 13,700 excellently prepared plant specimens to Kew, including about ninety new species, among them the excellent styrax.

LILIUM AURATUM

shaped flowers coat the undersides of the branches, which often droop at the slender tips. I also look upon Richard Oldham as a long-lost cousin, as my maiden name was Oldham.

According to Alice Coates' *Quest for Plants,* he had a horrid time. He came to Kew from Macclesfield in 1859, and the following year was appointed to the Succulent House. This was regarded as a penance, and indicated that he had already incurred the displeasure of Sir William Hooker, the then Director. Alice Coates says of him: '*He was one of those whom fate seems to have*

Of the many lilies I grow, and others I long to, *Lilium auratum* takes a lot of beating.

Don Elick, who lives in Japan, is very strict with us when he describes the total failure of the gardening press, '*which seems to think that the gold banded lily has something to do with what the Japanese call L. auratum; it has nothing of the sort. The lily's name in Japanese is yamayuri, simply 'mountain lily' ... for L. auratum grows in hills, and the hills round rural hamlets are invariably referred to as mountains'.*

Although this unique lily was found and described by von Siebold,

Lilium auratum by the terrace

much of his collections were lost, and it was not until 1860 that bulbs collected by John Gould Veitch flowered for the first time in England and were described by Lindley. After that it was rediscovered and sent home by several plant collectors, including Robert Fortune, who thought he had a first discovery. Don Elick tells us that of the many hundreds of bulbs dug in the wild, few survived, owing to the mishandling of the suppliers and ignorance of its needs by gardeners – but above all because of their inability to prevent the virus diseases that weakened it. Now we know that to be sure of virus-free bulbs they must be grown from seed, and given the conditions in which they thrive in the wild.

I was very lucky to be given two seedlings by my friend and neighbour Mike Graham; they were in black polythene pots and he told me to keep them in the greenhouse until November, and then plant them out. In this garden there is not a lot of choice for the ideal position, so they were put in a rather shallow bed by the terrace, which seems by pure luck to have suited them.

They have been there ever since, producing dozens of five feet stems covered in hundreds of indescribably beautiful and richly scented flowers, magically repeated every year. I always have a lily party at the end of July (which happens to coincide with my birthday) to celebrate my extreme appreciation of their efforts.

My lily bed has always been too shallow, and it was another

163

Tricyrtis formosana - The Japanese Toad Lily

ingenious idea of Bill to make it deeper: he thought if I bought a stone border – to cement on top of the low-edging border already there – we could fill it with leaf mould which I had been offered from a huge nearby garden. The trailer load he collected filled this bed to the top of the new stone, and there was enough over to cover my cyclamen and many other little plants, which like a nice thick mulch to regenerate and get them through the winter.

Another member of the Liliaceae to which I am much addicted is the *Tricyrtis,* the Japanese Toad Lily, of which Brian Matthews writes in *The Plantsman*. There are about twenty species, but considerable confusion as to which is which. They are presumably called toad lilies because of their spots, but a curious use for one particular species, *Tricyrtis imeldae,* makes one wonder. This was named after Mrs Marcos of the Phillipine Islands, where it grows,

and the local Tasaday tribespeople, eat the flowers and rub the juice from the flowers or leaves on their hands before setting out on a frog-hunting foray; it is said to be attractive to the frogs and make them less slippery. The Tasaday also liken the perianth segments to frogs' tongues. Tricyrtis translates as *'tri'* meaning three, and *'kyrtos'* humped, referring to the three outer petals which are swollen at the base and sacklike, (so says Mr William T Stearn in his *Dictionary of Plant Names for Gardeners,* a most invaluable book).

Of the two varieties that I acquired, neither flowered as expected. My first toad lily, called a Snake Lily, came from Burncoose Nursery in Redruth, Cornwall, labelled *Tricyrtis formosana stolonifera* and was supposed to have brown-purple spots on pinkish orchid-like flowers. The flowers were disappointingly small, but they are roughly as described, and now make a splendid tall clump every August. The second one I bought is *Tricyrtis hirta,* described as having creamy-white flowers with some pink and red spots. Gazing at a flower this very minute no creamy white is visible, just a mass of purply spots. It is half the height of the other and not the hoped for contrast.

Tricyrtis macranthopsis is a most desirable species, and especially as painted by Raymond Booth and described by Don Elick in their joint book *Japonica Magnifica*. Elick sees it growing in Japan where he lives,

164

and describes four different, but very similar species, *'all rare and desirable, all grow on vertical rock faces, in damp shaded ravines, often in the spray of waterfalls, and bear in the leaf axils of long trailing stems, waxy, tubular blossoms of surpassing loveliness'.* In Booth's painting every lance-shaped leaf is pointing down, and sheltering a brilliant yellow bloom, lined with tiny, discreet pink spots.

In 1855, *Curtis Botanical Magazine* shows a picture, very similar to my tricyrtis, and accurately states that, *'if this is not a plant which strikes the eye from its beauty, it can scarcely fail to do so from the peculiar form and colouring of the flowers.'* All the talk of *'vertical rock faces, damp shady ravines and spray from waterfalls'* is not very encouraging when trying to give these plants a home from home, but I have given mine some nice wire hoops to lean on as they do not appear to be able, or even want to, stand up straight.

Dr Wallich (1786-1854), its discoverer, thinks it may be identical with the *Uvularia hirta* of Thunberg; if so it is a native of Japan as well of Himalaya, *'where Drs Hooker and Thomson detected it, and whence they sent seed to the Royal Gardens of Kew.'* In Curtis, January 1st 1863, another illustration of *Tricyrtis hirta* announces the rediscovery of Thunberg's tricyrtis by Robert Fortune, *'who sent it from Japan to Mr Standish, in whose nursery at Bagshot it flowered last November. It grows four to five feet high, and the copious blossoms, which appear on the axils of all the*

upper leaves, and which are of a pearly white, dotted with clear purple, render it as singular-looking as it is beautiful'.

A bad attack of plantomania resulted from spotting an exquisite scarlet lily in my favourite Clematis Nursery, Peverils in Devon. It is called *Lilium grayi* and was found by Asa Gray on the slopes of the Appalachian mountains of Virginia in 1840. However, Gray was not satisfied that it was distinct from other lilies; it was not until after a second finding of it in 1871 that Sereno Watson, Curator of the Herbarium at Harvard, decided that it was and described it as a new species.

Liliium grayi was introduced into England in 1890, and flowered in an open border at Kew, being featured in the Botanical Magazine in 1892. A very fine specimen with thirteen flowers and buds was seen in the peat garden at the Royal Botanical Garden in Edinburgh in 1969. A grower described it as follows: *'the stems are slender, with nodding umbels of bell shaped reddish crimson flowers, sometimes arranged in two tiers, one above the other; they are spotted, maroon-black, on the inner surface, with chocolate anthers within the tube.'*

I saw it alone in stately solitude in Peverils garden; tall, scarlet and extremely elegant. One of its admirers writes that it strongly dislikes lime and prefers light shade, and particularly hates getting its feet wet. It recommended planting the bulbs on little hummocks, which serve to keep the bulb dry while allowing the roots to reach moisture. One nursery in the north of Scotland had the last two bulbs in the world; these should arrive just in time for me to plant in September, its psychological moment.

ERNEST HENRY WILSON

When Augustin Henry turned down the job, (of saving the valuable flora in China, which might otherwise disappear within fifty years) offered by Professor Sargent of the Arnold Arboretum, suggesting it would be more suitable for a younger man, it took a little time for Dr Thistleton Dyer, Director of Kew, to recommend a suitable candidate to Veitch. But he was worth waiting for. Ernest Henry Wilson (1876-1930), who came to be known as 'Chinese Wilson', turned out to be the last and greatest of Veitch's collectors. For eleven years he searched China for plants, finding some 65,000 specimens, comprising about five thousand species. He considers, *'that the Chinese flora is beyond question the richest temperate flora in the world ... there is no garden worthy of the name, throughout the length and breadth of the temperate parts of the Northern Hemisphere, that does not contain a few plants of Chinese origin.'*

Lilium regale will always be Wilson's abiding legacy; he found it in the Min Valley amongst the coarse grass and scrub, the home of many beautiful lilies. *'It luxuriates in rocky crevices'*, he says *'sun baked throughout the greater part of the year; it grows three to five feet tall and has slender leaves crowded on stems bearing several large funnel shaped flowers, red purple without, ivory white suffused with canary yellow, often with red purple, reflected through, and deliciously scented.'*

My half dozen specimens of this desirable lily, with which I should like to fill the garden, have to be content in a pot where they flourish, a seasonal reminder of Wilson and his determination to bring them back to delight his gardening admirers. He sent 600 bulbs to Veitch from Shanghai, which were shipped on board *SS Empress of Japan,* for Vancouver BC, and carried by express train to Boston Massachusetts, where they arrived April 20 1911. In July they produced a crop of flowers and in October a crop of seeds.

This Regale lily was responsible for a nasty accident Wilson suffered; when collecting it, he nearly lost his leg.

In 1910 he safely sent back 6,000 more bulbs to the Arnold Arboretum in Boston. These bulbs were dug, dried, packed and transported on men's backs and by riverway 2,000 miles across China to Shanghai. Quite a drama accompanied this activity when his sedan chair was swept from under him by a rock avalanche, which rolled him down the hillside. As he was extracting himself from this predicament a rock hit his leg, breaking it below the knee in two places. Wilson then devised a splint from his camera-tripod, and was about to continue his journey when another mule train came by. There was no room for it to pass so he had to lie on the path and let nearly fifty mules step over him; amazingly not one hoof touched him, though *'each one looked as big as a plate.'* *Lilium regale* only grows in the Min valley as far as anyone knows, and it was from this introduction that the Regal lilies in our gardens derive.

Wilson wrote an account of his four expeditions into China. The first two years were for Veitch, but the great firm was in decline and the next two journeys were made at the offer of Professor Sargent, on behalf of Harvard University, the owners of the Arnold Arboretum.

Wilson's book, *A Naturalist in Western China,* is written in a factual style and is not an inspiring read, but here and there has touches of imagination. I like some of his comments on the Chinese themselves; *'the Chinese do not see time from the Westerner's point of view, and for the traveller in the interior part of China, the first, last and most important thing of all is ever to bear this in mind.'* (I remembered this when the guide left me behind.)

He greatly admires their boatmen,

especially in the dangerous waters up river between Ichang and Chungking, where the sublime beauty of the gorges, the swift currents, and many rapids he often appreciated. *'Oriental methods are not occidental methods, but they succeed just the same'* he says, and notes that many accidents which have occurred on the Yangtsze have been caused by ignorant foreigners over-riding these Chinese boatmen who are *'careful, absolutely competent and thorough masters of their craft'.* He adds that the Chinese *'do not understand tents ... on all the main roads there are inns of sorts, usually very filthy, and in season abounding with mosquitoes, creeping things and stinks, the latter in fact being always in evidence.'*

This was Wilson's last journey in China, but he made two more fruitful trips to Japan, Korea and Formosa. In 1919 he became Assistant Director to the Arnold Arboretum, and when Professor Sargent died in 1927, Wilson succeeded to his post of Keeper.

After surviving the many hazards of travel in the East it was ironic that he should be killed in a motor accident in Massachussetts.

10

—MORE MUST HAVE— PLANTS

*'How could I possibly forget such a huge and important plant
as the ginger lily, Hedychium gardeneranum?
It is almost a member of the freak brigade,
its habit being to lie low for as long as its feels like it,
and then to burst forth without any warning
into the most sensational sight.'*

Hedychium gardeneranum is the most common of these extremely uncommon plants and I had planted its rhizomes behind a quite reasonably sized camellia backing on to my myrtle hedge, where it lurked for about eight years. Then the three massive stems suddenly erupted and grew several inches a day to about five feet, sheathed with tapered leaves and finally topped by very large clusters of almost orchid-like, brilliant yellow blooms with red stamens. They are excellent exhibits for a museum with their exciting behaviour, and although I believe they have been pronounced a pest in New Zealand, I can't get enough of them.

Their reputation leads one to believe they are tender in constitution, but my exhibits have shown no signs of it so far. Perhaps 'tenderness' is a relative term; I read somewhere that no plant should ever be

*Hedychium gardeneranum
– the Ginger Lily*

N.º 708

H. coronarium by Sydenham Edwards, Curtis's Bot. Mag. 1803
Inset: H. coronarium (?) against the myrtle hedge

Hedychium coronarium (?)

considered tender until one has killed it, personally, and at least twice.

Having discovered there were other varieties which might add distinction, I found *H. greenii* and planted it alongside, where its stunning orange flowers will stand out. I had come across a few specimens in a tunnel, unloved and neglected in a rather sad nursery that I went to by a mistake. The huge rhizomes – each jammed into a tiny pot – had fallen over, and the nurseryman seemed glad to get rid of them. Happily, the very long stems just fitted obliquely into my car. The nurseryman did not know if his white one was *H. coronarium* or *H. spicatum*. The former means 'snowy garland', which might be too delicate, and the latter has been likened to a flock of butterflies, but its poor habit of flowering (only one or two blooms at time) lessens its attraction.

Maybe the orange seed capsules which open to reveal succulent, fleshy red seeds in the autumn will redeem it, and with a bit of luck, mine could turn out to be *H. forrestii,* one of the hardiest, according to Edward Needham, who grows it among his collection of hedychiums in his well-hidden garden in Cornwall.

Tom Hudson, a friend and neighbour, has also given me a beautiful pale yellow variety which he found in China recently – it will be enjoyable to wait for them all to dazzle me at once.

DR NATHANIEL WALLICH

Dr Nathaniel Wallich writes about them in 1853: *'The genus Hedychium is exclusively East Indian, consisting mostly of exquisitely beautiful and sweetly fragrant plants, which flower in profusion during many months of the year and especially during the wet season … no plants are more subject to changes; this applies equally to their wild and cultivated state and is a constant source of trouble and perplexity to those who wish to study them in their native place of growth or in gardens; the dried specimens are still more difficultly examined, owing to the delicate fabric of the flowers and generally to their colours being lost. A good many species have in consequence been enumerated and described which have no reality'.* I really like that last sentence.

Wallich continues, *'I have myself been often deceived by the freaks and versatility of form and colours, in these lovely flowers, and even the stature and whole appearance of the plants I had before me, and have had successive drawings made of them, imagining that they were specifically distinct, whereas they were in reality one and the same plant, only arrayed in various fancy guises … this leaves the systematising botanist to grope his way through the maze as best he can.'*

GEORGE FORREST

Hedychium forrestii was found by George Forrest, who also introduced one of my absolute favourite and most valuable plants, *Pieris formosa*

forrestii. Forrest was sponsored by JC Williams of Caerhays Castle in Cornwall, and it was there that this plant was first grown from seed he collected in 1910. There are many varieties of pieris, but this one and its many hybrids stand out. Hillier describes it as *'one of the most beautiful of all shrubs, the young growths being brilliant red and the large, slightly fragrant flowers, borne in long conical panicles.'*

Pieris Formosa

From my bedroom window, which overlooks the west side of my front door, I can see several pieris, sometimes simultaneously, sending out their young foliage in varying shades of scarlet, red, deep pink to pale, and framed by the background camellia hedge. In the period when there are few flowers, this continuing sparkling clash lifts the spirit.

Sir Joseph Dalton Hooker (1817-1911) might have been the plant collector, (and, of course, plantaholic) that Banks would have most admired. Plants were the passion of his life and he studied plant geography and distribution with enormous industry, as well as geology, meteorology and palaeontology. Hooker greatly admired Baron von Humboldt, the founder of plant geography, whom Charles Darwin described as *'the greatest scientific traveller who has ever lived'*, and von Humboldt wrote of Hooker, *'what a notable traveller is Joseph Hooker. What an extent of acquired knowledge does he bring to bear on the observations he makes, and how marked with sagacity and moderation are the views that he puts forward'.* Hooker was inspired by both von Humboldt and Darwin, and wrote of the latter, *'To follow in his footsteps, at however great a distance, seems to be a hopeless aspiration'*, but it awoke in him a desire to travel and observe. It seems to have been a mutual admiration society.

There are two of their very special plants which have to be accommodated in my garden; one is the blue poppy, *Mecanopsis bailyii*, now known as *betonicifolia*, the first Latin name I ever learned. My grandmother introduced me to it in her garden in the Highlands of Scotland, and there are no words to describe its seraphic blue; it is simply inimitable. A native of East Asia, it has been collected by successive plant hunters early in this century, but, it is not easy to establish, and so far I have not succeeded.

The other is *Paris japonica* and another variety *Paris polyphylla*. The former is the gem of the genus and extremely showy – with large, pale, green leaves in a parasol arrangement, and creamy white stars rising from the centre of each leaf. The latter are quite sensational flowers, which grow in the same system of structured whorls; first leaves, then inside another whorl of floral parts in perfect symmetry, all in muted shades of green, purple and yellow. The main difficulty with these paris plants is that they like a bit of frost to act as a catalyst, something I cannot always guarantee, especially under the camellias where they grow in my garden. They are all to be found in just the sort of country in which Wallich was describing the hedychiums.

With botany and plant hunting in mind, Joseph Hooker trained as a doctor in the Navy, and in 1839 applied for, and was accepted as, assistant surgeon on an expedition whose scientific purpose was to determine the exact position of the South Magnetic Pole – with geography, hydrography, natural history and terrestrial magnetism all to be investigated at the same time. This was right up Hooker's street, and he was promised every opportunity of collecting plants.

Hooker's travels, on this four year voyage, took him through all the inhospitable islands and seas in the southern hemisphere, further south even than Cook, and he collected extraordinary plants including lichens, mosses and grasses. His correspondence with his father and Darwin, his diaries, and above all his *Flora Antarctica,* describe every detail of this fascinating experience, and on his return he was determined to leave the Navy and devote his life to botany.

His father, Sir William Hooker, became Director of the Royal Gardens at Kew in 1841. He and his father had always been very close, and Sir William never missed an opportunity to further his son's career. Hooker also kept in touch with Darwin, who questioned him on the many scientific and botanic subjects he studied on the four year voyage. Hooker longed to travel again, and wrote to his grandfather, *'I shall be ready to make any sacrifice to get to the tropics for a year, so convinced am I that it will give me the lift I want, in acquiring a knowledge of exotic botany'.*

At last a journey was arranged; in April 1848 he was to go to the Himalayas on half pay from the Navy, with whom he travelled to Calcutta, and thence to Darjeeling by palanquin, elephant and boat. Hooker was entranced by India from his first sight of it and much enjoyed travelling by elephant, describing how adept he became at *'stepping on a tusk, gripping at a broader ear; if I drop anything, hat or book he picks it up with his trunk and adroitly tosses it over his head into my lap'.*

Collecting plants as he went, he found it convenient to change from the elephant to a boat, *'not unlike a floating haystack',* forty feet long and fifteen wide, where he could spread out his papers and dry his plants – for instance, primulas and meconopsis he discovered in abundance – lovely decorative plants for shady places. He suffered from invasions of black ants which got into everything including the food, ticks penetrated his clothing, even in to his hair, and *'leeches, which get all over one's person, and which I have sometimes taken off a hundred in a day.'*

Both von Humboldt and Darwin had given him missions of research for them. For von Humboldt, it was to take temperature readings at different heights, to discover the altitudinal limits of individual plant families and to examine geological formations. For Darwin, it was mostly questions about animal habits, elephant, cheetahs and tigers, all of which Hooker came across. He described the indispensable yak, whose hair made ropes, which provided milk and meat, even its dung and bones were as fuel. He was delighted with a Tibetan mastiff, *'his glorious bushy tail thrown over his back in a majestic sweep and a thick collar of scarlet wool round his neck and shoulders, setting off his long silky coat to advantage.'* Later he bought a black puppy, a cross between the mastiff and a Sikkimese hunting dog, and this pet became his constant companion for many months. In one of his letters he says: *'he has grown a most beautiful dog, with glossy black hair, pendant triangular ears, a high forehead and jet black eyes, bold and erect, with such a tail, straight legs and arched back.'*

From Darjeeling he went by pony, climbing to about 7,000'. He made friends with Archibald Campbell and Brian Hodgson, after whom he named the matchless *Magnolia campbellii* and *Rhododendron hodgsonii*. This amazing family of plants, named from the Greek *rhodon*, a rose, and *dendron*, is vast, and mostly to be found in mountains and gorges bordering China, Tibet and Upper Burma; they range in size from tiny prostrate alpines to huge trees with enormous leaves. Hooker will always be remembered for his book *Rhododendrons of the Sikkim Himalaya,* describing the forty three species he found there, many of which were grown at Kew from the seed he sent home.

Among the smaller slow-growing species suitable for me is one mentioned before for its beautiful new growth, *R. yakushimanum.* Only introduced in 1934, it grows in the windswept, rain-drenched mountain peaks of Yakushima Island in the very south of Japan. Here in my garden there are three, growing in the vacant spot from where I moved the *R x* 'Winsome', and where the pieris just described also grows opposite the house. They have camellias behind them and a mass of *Omphalodes capadocica* around their

feet; small, herbaceous, perennial plants with the most piercing blue flowers. They are expensive to buy, but easy to divide, and seem to spread out naturally into mats. I first saw them growing thickly at the foot of a huge wall at Cawdor Castle near Inverness.

Omphalodes cappodocica

The leaves of *R. yakushimanum* are dark, shiny, green above and recurved at the edges, and densely brown beneath, and the flowers grow in a compact truss; pink and bell-shaped in bud, opening to apple blossom pink, and finally white. The new growth is almost silver when it first appears, but these plants are decorative at whatever stage of their development.

An irresistible rare species is *R. mallotum,* which I will grow anyway for a few years, until it gets too big. This was found by Farrer in 1924, but described by Peter Cox, when the latter found it again. It has the most mouthwatering foliage with deep, deep orange indumentum (the downy underside to the leaf), and has dark red flowers. It must have been a wonderful sight, as described by Peter Cox's father who was with Farrer, *'the entire Burmese side of the north of the pass was studded with it, rising squat and sturdy over a sea of Bamboo; it was particularly uniform in size, always about 16 ft in height.'*

Several generations of the Cox family have been plantaholics, right up to the present day known for their particular expertise on rhododendrons.

I followed the steps of these intrepid plantsmen up to Nepal on an International Dendrology Society tour, finding the *Pleione praecox*, the charming little purple orchid which does not need heat and will grow in a cold greenhouse. There, it seemed perfectly happy, growing directly on bare, overhanging rocks. At 16,000 feet, Hooker had found a pink flowered *Arenaria*, and two species of *Corydalis* – both the latter are delightful and make good under-planting. *C flexuosa* has a long flowering season of interesting intense blue flowers, while *C solida* is bright pink. They all have homes in the beds on either side of my dog, where everything is supposed to be recumbent.

THE CHETWAN NATIONAL FOREST

A great treat in Nepal was a magical visit to the Chetwan National Forest, where the rare white rhino prowls about, avoiding the leopards which lurk in the undergrowth. The International Dendrology Society had arranged for us to botanise while travelling on elephants, which is the most recommended way to carry out such an activity; it places one at the exact practical and desirable height for closely examining orchids growing epiphytically in the trees (only using their host for support), and at the same time journeying restfully at a reasonable pace, but safe from too close contact with jungle fauna.

One of our party managed to drop his camera case on the ground, but Indian elephants are quite brilliant, and it was a simple matter for one of them to pick up the case and toss it up to his 'mahout.' The latter try very hard to give their passengers a thrill, and they succeeded: there was a most exciting moment when we cornered a leopard. We travelled four to an elephant, and must have employed about six elephants spread well out in the forest. I suddenly heard the much too close sound of a feline growl from a leopard which was unable to decide which of the two adjacent elephants to attack. Our elephant was most unwilling to hang about and find out, but the mahout continued to urge his beast forward, causing it to trumpet and growl at both ends – simultaneously, while trembling violently in a most alarming manner. Luckily the leopard decided to retreat and soon we were continuing majestically on our way.

Hooker became President of the Royal Society in 1873 and was offered, but declined, the Honour of Knight Commander of St Michael and St George; he had a very good idea of his own value and would accept nothing less than admission to the Star of India. He could not resist one last, luxurious and prestigious expedition to America, to which he was invited by Asa Grey, Harvard's Professor of Botany. It

Parrotia persica, the Persian Ironwood

was the trees that really impressed him and he wrote to Brian Hodgson, *'you may travel for weeks in forests of 8 to 10 pines, spruces, silver firs etc of which most of the species are never under 150 feet and often 250 feet high and 20-30 feet in girth.'* Hooker travelled 8,000 miles by train and wagon during his three months stay, but with the exception of Yosemite Valley, *'no one place'* he said, *'nor altogether, had the interest concentrated in Sikkim, and its mountain scenery; it is a bagatelle compared with any little bit of the Himalayas or Alps, whether as regards beauty, bulk, grandeur or interest.'* There can never have been another man who had the right to sum up continents in such a way; no one else can have covered such an enormous variety of the area of our world, with such an informed eye.

PARROTIA PERSICA

Still indulging my passion for trees it was a treat to be given a plant of the *Parrotia persica,* the Persian Ironwood, although despairingly thinking of the two enormous specimens recently seen at the Westonbirt Arboretum. However, the GPO had been complaining about an old holly tree just by the road, interfering with their telephone lines, so when that disappeared, in went the little parrotia. It had to be accommodated, apart from anything else because of its history. It was found by Carl Anton Meyer (1795-1855), a German botanist, in Russian employ as director of St Petersburg Botanic Garden. Meyer found the parrotias as a shrub on his Caucasian trip, which he led under contract to the Russian government in 1829, and named the shrub after the German natural scientist and explorer Dr Friedrich Parrot (1791-1841).

The timber is the well known Transcaucasian ironwood; hard and durable and of a light pink colour at the core. It was introduced to Kew in about 1840, as a 25-30 year old pot plant, and flowered there in 1868. Its home is the warm, leafy, humid forest of Northern Persia, as well as the southern shores of the

176

Caspian Sea.

At times – and thank goodness that for me this is one of them – it has an interesting and helpful way of growing multiple stems, which results in a shrub-like plant, rather than a larger, upright, single-stemmed tree. Its young leaves are deep green, edged with red, but turn yellow and scarlet in the autumn. In spring it produces clusters of crimson stamens, but its flowers have no petals. It appears to be a sociable tree, happiest with neighbours, where it can catch the light to show off its rainbow colours; in my garden it will have *Stewartia malacodendron* to consort with, another brilliant, autumn, scarlet show-off.

Dr Parrot's chief claim to fame is his heroic climbing of Mount Ararat, being the second person in history to reach the summit – the first being Noah. Parrot published an account of his ascent in 1811, but a German chemist called Martin Klaproph, who visited the country a few years later, declared it to be impossible because the peak of that mountain is a cone of steep ice. It was, however, climbed by several people later, and after reading Dr Parrot's fascinating account of the climb, one can hardly doubt his veracity, especially as von Humboldt describes the traveller and philosopher as, *'constantly guided by the love of truth.'*

Without quoting his whole book *'Journey to Ararat'*, which I read from cover to cover one day in the Rare Books department of the British Library, one can feel the enormity of his undertaking, simply from an extract or two: *'The summit of the great Ararat lies in 39 42 North latitude and 61 55 East latitude …more than three miles and a quarter above the sea, or nearly two miles three quarters above the plain of the Araxes (river). The NE slope of the mountain, may be assumed at fourteen, the NW at twenty miles in length. On the former, even from a great distance, the deep gloomy chasm is discoverable, which many compare to a crater, but which has always struck me rather as a cleft, just as if the mountain had been rent asunder at the top. From the summit downwards, for nearly two thirds of a mile perpendicular, or nearly three miles in an oblique direction, it is covered with a crown of eternal snow and ice ... but upon the entire northern half of the mountain it shoots up in one rigid crest to the summit ... This is the silver head of Ararat.'*

Dr Parrot describes Little Ararat with equal grandeur: *'Its declivities are considerably steeper than that of Great Ararat; its form almost perfectly conical, marked with several delicate furrows, which radiate downward from the summit,'* and he makes a very neat drawing of it with his party in the foreground. Dr Parrot almost reached the summit the first day, but decided it was too late in the afternoon, tired as the party was, to risk the last assault. His young and less experienced companion slipped on the way down, and caused them both to fall and slide nearly a quarter of a mile, ending up dangerously close to the glacier edge. They reached *'our dear monastery'* (on which they had based their climb), *'and refreshed ourselves with juicy peaches and a good breakfast, but took special care not to let a syllable escape us, while among the Armenians, respecting our unlucky falls; as they would not have failed to discover there in the divine punishment of our rash attempt to arrive at the summit; access from which, since the time of Noah, has been forbidden to mortals by a divine decree; for all the Armenians are firmly persuaded that Noah's ark remains, to this very day, on the top of Ararat and that in order to ensure its preservation, no human being is allowed to approach it.*

An interesting legend tells of a monk named Jacob, resolved to convince himself by personal inspection, of the actual existence of the ark on the summit of Ararat, but he fell asleep several times and on waking found he had unconsciously gone down as much as he could ascend during his waking efforts ... at last an angel appeared to him in his sleep, to tell him that his labours were in vain, as the summit was unattainable.

After several days of arduous climbing, deteriorating weather and the glacier ice which necessitated the laborious cutting of steps, Parrot came to the place in the valley between the two Ararats, where the remains of the Ark were supposed to lie. Here accumulated coverings of ice and snow are often more than 100 feet thick, quite sufficient to cover the Ark, should it still be there, as it was only thirty *'ells'* high.

At last, *'on calculating what was already done and what remained to be*

Big and Little Ararat

ARARAT FROM SYRBAGHAN.

done, on considering the proximity of the succeeding row of heights, and casting a glance at my hearty followers, care fled, and 'boldly onwards' resounded in my bosom. I pressed forward round a projecting mound of snow and behold! Before my eyes, now intoxicated with joy, lay the extreme cone, the highest pinnacle of Ararat; at about a quarter past three on 27th September 1829, we stood on the top of Ararat.'

THE HAMAMELIS

Leaving Dr Parrot exulting on the top of Mount Ararat, I must describe another tree of the same family, the *Hamamelis,* which I mentioned before growing under my conker tree, and which has been known as the most important of the family since the 16th century. Dr Rudolf Josef Dirr wrote about it in his book of the same name in 1994. This book caused me considerable trouble, as I had hunted high and low in all libraries and found nothing about this interesting family of trees, and then suddenly there was all this wonderful information, but tantalisingly in German of which I could not understand a word. A kind friend, who had spent a lot of time in a kind of Le Carré job in East Germany, was persuaded, with several bottles of Famous Grouse, to translate the most important bits for me, and in no time, there before me, and beautifully typed, was exactly what I had wanted to know.

The Hamamelis is known as the witch hazel, probably from the use

Hamamelis mollis – The Witch Hazel

of its branches as divining rods, often regarded as a mystical or magical phenomenon. The name *Hamamelis* was first given by Hippocrates to the Medlar tree, but in 1742 Linnaeus gave the name to the witch hazel genus. There are several forms of this tree, but my favourite is *Hamamelis mollis;* Charles Maries found this when travelling round China for Veitch in 1877-79. He brought seed back to England, and allegedly just one plant from this was found in Veitch's Coombe Wood Nursery, which lay there unobserved for nearly twenty years. One of its descendants joined my collection about twenty years ago, it is very slow growing but already far too big – I prune it judiciously and enjoy it.

Two more 'must have' small trees are related to the camellia, *Stewartia pseudocamellia,* the Japanese

179

Stewartia and *Stewartia malacodendron,* the Silky Camellia; they are both slow growing, valuable for their late summer flowering, and with brilliant autumn colour and ornamental bark. The latter grows near the same wall as my parrotia. It has white flowers with striking blue and purple stamens, and when visiting Peter Chappell at Spinners nursery in Lymington, late last year, it was just the perfect time to see it in its vivid scarlet winter clothing, and I bought a small plant of it. The former, *Stewartia pseudocamellia,* comes from Japan. It has pretty arching branches and throughout July and August has yellow-anthered, cup-shaped, white flowers. It still hasn't finished its show off, which it does with leaves turning yellow, purple, red and finally flaking its bark for us. The plant was named by Linnaeus after John Stuart, Earl of Bute (1713-1792), (he spelled it erroneously as Stewartia), who was responsible with Princess Augusta, mother of King George III,

for a good deal of the early planting of Kew gardens.

Located nearby in the garden is my *Lomatia ferruginea,* which one cannot be without and is greatly admired, the plant that Lobb and Comber introduced from Chile. This was named after the Greek word *'loma',* or edge, for the winged edges of its seeds, and *ferruginea* for the russet colour. It fitted in where an untidy old conifer – a relic of a previous era had been removed, and most of its old stump dug out, thereby creating a valuable space. Behind it grow my hamamelis and a large *Camellia japonica* Adolphe Audusson; there is room here for the little lomatia, and some shade-loving plants as neighbours. It will be close to the rather unsalubrious position to which I banished my disappointing hypericum, which is now producing another flush of brilliant yellow flowers just to show me it does not care.

I am trying out some roscoeas, uvularias and paris there as well.

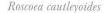

Roscoea cautleyoides

ROSCOEAS

The roscoeas belong to the Zingiberaceae, a family already a favourite because of the hedychiums, the ginger lilies, both showy and enthusiastic. Not many of this family can live outdoors in a temperate climate. They were found and sent home from Nepal in the early 1800s, by Dr Wallich of the Calcutta Botanic Garden to William Roscoe (1753-1831), who was the founder of the Liverpool Botanic Garden, and named after him. They were quite popular about 1820, then forgotten about until 1886, when an article describing them as *'good greenhouse plants'*, was promptly contradicted by several accounts of gardens in which they were happily growing outside.

They are written about in *The New Flora and Silva* by J M Cowan of the Royal Botanic Garden Edinburgh, who says they are attractive garden plants to grow, in any good, moist, loamy soil in a shady bed, and adds that where they are left alone, they will come up from year to year with very little attention – my favourite sort of plants.

They vary in height from 2 inches to 2 feet 6 inches; the flowerbuds are concealed by the upper leaves, and where there is more than one, the flowers usually expand singly. These are large, shaped like an orchid, either violet, violet-purple, pink, yellow or (rarely) white in colour. It has a unique structure among garden plants: a large lip conceals two other segments behind it, while the upper lobe, standing erect, is shaped like a hood, with two small petal-like growths inside it, one on each side of the stamen.

There seem to be two species which sound quite worth growing, *R. humeana,* which was found by Delavay but introduced by Forrest in 1912 and also by Joseph Rock. It is described as *'the finest in cultivation'*, and has large violet and bluish purple flowers; the other is *R. cautleyoides* which can be *'of quite singular loveliness, its flowers of a yellow unparalleled in the garden, uniform, soft and clear'*, but they can also be yellowish purple.

Helen Dillon, who grows it in Dublin, says in her book *'Garden Artistry'*, that the former is a *'neat plant with glowing purple flowers in early summer.* The latter she says *'multiplies happily with clear lemon flowers from sheaves of shining green leaves.'* This should show up my hypericum nicely. William Robinson describes the uvularia as *'a graceful perennial allied to Solomon's Seal, bearing yellow blossoms.'* *U. grandiflora* is the only one worth growing he says. This attains a height of 1 to 2 feet and its numerous slender stems form a compact tuft, with flowers long and yellow, drooping gracefully.

It comes from North America and is named after the 'uvula', which hangs in our throats, in reference to the hanging blossoms and fruit of the plant. The possible purple of the roscoea will blend well with my dactylorhiza.

11

——THE FLORA OF—— 'DOWN UNDER'

'It does seem the ultimate in plantaholic lunacy to have to include the Antipodes in my travels, but the Chatham Island forget-me-not requires this enterprise, and it took me all my time to arrange a trip – not that I actually reached the Chatham Islands, in spite of my efforts, but I at least made a dashing attempt. I must also admit to be being seriously influenced by a deep desire to explore in Banks' footsteps.'

The Chatham Island forget-me-not, *Myosotidium hortensia,* grows naturally nowhere else in the world, and is now threatened with extinction. It is a hugely memorable plant, with massive, shining, heart-shaped, dark green leaves over a foot broad, thick and succulent and strongly ribbed beneath, standing proudly on stout stalks, crowned with brilliant blue; the *New RHS Dictionary of Gardening* describes them unattractively as *'dense corymbose cymes.'* With almost hydrangea-like, flowers in spring; these are sometimes called 'Chatham Island lilies', but are not in the least like lilies. Unsurprisingly, they are like massed blue forget-me-nots,

Myosotidium hortensia, the Chatham Island forget-me-not

and there is an even rarer white form. Mr Cheeseman wrote of the plant in his *Illustrations of New Zealand Flora*, published in 1914: '*Its peculiar habit and appearance so widely different from that of other Boraginaceae, its beauty as a garden plant, and above all that such a distinct genus should be confined to the tiny group of the Chatham Islands, where it is far removed from any near allies, and where no key exists as to its pedigree and past development, are facts which necessarily involve many questions of importance.*'

This rarity was introduced into England by Mr Watson of St Albans, who exhibited a living, flowering plant at a meeting of the Horticultural Society in March 1858, where it attracted much attention. It used to grow all round the main Chatham Island, forming a broad belt on the seashore, often in an unbroken line for miles at a time just above where the dry seaweed marks the high tide limit. Now it struggles to exist against an invasion of sheep, which devour its leaves, and worse still pigs, intent on rooting up and eating its fleshy rhizomes.

Luckily, among its admirers, are those who have naturalised it in many parts of the world. I could see that to grow it was going to be a great challenge, but one to be taken up at once. I would indulge its foibles one by one; masses of light, sandy soil and specially collected seaweed from my local beach.

First I acquired little seedlings (quite a few nurseries sell them) and tried them in the glasshouse, where they were curiously sensitive to their position and looked better in the shade, with not too much water. However, they never looked really happy, and when I saw them growing enthusiastically outside in a sheltered garden in County Carlow, Ireland, I thought to myself why not try that here in Cornwall? I duly made them a suitable bed, sheltered by a camellia hedge, and added some sphagnum moss I had left over from the orchids for good measure; and there they are. They have one of Bill's most successful tunnels, designed to let the air flow through the ends, and with sides to be rolled up and down according to the weather. All survived one winter and flowered brilliantly; now let us see if they can do it again.

PINPOINTING CHATHAM ISLANDS

Now committed to this enormous new adventure to visit Down Under and see what, if anything, the sheep and pigs had left of these unique forget-me-nots, I consulted the huge *Times Atlas of the World* fortuitously given me by my brother in America, to pinpoint the exact position of the Chatham Islands.

It was quite a shock to find that they were probably the smallest and furthest away dots in the whole world, and glaring me in the face was the indisputable fact that Australia, that huge land mass, was slap bang on my way.

Terra australis incognita described it perfectly, but if I once more adapted my methods to the circumstances, I might manage to insinuate a few lectures into that vast continent. It would give me the opportunity to find out how some of my other southern hemisphere plants grow in the wild, (perhaps upside-down?), and to see Botany Bay and visit Young Nick's Head in New Zealand, the first land sighted by Cook and Banks, which they thought was the Southern Continent. From there I would pause long enough to hop over to the Chatham Islands.

Imagery of New Zealand had long been in my mind, fired by the many stories I had heard from my Tregrehan friends, only a few miles from where I live. In 1840, a scion of this family had run away with the coachman's daughter and settled in New Zealand, and ever since there had been close communication in spite of the immense distance – and especially of the horticultural kind. All sorts of information had been exchanged over the years, not to mention seed winging its way to and fro. The young emigrant started to build what became one of the biggest sheep and cattle stations in the North Island, and from his first modest homestead the family grew into a fine colonial mansion. In the meantime the garden was developed, always to reflect that of his old home in Cornwall.

I stayed there and managed to scour this magical garden, filled with every variety of desirable plant, grown with the advantage of a more clement climate. The omens were against me that time; terrible weather, volcanic eruption, closing of roads and airports, and it was impossible to explore the country or get to the tantalising Chatham Islands. However, examining this beguiling garden again, which had been created with such long ago homesick yearning – *ça vaut le détour* – as the Michelin Guide would say.

Banks is revered all over Australia, so my lecture about him would be very suitable; my only fear was that they would know more about him than I did. In due course I was thrilled to be invited to Perth, Adelaide, Brisbane and Melbourne, which were neatly placed for my sightseeing, and my friends invited me to stay in New Zealand. My hosts were always wonderfully kind, looking after me and taking me to the many obscure places I wanted to see. Then there was the replica recently built of the *Endeavour*, and I was invited to go out for 'a day sail' in her round Sydney harbour – what a treat. Every time we went under that magnificent harbour bridge they fired the cannon using real gunpowder and a proper ramrod – it made a fantastic bang.

THE GRASS TREE

The Swan river, forever stamped on my memory with its beautiful black swan inhabitants, flowed past the colonial house in Perth where I stayed and started my tour. Here

Xanthorrhea, the Grass Tree or Blackboy

Xanthorrhea australis

grew a most extraordinary plant – another member of the freaks brigade – *Xanthorrhea,* the grass tree.

It was Reginald Farrer who is supposed to have referred to some plants he discovered as being related to the Strewwelpeter family. This seems a perfect description of *Xanthorrhea,* the colloquial names of Black Gin and Black Boy being no longer politically correct. *Xanthorrhea* looks like a very untidy old man, in great need of a haircut.

Botanists have now lumped together all grass trees which are unique to Australia into the Liliaceae family, and one cannot help wondering whether such elegant plants as the lapageria would care to acknowledge such untidy cousins.

BLACK GIN

Black Gin, *Kingia australis* (named after Captain Philip Gidley King, Royal Navy and Governor of New South Wales 1800–1806), is distinguished by its many drumstick-like heads of flowers, which are quite different to the solitary tall flower spikes of the other grass trees. The Kingia trunk is black, up to 3 metres high with a tufted head and rush-like leaves, the older ones reflexed or drooping; the leaves are square in section like matchsticks, flattened at the base and cemented together with resinous gum. They taper from 3 millimetres to needlepoint, upright at the crown, curving down as they age to form the dried skirt which hangs decorously round the trunk. The flower spikes shoot vertically from the centre to 3-5 metres tall, even on quite small plants – vivid green at first, creamy as they open – the flowers begin at 60 centimetres up the stem, completely surrounding the spike to its apex. They are sweetly scented and always open north side first – a good compass indication – but flower sporadically and rarely bother to do so two seasons running.

30 CENTIMETRES IN 120 YEARS

The Black Gin grows very slowly, perhaps 30 centimetres in 120 years, and mystery surrounds the age they achieve although it is thought likely to be over a thousand years. They are affected by bush fires, which destroy the leafy skirt, but seem to induce more vigorous growth at the crown.

The grass trees, or Black Boys, of Australia occur in fire-swept scrub, and are called 'Black Boys' in allusion to the charred blackened stem. This is made up of fibrous leaf bases, gummed together with resin which dries hard. The flowers are lily-like on pendulous racemes, and are closely related to the Black Gins but much more common – growing throughout different parts of temperate Australia. They rarely have more than one slender stem of 5-6 metres high, which will send up to twenty shortish, scaly stems from its crown of leaves, terminating in pom–pom like flower heads,

resembling the globe artichoke. They are bright, yellow green when young, turning brown and drooping with age and have slightly flatter leaves. The Black Boy will die if it is knocked down, but the Black Gin will grow new roots from a horizontal position; they all have hermaphrodic flowers but set very little seed.

J H Maiden, in his book *Useful Native Plants of Australia* published in 1889, describes the resin from the species *australis,* saying it is *'found in masses of irregular globular shape, within the body of the tree, exuding in large tears and drops near its roots; it is a dark red, friable substance, the purer homogenous specimens exhibiting a most brilliant ruby colour, when crushed into fragments; it fuses readily with the same deep colour and exhales the characteristic odour of gum benzoin and dragon's blood under such circumstances.'*

ARCHITECTURAL INTEREST

The grass trees of Australia are especially valuable as architectural plants in a garden where the climate is hot enough to grow them outside. They are available from Australian nurseries in very small tubes and each incipiently, untidy plantlet reaches just to the top of its barrier, promising on its label to grow a dark trunk in twenty years at 1 millimetre per year; it is described as fragrant but says nothing about Dragon's Blood. I bought a little tube and after about five years, my grass tree is certainly bushier, potted up out of its tube, but I have given up measuring its millimetres.

When I came upon, quite unexpectedly in my local nursery in Cornwall, several young (about seventy years old), grass trees in pots, with tall spikes very like bulrushes about a yard in height, I was severely tempted to buy one, even though it cost nearly £60. It was called *Xanthorrhea johnsonii,* (I have yet to discover who Johnson is), and alongside was a notice which said, *'These very ancient plants originate in Queensland, Australia. They are very tolerant of a wide range of conditions and add a completely new structure to our British gardens. It is capable of living hundreds of years and it is believed that a metre of trunk can represent 200–300 years of growth. Their charred black trunks are the result of earlier bush fires, a phenomenon they are designed to cope with.* The accompanying instructions said that *'although it would tolerate a light frost in their native habitat they should be treated as spectacular tub plants, for the patio in summer or as conservatory plants all the year round. Repotting will not be necessary for a number of years.'* However well designed they are, I have absolutely no intention of producing a bush fire to test them. Needless to say I bought one – imagine my shock and horror when the tip of the flower broke off getting it out of my car. I mourned it for several weeks while contemplating my mortal span, then decided to go back to the nursery and describe my dilemma. My idea was to part

exchange it for another flowering specimen as, even if it took several generations of nurserymen for it be noticeably bigger, it was still a valuable plant and another sporadic flower might appear before he collected his pension. To my delight the nursery offered to exchange it for an identical plant with a flower, at no extra charge, remarking that there was plenty of life in my plant, which was otherwise undamaged. Now I can watch its every move and await the lily-like pendulous racemes or pompom artichoke-like flower heads.

Leaving Perth, Western Australia, I discovered the difference between International and Domestic Airports. Too late as I saw my taxi disappearing, did I realise that the cleaner and his Hoover and I were the only occupants of this vast airport, from where I was hoping to catch the very early flight to Adelaide. Normally being at least two hours earlier than is necessary, a situation like this throws me into panic, but the cleaner was in life-saving mode and sent for another taxi, which took me to the not too distant Domestic airport. Soon I was in my jumbo jet, relishing the comfort at not having to suffer the fate of Mathew Flinders (another of Banks protégés who comes in later) in his painstaking survey of the coast. I had the Great Australian Bight at a glance with all the inlets, gulfs and river mouths and above all Encounter Bay just south of Adelaide, so called because this is

187

where Flinders overtook the French. I was particularly thrilled to stand on this southerly tip of Australia – next stop Antarctica – and conjure up a picture of those sailing ships meeting after their long, lonely and dangerous voyages into the totally unknown.

THE FATHER OF AUSTRALIA

Not for nothing is Joseph Banks known as the 'Father of Australia'. His first landing with Captain Cook in New South Wales in April 1770 was his introduction to a new country, and during the years which followed he did his best to organise further expeditions to explore this *'island continent'*, if indeed that was what it was. So little was known of it in our country, that the first convicts thought if they escaped westwards they would end up in China. It was thought that there could be a split down the middle, between the Bay of Carpentaria in the north and the Great Australian Bight in the south, making two vast islands, but no-one had been back to discover if this was true.

All our best ships were dedicated to fighting the French, but in 1787 one of the most extraordinary and daring expeditions was mounted by the Pitt Administration in London, to form a Penal Colony in New South Wales. The background story to this episode in our history was our loss of America after the American War of Independence. We had been used to selling our convicts as slaves to America; this arrangement suited everyone as the convicts were well treated and freed at the end of their sentence, after which they could begin a new life there – or they could come home to England.

The Bunbury Commission was set up to look into the possibilities of creating a Penal Colony, and when New South Wales was discussed, Sir Joseph Banks was summoned to give his opinion. Not only was he one of the few people who had ever been there but also as luck would have it, he was a botanist and even more important, an English farmer. Banks reported that, *'beyond the coastal marshes the soil was light, white sand; there were areas of much richer, deep black soil, which bore besides timber, as fine meadow as ever was seen and vast quantities of grass.'* He considered it *'sufficient to support a very large number of people,'* did not doubt *'our oxen and sheep, if carried there would thrive and increase,'* thinking the climate similar to that of Toulouse in the South of France. The inspired way in which he assessed the Botany Bay region's potential to become a neo-Europe, and the way in which he equipped the first colonists to realise this, explains the central role he played in the Colony's first 17 years.

The lists he drew up of the seed and plants they were to take make fascinating reading. It was not to be simple prison fare; one must imagine that he hoped many other Colonists – perhaps people displaced from America – besides convicts, would settle Down Under to enjoy the artichokes, horseradish, garlic, the long orange carrot, the swelling parsnip, celeriac and asparagus, not to mention the apples and pears, nectarine, apricot and peaches, mulberries, raspberries and strawberries that he included. He sent the First Fleet via Brazil especially because citrus trees could be embarked, as could bananas, cocoa, coffee, tobacco, even ipecacuanha and the coccineal insect. (You may remember that Francis Masson mentions seeing the cactus with this scale insect in the Captain's cabin *'which looked like a small greenhouse'* at Cape Town). Banks had something of a bee in his bonnet about this insect, but was determined to send it wherever a textile industry was to be established.

The news of this amazing Penal Colony set up by the British must have fired Napoleon's ambition for France, and his passion for the advancement of science that led him to send an expedition to the South Seas, commanded by Nicholas Baudin in 1800. Napoleon personally ratified this expensively fitted out expedition, which consisted of two ships, *Le Geographe* and *Le Naturaliste*, with twenty two scientists of all kinds, astronomers, geographers, minerologists, zoologists, draftsmen, botanists and gardeners. This French venture was commanded by the well-qualified Nicholas Baudin, and it was largely the news of it that at last persuaded the British Government to give in to Sir Joseph Banks' petitions, and grudgingly provide the battered old hulk, renamed *HMS Investigator*.

Banks had longed, ever since his own first visit, to send a proper expedition, equipped with naturalists and other scientists to circumnavigate and survey the whole continent. It was not until this very year of 1800, thirty years after Banks himself had landed at Botany Bay (1770), and thirteen years after the arrival of the First Fleet (1788), that he could at last realise his plans. The ship was in a dilapidated state but to Banks and Matthew Flinders (1774–1814) she was the answer to prayer.

MATTHEW FLINDERS

Flinders, also a native of Lincolnshire, was a young man after Banks' heart; inspired as a small boy by the Endeavour voyage, he had moved heaven and earth to join the Navy, with the sole purpose of further exploration of NSW. He sailed with Bligh on his second (and this time successful) breadfruit voyage, learning from Bligh – who had in his turn learned from Captain Cook the mastery of skills such as seamanship, surveying, cartography, navigation and, above all, how to preserve the health of his men.

With Banks' help Flinders was now appointed to lead this enterprise at the age of 27. His brief was to circumnavigate and survey the whole continent, and if possible, to catch the French. Before he sailed, Flinders dashed back to his home town of Donnington in Lincolnshire, and married his childhood sweetheart Ann Chapel. Together they lived on board the *Investigator,* while she was making ready for the voyage and, but for an unlucky inspection, he would probably have taken her with him. The inspector however, noticed she was not wearing her bonnet, and guessed she was not a casual visitor; Flinders was given the choice of sending her home or abandoning his life's ambition; their letters to each other are heartrending and little did they realise it would be ten long years before he returned.

ROBERT BROWN

It was a brilliant choice to send with Flinders another enthusiast of similar age as naturalist, Robert Brown. Brown was born in Montrose in Scotland in 1773; he was a schoolboy naturalist and early plantaholic, and at 18 read a paper on *'The Botanical History of Angus'* before the Edinburgh Natural History Society. He became a medical student at Edinburgh University, joined the Army as an Ensign in the Fifeshire Regiment of Fencibles and served in Ireland as a Surgeon's mate. He wrote a manuscript of 843 neatly written folio pages describing plants collected in 1794-98, and was elected an associate of the Linnean Society of London. In this close-knit community of botanists, Banks

heard of his availability, and wrote a letter offering him the post of naturalist in *HMS Investigator* at £400 p.a. signing it *'Yours Sir with real esteem and regard.'* This was a chance for Brown beyond his wildest dreams. Banks mustered just five young men as scientists for the voyage, including William Westall, a topographical painter, John Allen a miner, John Crossley astronomer, and Peter Good as gardener. He himself masterminded the expedition, and worked tirelessly on every detail.

FERDINAND BAUER

Banks chose Ferdinand Bauer to go as natural history painter on the voyage. An Austrian nearly twice the age of the others, he and his brother Franz were, and are, considered two of the finest botanical artists of all time. Franz was the first resident artist at the Royal Gardens at Kew, and worked there for Banks for 50 years. There were five brothers, whose father was court painter to the Prince of Lichtenstein. Ferdinand was trained as a miniaturist, and learned to paint with the aid of a microscope, thus producing not only the most beautiful works of art, but perfecting a method of presenting the reproductive parts of the plant and the minutest detail of its seed and pollen. Brown describes Bauer as indefatigable in his work during the voyage, and he brought home over 3,000 paintings.

Callistemon pallidus, the lemon bottlebrush

Brown himself was no slouch; altogether including the Flinders' voyage, he spent four years exploring Australia and Tasmania for plants, returning in 1805 with 4,000 specimens. He collected nearly a quarter of all Australian orchids, as well as 187 new genera and over 1,000 species, among them acacias and callistemons. The latter has a special glory with its long spikes of flowers without petals, just a mass of clustered stamens arranged in formal rows like a bottlebrush, its unofficial name. Its proper name means 'beautiful stamens' in Greek. Two varieties make a strong contribution to my garden museum in early summer; *Callistemon citrinus,* which is the crimson rather pendulous bottle-brush, stands next to *C. pallidus,* a yellow and very upright variety. *Boronia heterophylla,* another plant I owe him, is a delight with its miniature leaves and brilliant puce, exquisitely scented, tiny flowers which fills the greenhouse with

fragrance. I won't grow *Boronia megastigma,* Brown Meg as she is called, although she has the same heavenly perfume, she is quite ruined by being such an ugly colour.

GEORGE HIBBERT

The hibbertias which Brown also introduced are named for George Hibbert, a patron of botany at that time – and there are two that I have grown. *Hibbertia scandens* will only grow inside and climbs away with pretty, rather evil-smelling yellow flowers. The other one *H. aspera,* flowers on the wall outside my greenhouse; it will take a very slight frost but the leaves protest by going very dark green. It is absolutely covered in yellow, primrose-like

Hibbertia aspera

191

flowers, for weeks in the spring – very good value.

I am very proud of my flourishing tree fern *Dicksonia antarctica,* also attributed to Robert Brown; I did not manage to see this in the wild, but saw the New Zealand variety all over that country. It has to have a six feet span in all directions, and I can just give it this in the shady grove near my conker tree. It keeps its tiny, infant fronds tightly furled in the centre, which develop through the winter, and provided they are

had bought a magnolia which I decided to fit in at the bottom of the garden, but after about two years I discovered to my dismay that it was wrongly labelled and would be impossible to grow where I had put it. I tried to persuade the nursery to exchange it but they refused, telling me that if I dug it up now I would kill it. I rang another friend who had recently imported some tree ferns, told him my problem and asked if he would do a swap. He told me that my magnolia was probably only

Dicksonia antarctica – the tree fern

protected by fleece they will survive a few degrees of frost. It is a most rewarding plant to watch as soon as the spring arrives; several inches of baby fronds unfurl daily. It is extremely thirsty and has to be nearly drowned to be satisfied. I was very lucky to acquire it as they are not easy to find. It happened that I

worth about two thirds of his tree fern, which cost about £120, so we did a deal. The magnolia moved without difficulty. I probably have more experience in moving plants than most people, (as I never stop) and it is now flourishing in its new home. In exchange came the expensive log – the tree fern – hard to tell which end to plant. It puts on a new ring of elegant, feathery ferns every year, and is the glory of the garden. Bill proudly says it is the only one in the village.

OTHER FAVOURITES

Prostranthera lesianthos will just about survive in a sheltered position by the greenhouse but is not very long lived. It grows to a small tree and has the prettiest small white leafless racemes, sometimes tinted lilac. *P. rotundifolia,* the mint bush, has small purple flowers – they both have little lips. *Correa reflexa,* the Australian fuchsia makes a neat little hedge; it first became known when Joseph Banks and Daniel Solander collected seed and herbarium specimens of it at Botany Bay in May 1770. It is described by two botanists in 1798, who both named it after the Portuguese Ambassador and botanist Jose Correa de Serra. The *correa* is endemic to Australia and is found in all States; there are eleven species which are inclined to hybridize with near neighbours; mine is a low-growing shrub with small, tubular red flowers, reflexed and seemingly lined with yellow. It does not show off at all where it grows in the 'recumbent bed' in front of the dog, and I have to bend down and lift up the leaves to find its little blooms, which flower late in the year almost up until Christmas.

The nearest plant I grow to an annual is the Australian *Scaevola.* This comes from the Latin word *scaevus* meaning left-handed, referring to the fan-shaped, one-sided corolla. There are granite troughs around my terrace, and in three of these grow the little purple scaevola which flowers from May until the autumn, when it has to give way to spring bulbs. It is sometimes obtainable from better nurseries, and is in fact a small shrub, requiring no attention but water; I saw white ones growing wild in New South Wales.

The French officers, rescued by Flinders who directed them from Encounter Bay to Port Jackson (later Sydney), wrote interesting letters home in 1802, in which they described the state of the Penal Colony about twelve years after its beginning. They were particularly surprised by the good stone buildings, the excellence of the roads and the fine garden at Government House, Port Jackson, where *'the Norfolk Island pine grows by the side of bamboo from Asia; further on is the Portugal orange and the Canary fig, ripening beneath the shade of French apple trees; the cherry, pear, peach and apricot are interspersed among the metrosideros, correa, melaleuca, casuarina and eucalyptus and a great number of other indigenous trees',* but the profligacy of the peach tree was of particular note. From Sir Joseph's lists we know that he sent six species of peach, but by this time there were perhaps as many as 160,000 peach trees growing in the Cumberland plain; *'we may see'* wrote Peron, a French officer, *'whole fields covered in peach trees, and their fruit is so abundant*

193

that great quantities of it are dried: several of the colonists prepare from it an agreeable kind of wine, others distil from this wine a good-tasted spirit; and it is not unusual to see the farmers fatten their pigs with peaches.' That really impressed the French.

EUCALYPTUS

One of my first and worst mistakes was to plant the wrong sort of eucalyptus – one of the many which grow huge and fast. Every year I topped it to stop it going straight up to heaven and to make it bushy; I loved it for its foliage and it hid my garage from the house, but I could see it was not controllable and would have to go. It was a nightmare to dig up, obviously trying to get back to Australia through its roots, and it took Bill and all his sons' extreme efforts, (plus towing by car) to drag it out.

As Stirling Macoboy says in his *What Tree is That? 'in Australia the ubiquitous Gum Tree is king.'* There are over six hundred species, and although you see them growing in almost every part of the world, all but very few have come from Australia. I saw one of these in North India, *Eucalyptus deglupta,* the Mindanao Gum, which comes from the Phillipines and has the most amazing rainbow bark. I would love to grow *E ficifolia,* the red flowering gum, and now that I have recovered from my bad eucalyptus experience, I shall set about acquiring one. It is described as *'a superb small tree of lax habit, with scarlet or flame coloured flowers, in large corymbs, at the ends of the branches – very tender'.* Just up my street.

Most eucalyptus have white flowers, but it is their fragrant silvery-blue leaves that are so attractive. They vary greatly from spear to heart-shaped, and in the delicate, juvenile foliage – often quite different to the more mature, they always abound in that magical, glistening azure which provides the shimmering haze floating over the Blue Mountains of New South Wales, making them romantically inaccessible but necessary to explore.

Botany Bay was one place I really wanted to see. You would think there would be a path beaten to the spot, but I had left it rather late, and though I set off several times in buses which promised to get there, they all seemed to peter out long before arrival. I found my best view of it was from the air when my jumbo jet, on its way to New Zealand, flew so low over it I could see the memorial which marks the spot where Banks and Cook first landed.

12

FURTHER 'DOWN UNDER'

'After my first visit to New Zealand (which followed on from this Australia tour), and when all my plans were thwarted by the elements, I had vowed never to return, but events took a different turn when one day I was stopped in my tracks by an advertisement in the Times, which described a trip round New Zealand by sea. That's more like it, I thought.'

Immediately on spotting the advertisement I envisaged the possibility of seeing all the plants and places I had failed to see, and I could have another go at the Chatham Islands. The ship was small, about 3,000 tons, just ten times the size of *HMS Endeavour,* but no way did I intend to endure the sufferings and indignities of the 18th century travellers; this would be a luxury voyage of discovery – hideously expensive, but the opportunity of a lifetime – and it would make up for the unsuccessful previous sortie Down Under.

The ship was called *MV Oceanic Odyssey* and she belonged to a firm I

had never heard of called Noble Caledonia. All the names seemed good omens, and I decided that I still wanted to see Young Nick's Head and some of the other memorable places at which they touched, just as Cook and Banks did from the sea. Not only could I do my own pilgrimage, but the package promised visits to national forests, conservation areas, and botanic gardens, as well as whaling stations, sites of flightless birds and above all, several species of that most mysterious bird, the albatross. Luckily one whole day was dedicated to sea bird watching and I was able to photograph these

Albatross

enormous and beautiful creatures fighting over some fishy delicacy they both coveted.

The outward flight, about twenty four hours (that is, dinner three times in a row going out, and breakfast the same on the return), was direct to Auckland (I don't think much of stop-overs) where we joined the ship next day.

It makes one's mouth water to see the size to which some of the plants grow in a favourable climate like New Zealand.

How I would like to have a hedge of that exquisite *Metrosideros excelsa*, almost the first plant I saw, still just in flower in February, the end of their summer. When you see huge bushes of it growing wild, happy and exultant with its brilliant scarlet flowers, spreading away as far as the eye can see, you cannot think of it confined and reluctantly creeping out of a flowerpot – sheer cruelty to plants.

My day trip by air to Chatham Island – an hour each way, and booked in advance – was going to be touch and go. Needless to say the ship's itinerary was arranged well ahead, with the weather the only flexibility.

As the exciting day approached the forecast grew worse, and sure enough, the Captain called us all into the saloon to tell us that our schedule had been changed, because of a cyclone which was on collision course with us. This of course meant the cancellation of my visit to the beautiful forget-me-nots. Was I really going to have to make a third visit Down Under to achieve my goal, or must I accept that perhaps my stars do not permit my visit to the Chatham Islands?

NEW ZEALAND'S RICHES

New Zealand has a wonderful selection of indigenous plants, many of which were first seen by Joseph Banks and Daniel Solander on that famous voyage of discovery in *HMS Endeavour: Clianthus puniceus,* the Lobster Claw plant as described earlier, which is sadly no longer found in the wild and the *Phormium tenax* – a favourite plant of Banks – who spotted the industrial potential of its tough fibrous leaves as early as 1769, when he first saw it at the place they named Poverty Bay; he had it established at Kew by 1789 . It used to be an interesting architectural plant in my garden with its stout strap-like leaves, but its aesthetic value is limited and it had to give way to another New Zealand spectacular, *Hoheria* 'Glory of Amlwch', when it became too big and

became *de trop.* This little tree is well named, being a cross between *H. sexstylosa x H. glabrata,* and has the virtues of both. It is semi-deciduous, the former being evergreen and the latter deciduous. I grow it where the eucalyptus used to be, and its delicate, pale green pointed leaves are a delight. It is profusely covered in summer, with small, snow-white, honey scented flowers; I am afraid no flax plant can compete with that however tough its fibres. There were opportunities of stalking this little tree in an open woodland area on the forest edge, but I did not see it flower.

WILLIAM COLENSO

Hoheria sexstylosa was attributed to an interesting plant collector, the Rev William Colenso. He was a Cornishman and cousin to a famous Bishop in Natal. Born in 1811 in Penzance, educated there and later apprenticed to a book-binder, when he was twenty three he was chosen by the Church Missionary Society to take a printing press out to New Zealand. When the Maoris discovered that a missionary printer had come out to make books for them, they were delighted. They already had a few lesson books printed in Sydney, and Colenso relates how *'No hero of olden times was ever received by his army with*

Hoheria 'Glory of Amlwch'

197

greater *éclat: they appeared as if they would deify me'*. For sixty five years he worked as a missionary, and an investigator into ethnology, the Maori tongue, zoology and botany.

As a missionary amongst the natives in the very early days of the colony, Colenso travelled in the wilds and came face to face with nature. He was the first European to cross the Ruahine Mountains, and here he found alpine vegetation in all its glory. In his own rapturous words he describes the scene: *'When we emerged from the forest and the tangled shrubbery at its outskirts onto the open dell like land just before we gained the summit, the lovely appearance of so many and varied beautiful and novel wild plants and flowers richly repaid me the toil of the journey and ascent, for never did I behold at one time in New Zealand such a profusion of Flora's stores. In one word I was overwhelmed with astonishment, and stood looking with all my eyes, greedily devouring and drinking in the enchanting scene before me ... Here were plants of the well known genera of the bluebells and buttercups, gowans and daisies, eyebrights and speedwells of ones native land, closely intermixed with the gentians of the European Alps and the rarer southern and little known novelties ... But how was I to carry off specimens of these precious prizes, and had I time to gather them? However as I had no time to lose I first pulled off my jacket, and made a bag of that, added my shirt and by tying the neck got an excellent bag, while some specimens I also stowed in the crown of my hat.'* Before Colenso's

time little was known of the alpine plants of New Zealand, and he collected most industriously, sending large quantities to Kew.

CLEMATIS INDIVISA

A delectable evergreen species of clematis I have to remind me of New Zealand is *Clematis indivisa*. It likes to grow up forest trees, but sadly I did not manage to find it. I believe it will grow outside here, but I like to see its delicate, greeny-white flowers, bursting with life and covering the back wall of my green-house in very early spring – perhaps under the illusion that it is safe in its own country. If the sun comes out, there are few more enjoyable occupations than to sit in late winter, with all doors closed and as protected as the plants, admiring not only its lavish display, but that of many other intrepid early blooms. Banks must have esteemed it also, since he gave it to Sydney Parkinson to paint.

GRISELINIA LITTORALIS

Griselinia littoralis is not the most exciting New Zealand plant, but it does have the prettiest pale, broad leaves, when it can thrive near the sea. It was named by Raoul Edouard Fiacre Louis (1815-1852) who was the medical officer in the French frigate *L'Aube*, during the stay of that vessel in Akaroa in 1840, and was described by him in the *'Annales des Sciences Naturelles'*. At that time it seems to have grown abundantly in the hill country forests, but now only a few, old living specimens remain.

Nearly all younger plants are epiphytic on tree ferns, the only mode of life, which protects them from deer. Many of them have been unable to develop a sufficient trunk to stand, and when the supporting tree fern dies, they fall within browsing level and are destroyed. *Griselinia littoralis* does not now occur anywhere in the primitive lowland vegetation, so I was unable to find it, even while admiring the tree ferns. Usually it forms a handsome evergreen tree from 40-60 feet high with a conspicuous spreading head, and it differs from *Griselinia lucida* in being usually terrestrial, while the latter is almost invariably epiphytic. The trunk is often crooked and gnarled from 2-4 feet in diameter, with light brown, rugged bark, and it produces tiny flowers in axillary panicles in October. It makes a very strong quick-growing hedge, and I had recourse to it in my garden, where I needed an extra barricade.

YOUNG NICK'S HEAD

Having totally failed to see Young Nick's head or Cape Kidnappers, so tantalisingly out of reach on my first visit to New Zealand, now, on my second foray Down Under, I made a point of accepting the Captain's invitation to any passenger interested in inspecting the bridge. Anticipating that I might need a lot of advice on this cruise, I made friends with the lowliest of officers on watch, and discovered that we would reach Young Nick's Head at 4am, when it would be pitch dark and about 40 miles off shore. Nevertheless he promised to telephone me at the moment it was in sight – and when he did, I could see from my cabin there was a distant light flashing in the gloom, and although it was not the most favourable of sightings, it was good enough for me.

I felt a true thrill, imagining Young Nick peering from the mast head, and the excitement of Banks and Cook and everyone on board the ship, as they heard his cry of *'Land!'* at this very spot. It was first sighted by young Nick, aged 12, at 2 pm on 6th October 1769 and it was from the masthead of *HMS Endeavour* that this land was mistaken for the Southern Continent, or *Terra Australis Incognita*. Knowing that they were approaching the position given for New Zealand by Abel Tasman, Captain Cook was on the lookout for signs of it: *'seaweed began to float by'* he says in his log, *'one or two pieces of barnacle-covered wood, everyone noticed the seal asleep in the water and reflected that seals do not go far from land.'* October brought one or two calms, in which Banks was off shooting birds and netting jellyfish; expectation was rising. There was a gallon of rum promised to the first person who should sight land, with the further promise that his name should be given to some part of the coast.

199

'Now', wrote Banks in his diary *'do I wish that our friends in England could by the assistance of some magical spyglass take a peep at our situation; Dr Solander setts at the table describing, myself at my bureau Journalizing, between us hangs a large bunch of sea-weed, upon the table lays the wood and barnacles; they would see notwithstanding our different occupations our lips move very often, and without being conjurors might guess that we were talking about what we should see upon the land which there is now no doubt that we shall see very soon.'*

CAPE KIDNAPPERS

Our Australian Captain did a great deal to make the voyage as interesting as possible, and when I was looking through his enormously magnifying binoculars, he offered to take the ship closer in to my next choice of Cape Kidnappers, which was much more successful. The Cape was so called because a young Tahitian named Tupia had wanted to accompany Cook in the *Endeavour* when they left the Society Islands, taking his son Tiata of about twelve. In the event they were very valuable in helping interpret to the Maoris when they found the language incomprehensible. A good deal of barter took place alongside, between the natives in their canoes and the sailors, and at one point Captain Cook noticed a large armed boat, *'wherein were 22 men ... one man had on him a black skin something like a bear skin which I was desirous of having*

that I might be a better judge what sort of an animal the first owner was. I offered him for it a piece of red cloth which he seemed to jump at by immediately putting off the skin and holding it up to us ... but he would not part with it until he had the cloth in his possession and after that not at all' . The armed boat returned later with some fish, and when Tiata went over the side to fetch it *'they seized hold of him… and endeavoured to carry him off; this obliged us to fire on them which gave the boy the opportunity to jump overboard, we brought the ship to, lowered a boat into the water and took him up unhurt.'*

Captain Cook continues this epic tale with, *'Two or three paid for this daring attempt with the loss of their lives and many more would have suffered had it not been for fear of killing the boy. This affair occasioned me giving this point of land the name Cape Kidnappers. It is remarkable on account of two white rocks in form of Hay Stacks standing very near it; on each side of the Cape are tolerable high white steep cliffs'.* Cook gives the exact position and its relation to Hawkes Bay which he named on the same occasion.

Now, everyone on board wanted a better look at Cape Kidnappers, which we reached in fine weather and in broad daylight, although mysteriously, no-one could see the Hay Stack rocks, even though the *'tolerable high white cliffs'* were just as Captain Cook described. Perhaps the earthquake of 1930 or some other earth movement can account for their absence. It is recounted that 3,000 hectares of new land were thrown up from the sea during this disaster.

Not only the Captain was interested in my frequent visits to the bridge, but some of the passengers also wanted to know what I was up to. In the end, the management of Noble Caledonia asked me to give my Banks lecture in the main saloon, on a day when we were at sea, so without any notes or slides I did my best, which included reading some of Cook's log and Banks' diary, which I had brought with me to study when we reached the salient points. My reward was to be any bottle of wine I chose from the ship's wine menu, but my audience was more generous and took me out to dinner when we reached Hobart, Tasmania.

DUSKY BAY

The one other place of great interest to me was West Cape, the most South West point of the South Island. Cook says, *'This Bay I have named Dusky Bay ... it is about 3 or 4 miles broad at the entrance, and seems to be as full as deep, in it are several islands behind which there must be shelter from all winds provided there is sufficient depth of water. The north point of this bay, where it bears SEBS is very remarkable there being off it five high peaked rocks, standing up like four fingers and a thumb of a man's hand on which account I have named it Point Five Fingers.'* I particularly looked forward to this after the disappointment of the Hay Stacks.

Cook goes on to describe *'the southern most bore due south distant five or six leagues and as this is the western most point of land upon the whole coast I have called it West Cape. A little before noon we passed a small narrow opening in the land where there appeared to be a very snug harbour; inland behind this opening were mountains the summits of which were covered with snow which seemed to have fallen lately and this is not to be wondered at as we have found it very cold this two days past. The land on each side of the entrance riseth almost perpendicular from the sea to a very considerable height and this was the reason I did not attempt to go in with the ship as I saw clearly that no winds could blow there but what was either right in or right out. This is westerly or easterly and it certainly would have been highly imprudent in me to have put into a place where we could not have got out but with a wind that we have lately found does not blow one day in a month. I mention this because there are some on board who wanted me to harbour at any rate without the least considering either the present or future consequences.'*

This last sentence is the only time there has been any suggestion of disagreement between Cook and the gentlemen.

Here, Banks writes that the ship *'stood along shore with a fair breeze and passed three or four places that had much the appearance of harbours and much to my regret who wished to examine the mineral appearances from which I had formed great hopes.'*

It is interesting to compare the following two descriptions of the same place by Sydney Parkinson, the artist, who says: *'On the 16th we sailed along the shore of the land we had passed the day before, which appeared as wild and romantic as can be conceived. Rocks and mountains whose tops were covered with snow, rose in view one above another from the water's edge; and those near the shore were clothed with wood, as well as some of the valleys between the hills whose summits reached the clouds.'*

Another of his shipmates writes: *'The land on this part of the coast afforded a most dreary prospect, and consisted of high mountains covered with snow and falling by the steepest descent immediately into the sea, without the smallest beach or landing place.'*

Banks now had the last word before they sailed for England: *'We are now on board of two parties, one who wished that the land in sight might, and the other that it might not be a continent; myself have always been most firm for the former tho sorry I am to say that in the ship, my party is so small that I firmly believe that there are no more heartily of it than myself and one poor midshipman, the rest begin to sigh for roast beef.'*

The cyclone had ruined this prospect also, so we sailed on to Tasmania, missing the wonderful scenery and Point Five Fingers.

That piece of ocean is not a shipping lane; indeed it must be one of the loneliest and least frequented seascapes – with rolling grey waters from one horizon to the other – looking no doubt exactly the same 200 years ago.

It was easy to imagine the thoughts of our intrepid sailors, avid as they were for *'roast beef'* as they continued their voyage of discovery, followed only by the legendary albatross which glide and fly faithfully astern – perhaps the ancestors of those which followed me.

—HYDRANGEAS AND— JAPANESE CHERRIES

'The wishy washy colours of the large globose heads produced by hydrangeas, so prevalent in the coastal areas of Cornwall, never attracted me much, but there are some interesting varieties well worth accommodating, some of which have lovely autumn coloured foliage.'

My latest acquisition and almost favourite is *Hydrangea serrata* 'Tiara', planted under the tree fern, which in turn benefits from the extra shade of the conker tree. It is a dwarf shrub, not supposed to exceed a metre, although you can never tell in Cornwall, where plants do tend to forget their rules. It has flattened corymbs of blue or white flowers, surrounded by a pretty circle of white, pink or bluish florets made of

delicate little petals, often deepening to crimson in the late summer.

It is next to another much larger, pale pink, flowering hydrangea called *H. 'Hovella'*, which I fell for at Hampton Court flower show, never having seen one this colour before. Its flowers are just now turning from pink to green, and which will end up cherry red; this desirable habit of changing their clothes makes them doubly valuable. I have made a

Hydrangea serrata 'Tiara'

Hydrangea x 'Hovella'

hedge of them all, adding *H. quercifolia,* which has long, pointed, white flowers, the florets much condensed into this most interesting shape. Its oak-like leaves – hence 'quercifolia' – also turn brilliant colours.

However, the hydrangea I grow most of has quite different flowers and is called *H. 'Ayesha',* described by Hillier *'as a distinct and unusual hydrangea of puzzling origin.'* This also makes a good hedge, having big, bold leaves of glossy green, and there is one hedge of these, with five plants squashed in behind the big euchryphias, just outside my office. Its flowers are densely packed and composed of thick-petalled, cup-shaped florets, much more like a large lilac in texture; some bushes produce quite a definite pink and white colour, others blue and white. They are much less ethereal than other hydrangeas, and their great virtues are the love of shade, the long flowering period into late autumn, their habit of forever changing both flower and leaf colour, and remaining decorative when the colours fade and they begin to look as if they have all been carefully dried.

MR H B

Shirley Hibberd, the 19th century horticulturalist thought of the hydrangea as a pet *'because it responds so willingly to any treatment its owner may think fit to give it',* but Loudon remarks that he thinks of it as *'particularly suitable for persons who have little else to do than attend to their garden or greenhouse as it requires so much watering'.* The very idea of making a pet of a plant whose name means 'water vessel' does not attract, but it is a sobering thought that this pet will drink *'ten or twelve gallons of fluid daily in warm weather.'* It would be invidious to single out any of the plants that I do think of as pets, but my more or less fervent descriptions of them will leave little doubt.

Hydrangeas have an interesting history, being intimately connected to several of my favourite people. The first garden hydrangea was the white flowered American *Hydrangea arborescens,* obtained by Peter Collinson in 1736. William Bartram discovered *H. quercifolia* during his travels in Carolina, Georgia and Florida in 1773–1778. It was when visiting Rosemoor Gardens in Devon that I saw a splendid hedge of them, growing against woodland at the bottom of a steep hill, which gave me the idea.

Mr Michael Haworth-Booth wrote the standard work on the genus early in the 20th century, and Sir Compton Mackenzie, in reviewing it, writes: *'This is a model flower book, for the lightness with which Mr H B wears his wide botanical and horticultural learning enables him to impart it most attractively.'* This sounded promising, and lucky for garden history Mr H B was not daunted by the conflicting data he found, the further he investigated the subject. No one book agreed with another, and as soon as he had one variety properly identified and classified, more complications would appear. It was the plants themselves that saved the situation, and for the next twenty years he grew all the varieties he could find. As he says, he *'studied their forms and foliages, the port and color of their flowers, their reactions to their individual conditions of soil and aspect began to send me a stream of messages of visual signals, definite and true. They interested me until I was enslaved and I knew I must devote myself to straightening out the tangle somehow.'* Another plantaholic described.

THE ORIGINAL

The original wild prototype species, from which the garden variety is derived, has been growing since time immemorial in thousands on the very shores of Japan, sometimes on lava rocks but always under the full influence of the sea. The Japanese cultivated these plants in their gardens and noted that one day, a sport, or freak seedling appeared. Instead of having a ring of large showy flowers around the little true ones in the centre, it produced a ball-shaped head, almost entirely composed of the big sterile flowers. This was the origin of the globose-headed hydrangea, called *Hortensia* by the French, but known in England as *Hydrangea,* 'Sir Joseph Banks.' What a pity they had to name this very dreary plant after Sir Joseph. In both cases, the large ray flowers are for ornament only, to attract the notice of the bees and insects, who transfer the pollen from one of the little true flowers to another. Carl Thunberg had brought herbarium specimens of both this maritime hydrangea and a woodland variety in 1784.

A living hydrangea was brought to Kew from China, by the agency of Sir Joseph Banks in 1789. Its strange green flowers excited the curiosity of all, even in the Customs House. This variety is identical to the coarse, strong growing, rather tender, weak-coloured hortensias still to be found on the coasts of Cornwall today. I note with interest that even my *H. ayesha* has a tendency to send out a sport of the ugly globose bloom occasionally – it is very quickly beheaded.

Carl Thunberg's original herbarium specimens, labelled *Viburnum macrophyllum* and *V. serratum,* (*Viburnum* was later changed to *Hydrangea*), were available for Mr H B to study from Uppsala, and he scoured the countryside, gardens and nurseries to investigate live specimens, as well as spending long, exhausting days in great libraries. He found von Siebold's wonderful *Flora Japonica* a landmark in hydrangea history, written in 1840. Mr H B also studied the great E H Wilson's scholarly note (1923) on the hortensias, and decided Wilson was mistaken in his deductions, and that this was one source of the confusion. He was particularly baffled by the extraordinarily distinct character of Sir Joseph Banks' original clonal Chinese variety, introduced in 1789. This closely resembled the maritime hydrangea, found by Thunberg and Wilson, which only flourished by the sea, and flowered only from the terminal bud, and not from every side shoot as did the woodlanders. He decided that *H.* 'Sir Joseph Banks' was a globose sport of Wilson's pure maritime species. There was still a mystery, because Wilson's maritime species had not been imported into this country. It was only after finding wild plants of the latter, growing happily on the cliffs near Shanklin, Isle of Wight and examining them carefully that Mr H B decided that they were branch sports; that is reversions to the original maritime hydrangea. He then renamed this *Hydrangea maritima.*

I was intrigued by the French name hortensia for the mop head hydrangea, which seems to have been chosen by Commerson, who travelled as botanist with de Bougainville (you may remember) accompanying him on his voyage around the world in 1766. Could it be coincidence that Mademoiselle Baret, mentioned earlier – she, whose gender was revealed by the Tahitians – his valet and lifelong friend, was also called Hortense?

Enter again Mr Haworth-Booth, who after his long research comes to the conclusion that most garden hydrangeas are hybrids, the result of centuries of selective breeding for garden decoration by the Japanese.

H. petiolaris, a very vigorous Japanese climber, which grows on the wall behind my *Magnolia grandiflora,* is visible from my office window. It has self clinging rootlets like those of the ivy, and takes some time to get going, but flowers well in the summer.

One frequently meets new plants in other people's gardens, and this happened with *Dichroa febrifuga,* an evergreen relative of the Hydrangeaceae family. It resembled *H. aspera* but its flower was pointed and in texture more like *H. Ayesha.* Difficult to acquire and fussy about the favoured position found for it, it looked very sad after one of the wettest spells that winter, practically drowned, so it had to be consigned to the convalescent bed – out of sight and, with difficulty, replaced. The new one has a flower, but it does not seem to come out properly; perhaps it can be encouraged to do better in the future. Meanwhile the first plant has recovered and has much bigger leaves. Glyn Church, whose book *Hydrangeas* mentions the dichroa as a recent introduction from North Burma, recommends *Dichroa versicolor,* another variety, whose '*rich denim blue flowers are produced more or less all the year round.*' I bought my second plant from a local nursery, well known for mislabelling its plants – could the large leafed one turn out to be *D. versicolor?* What a bit of luck if it is.

Mr H B mentions another garden variety, 'Beni-kaku', as the *H.*

japonica of von Siebold. It has large ray flowers, whose sepals are markedly serrated, but have the most extraordinary colouring. Many hydrangeas are well known for their chameleon habit of colouring, depending on how much aluminium is in the soil, but this one, irrespective of whether the plant is growing in neutral to limy soil or acid, produces ray flowers that bloom pure white and turn crimson only owing to the effect of sunlight.

VIBURNUMS

Viburnums follow very well after hydrangeas, Carl Thunberg having originally named them as such. They are a most valuable addition to any shrub collection, the only problem being to choose the best for a variety of reasons. Two new ones have joined my museum from Peter Chappell's mint selection in his Spinners Garden in Lymington. My long search for *Viburnum furcatum* ended on his doorstep, after I had read of the plant's virtues in Roy Lancaster's article in the *RHS Garden* Magazine in October 1998.

Lancaster describes this viburnum as one of a forgotten band of viburnums, but one of the best hardy ornamental shrubs, suitable for lime-free soil. It has huge, heart-shaped, deeply veined leaves with coarsely shaped margins, which turn from pretty pale green to deep wine shades in the autumn. In May its blooms are of lace cap form, with corymbs of small white scented, fertile florets, ringed by quite large, conspicuously white, sterile flowers, after which the red berries appear, which turn blackish when ripe.

E H Wilson mentions this plant in his book, *More Aristocrats in the Garden*, as *'conspicuous from afar, midst the forest undergrowth, suggested of suspended snowflakes.'* Nevertheless, in spite of dedicated care, it was determined to die on me, and when next I have the energy to go to Lymington, I will replace it. Peter Chappell introduced me to eye catching *Viburnum setigeron*, whose leaves are constantly changing colour, from metallic-blue-red, through shades of green to orange-yellow in the autumn. This was another plant collected by the intrepid William Mesny during his travels in China. *Viburnum carlesii* was found by William Richard Carles who was the British Vice Consul in Korea, and who made several trips into the almost unknown interior, and sent home dried specimens of it to Kew in 1885. It was notable for its delicious scent, but was surpassed in every way by its hybrid, *V. juddii*, named after William Henry Judd, the propagator of the Arnold Arboretum where it was bred. My plant of the latter is an annual delight when its winter-bare branches suddenly burst into leaf and scented flowers.

THE HYPERICUM

Another plant I have spent a long time despising is the hypericum, but

I was interested when visiting that rarest of gardens, Ray Wood at Castle Howard, which has recently been reopened to the public. Here I found a highly desirable specimen called *Hypericum augustinii,* with the most beautiful, quite large and brilliant yellow flowers with a wax-like lustre. One literally had to touch them to see if they were real.

Lin Hawthorne, the Curator, told me how the great gardener and botanist, Jim Russell, had recreated Ray Wood, about twenty years ago; an amazing achievement of planting a north facing slope in North Yorkshire with hundreds of rhododendrons and azaleas brought up from his collections in Surrey, and flourishing as if they were in their native habitat. Some of his plants were from layers taken from original introductions of the plant collectors, who travelled in the last hundred years or so. His labelling was uniquely informative. July is the time for hypericums but in the spring, Ray Wood is in its full glory and worth a pilgrimage to see. Lin gave me some seed from the hypericum, for which I was grateful, as there is no mention of it in the *RHS Plant Finder.*

All sorts of legends are attached to the hypericum or St John's Wort. It is supposed to keep evil spirits at bay, and flowering as it does at the summer solstice, it was named in honour of St John, whose feast is 24th June. It is also supposed to have protective powers against lightning, witches and the evil eye.

Augustine Henry found a very fine form of it in Ichang, China, *H. patulum* var. *henryi,* which he sent to Kew in 1898, and *H. patulum* var. *forrestii* was collected by George Forrest in Yunnan. The finest hybrid is the famous 'Hidcote Gold', raised at Hidcote in the 1940s by Major Johnston, from seed collected some say in a garden in Kenya, others in China, (so says Alice Coates in her *Garden Shrubs and their Histories*). It is shapely, robust, semi-evergreen, perpetual flowering, indifferent to 30 degrees of frost, has all the hypericum virtues, and was given an Award of Merit in 1954.

ROWALLANE HYBRID

H. hookerianum was found in Assam and introduced by Thomas Lobb, when collecting for Veitch in 1848–51. Reginald Farrer collected seed on his last expedition to N Burma in 1920, and descended from this is another famous garden variety called 'Rowallane Hybrid'. There is close rivalry between this and 'Hidcote Gold' for the title of 'King of hypericums'; the former has the larger flowers, but is much the less hardy.

Charles Nelson, in his book *An Irish Flower Garden*, describes it: '*as much as two metres tall, the shoots arch gracefully, the tips laden down by the large flowers. Its leaves, arranged in opposite pairs, are ovate, dark green above and paler grey green underside; the flowers which appear in groups of three at the ends of the shoots and side branches are about 5cms across, a bowl of brilliant yellow like a giant buttercup. The petals have a silky sheen inside, the numerous orange stamens are grouped into five fluffy clusters and the prominent ovary and style are green.'* It flowers from June until late autumn, being covered in flowers all this time if it is happily planted. It is a self-sown seedling believed to have been the result of cross pollination between two Himalayan St John's Worts. There is another enthusiastic description of it in an advertisement when it was newly bred: *'not only is the saucer shaped flower at least one inch larger than any other variety of hypericum, but it received a severe test for hardiness during the spring of 1938, when it successfully endured drought followed by hard frost and east winds.'* Strong plants about 2 feet were offered for 5 shillings each and a few larger specimens at 7 shillings and sixpence. A plant of H. 'Rowallane Hybrid' was also available in Peter Chappell's garden, 'Spinners', but not at this knock down-price; however, fetching it gave me a chance to investigate his garden, which is known to be full of rarities, (and thus great temptations). The hypericum has not lived up to expectations so far, and has been moved to a less prestigious position. Perhaps I was right to despise them after all.

Before proceeding to the Japanese cherries, this is the moment to return to the unsalubrious bottom of the garden, (the less prestigious position just referred to), where plants which were out of favour for one reason or another had been found a temporary home. It was hidden by the twelve foot camellia hedge, which curved towards the newly installed small greenhouse for the lapageria seedlings; here was an opportunity for a surprise corner and more Must Have plants.

THE SURPRISE CORNER

I hankered after bamboos: not that any of them seem to be called bamboos any more, and the more you read about them the more it appears that no-one really agrees with anyone else. It is said that they die after flowering, though some flower for thirty years without stopping; other varieties threaten invasive behaviour which will speedily form such thickets and root clumps as to be completely ineradicable. There are four especially desirable bamboos, without known vices, which would grow to 3 metres or more inside my most easterly wall, and disguise the ugly buildings beyond. Two *Phyllostachys* (referring to the leafy inflorescence of these bamboos) *nigra* would grow towards each other, their beautiful narrow pale green foliage arching gracefully like magic wands on their exotic black stems, and between them, to make sure of no gaps, would be *Fargesii murielae*, found by Ernest Wilson in China and named after his daughter Muriel. Also irresistible was *Fargesii nitida;* these last two are the most

Cestrum elegans in flower on Christmas Eve

elegant and ornamental of all bamboos. They are named in honour of an intrepid French missionary and naturalist who travelled in Central China.

Fortuitously at this moment I had decided that *Crinodendron patagua,* the white flowered lantern tree, was outgrowing its position on the terrace and would be perfect for the south east corner of this fast-developing little area. It was extremely difficult to extract, having insinuated its roots into all its nearby neighbours and beyond, but it graces its corner well. Between it and forming an L with the bamboos, I have put another camellia hedge of varieties I longed for but had not managed to fit in, and in front of these are some *Amaryllis belladonna.* Now there is the centre rhombus-shaped bed, which used to have spinach (fought over by me and the slugs, and always won by the slugs) and runner beans, which Bill knows I like.

Now I think I will fill it with *Echium wildpretii* in the centre and lots of *Convolvulus cneorum* surrounding them, which will make a pretty silvery patch. *Cestrum elegans,* which had been growing in the shelter of my big camellia hedge, has had to be moved and is now leaning against the myrtle hedge in full elegant flower, two days before Christmas.

THE JAPANESE CHERRY

I described earlier how the splendid Japanese cherry was intended to become an umbrella, over a congestion of camellias. I had planted it on the boundary to make use of every inch of my territory; the neighbour here has no interest in his garden but has a very untidy and weed-like tree, known locally, according to Bill, as a 'withy,' which was interfering with the cherry, and spoiling my view of it. It took a long time, but at last I persuaded him to let Bill, who was longing to get at it, trim it and replace it with some myrtles, which I gave him. The Japanese cherry is a ravishing addition to this corner of the garden, with its late flowering myriads of fimbriated blossoms, brilliantly replacing the fading camellias.

When I bought this handsome plant from the Duchy Nurseries it was called Mayako, and I chose it because it wasn't too big and it flowered later than any others; I tried to discover its origins but it seemed to have disappeared from the catalogue and the nurseryman told me it was now sold under the name of *Prunus shogetsu.* It was all

Prunus Shimidsu Sakura

explained by Collingwood Ingram, (known as 'Cherry' Ingram because of his addiction) who was an amateur botanist and gardener of renown for most of the 20th century. He dedicated his waking hours to the study of these beautiful trees, and says, *'the Japanese – who are generally supposed to be the most aesthetic race in the world – rightly regard their flowering Cherries as the most precious of their many floral treasures. The blossoming of the Cherries is made the occasion of a national holiday, and high and low alike make an annual pilgrimage to the more famous groves and plantations. It was from the district of Yoshino, in the province of Yamato, that in 1735 the Shogun ordered 10,000 of these trees to be transplanted to a grove near Tokyo, some of which are still flourishing at 60 to 70 ft tall.'* Collingwood Ingram laments that such planting of these magical trees is not copied in England, though, as he says, most of the species are perfectly hardy and could easily be grafted onto our native *P avium*.

He writes in considerable detail about my most beautiful *P. 'Shimidsu Sakura'*, which means 'moon hanging low by a pine tree'. He blames himself for wrongly naming it in 1925, a after deciding it was not *P. 'Mayako'* or *P. 'Shogetsu'* (its second mistaken name), because the flower described was *'light pink, with long slender flower stalks (about 8 cm), the infloresence being held in an upright position.'* He therefore had to rename this cherry which he says, *'is characterised, especially towards the end of the season, by the extraordinary length of its lax and completely pendulous corymbs;indeed, the three to six flowered infloresence is often 6 or even 7 inches long, the pedicels in particular being notably elongated ... The foliage normally appears at the same time as the blossoms, which partially explains the phenomenal length of the flower stalks.'* He continues: *'pink tinted in the bud stage, the blossom becomes snowy white when fully open. They are semi-double and fairly large, measuring nearly 5 cms across. The individual flower being of a flatly open shape, with the petals frilled at their edges, suggests to the fanciful mind, a miniature ballet-girl's skirt, while the small leafy carpels, to be seen in the centre of the blossom, might be likened to two tiny green legs.'* Every word he says is true.

Mr Ingram adds, *'I propose to honour the memory of Kengo Shimidsu – a man whose passionate love for these trees saved many of the finest varieties, including this one – from extinction during that critical period in the last century (19th) when their cultivation was being wholly neglected in the land of their origin.'* So now we know.

—THE PLANTAHOLIC'S— MAGNET

*'To have lived in the days when only
a few decorative plants
were known, and when single tulips were planted a few feet
apart because they were so precious and rare,
must have been the inspiration of
the incipient plantaholic.'*

Some of the young plantaholics I have already described were lucky enough to be discovered by Joseph Banks or some other travelled plantsman, who knew the world was waiting for them to go out and search for the thousands of varieties of heavenly plants which they had glimpsed in the distance, or of which they had heard entrancing descriptions. Some of them would have been employed and told what to look for, and they would not have known what they would find. But when they saw it, they would recognise it for its value. What made them successful was

their taste and judgment. Every single plantaholic would have his own opinion of what makes such a plant, a subject which would no doubt provoke fierce arguments.

To be chosen in the first place, they would have to be men of knowledge and experience. But what yardstick did the successful plant collectors use, I wonder? The question was interestingly argued by two erudite men in *The New Flora and Silva,* which publication sadly died in August 1940. Mr H Armytage Moore writes that a collector's choice must be guided by *'the plant's soundness of constitution, adaptability to existing conditions of soil and climate, beauty of flower foliage and/or fruit, attractiveness of habit, carriage and display of flower and fruit and character of foliage, the whole conveying a general air of good breeding, appropriate to an aristocrat of the garden. Quality, distinctiveness and individuality can stand out conspicuously in the plant as in the personage, and are clearly discernible to the trained eye. Comparisons may be odious amongst people, but they are of distinct importance in the plant world.'*

He goes on to give some examples from his own garden, among which are *Magnolia wilsonii, Embothrium longifolium, Euchryphia glutinosa* and *Rhododendron falconeri*, all of which are uncommon, to say the least.

A SHARP RIPOSTE

Mr E H M Cox, Editor of *The New Flora and Silva*, writes in reply, that he is much intrigued by Mr Armytage Moore's views, with most of which he agrees, but he says *'personally I should define a good plant as one that possesses beauty that can be appreciated not only by the trained eye but also by vast numbers of lay gardeners. Why'*, he says *'are quality, distinctiveness and individuality only discernible by the trained eye? I think the expert gardener is one of the poorest judges of quality; he looks for differences where none exist, novelty is a shibboleth; and he often turns the blindest of eyes to anything that many thousands of people call beautiful, simply because it is beloved by the herd. The expert gardener*

is often a plant snob of the deepest dye.' It is a treat to be embroiled in this delightfully sharp encounter.

There is another aspect which E H M Cox suggests: *'that gardeners are inclined to forget that plant hunting is a very old occupation, and that only at a comparatively late date has the intensive production of new plants of purely ornamental value been wedded to the purely scientific collection.'*

He describes two collectors with different methods: Reginald Farrer, with whom Cox also travelled, who set out to collect *'the cream of plants of horticultural interest, skimming the country and ignoring the purely scientific,'* and George Forrest, *'who works thoroughly a particular area and does not neglect the scientific side of botanical exploration, while keeping a weather eye open for plants of real garden value'.* Cox adds, *'I know from my own experience just how difficult it is to judge the garden value of plants; in the wild and in their own setting they may seem much more desirable than their progeny in the more sophisticated surroundings of a garden.'*

Cox refers to this in October 1938, *'when everyone in the gardening world had suddenly gone, what Americans call haywire, over Chinese plants, looking with a prejudiced eye on anything that did not come from East Asia.'* He cites an example of a *Primula sonchifolia*, which he and Farrer found in Upper Burma, about which they both wrote paeons of praise in articles spreading its fame, until one day, seeing it flower for the first time in a garden, it showed most clearly it did not like cultivation. Suddenly also its colour and form, so perfect in its natural habitat, seemed *'a little coarse and to have the appearance of mutton dressed as lamb.'* He lays down certain criteria for a successful and popular plant, which besides the obvious ones of good colour, early flowering, and genuine hardiness, must be easy to propagate, and thus available to be sold at a reasonable price.

That is where Mr Armytage Moore's aristocrats fail; popularity is an indicator because you would think that all such plants would be popular, but many of them have not had a chance to be popular, being often unobtainable. If you look at it the other way round, are all popular plants good?

With the plethora of garden plants even then, the RHS started to bestow the Award of Merit, with the good intention of marking an exceptional plant, but which Mr Cox says *'is now* (1938), *becoming a laughing stock.'*

He adds that *'immediately after the war* (the Great War), *there was a music hall joke about the only man left in London without the OBE. The analogy is obvious.'*

Not so the Award of Garden Merit of which he approves. In fact he recommends spending 4 shillings on a small book published by the RHS, and called *Some Good Garden Plants.*

A NEVER ENDING PASSION

There is no end to this story because a Living Plant Museum can never be complete; especially as I cannot resist gaily squeezing in just one more prize possession, where I optimistically spotted a space or more likely made one by moving something that had disappointed me. What a relief it is when I occasionally trot round gardens or flower shows or look at gardening programmes on television, to find there are so many plants that nothing would induce me to grow. Any addict, however, will know that having fallen into temptation yet again, it is the researching and finding something unknown or unexpected about a special plant's collector that is as exciting as finding the plant itself.

It's the hunt that is the fun, and if you are exhausted by the physical aspect of this activity, there is another enjoyable pastime which feeds the habit between quests, and for which the indispensable good weather is not required – that is, having a pile of age-old gardening magazines to browse through, such as the *New Flora and Silva, Gardener's Chronicle, The Plantsman, Curtis Botanical Magazine* and others, bulging with the best-informed brains of the day, new ideas and opinions. There lies inspiration, and of course temptation but, with a bit of luck, some other irresistible plant like the red echium will fly into sight.

INDEX